Coming Out
and Disclosures
LGBT Persons Across the Life Span

Ski Hunter, PhD

Routledge
Taylor & Francis Group

NEW YORK AND LONDON

First Published by

The Haworth Press, Inc., 10 Alice Street, Binghamton, NY 13904–1580.

Transferred to Digital Printing 2009 by Routledge
270 Madison Ave, New York NY 10016
2 Park Square, Milton Park, Abingdon, Oxon, OX14 4RN

For more information on this book or to order, visit
http://www.haworthpress.com/store/product.asp?sku=5423

or call 1-800-HAWORTH (800-429-6784) in the United States and Canada
or (607) 722-5857 outside the United States and Canada
or contact orders@HaworthPress.com

PUBLISHER'S NOTE
The development, preparation, and publication of this work has been undertaken with great care. However, the Publisher, employees, editors, and agents of The Haworth Press are not responsible for any errors contained herein or for consequences that may ensue from use of materials or information contained in this work. The Haworth Press is committed to the dissemination of ideas and information according to the highest standards of intellectual freedom and the free exchange of ideas. Statements made and opinions expressed in this publication do not necessarily reflect the views of the Publisher, Directors, management, or staff of The Haworth Press, Inc., or an endorsement by them.

Cover design by Jennifer M. Gaska.

Library of Congress Cataloging-in-Publication Data

Hunter, Ski.
    Coming out and disclosures: LGBT persons across the life span / Ski Hunter.
        p. cm.
    Includes bibliographical references.
    ISBN: 978-0-7890-2689-7 (hard : alk. paper)
    ISBN: 978-0-7890-2690-3 (soft : alk. paper)
    1. Coming out (Sexual orientation)—United States. 2. Social work with sexual minorities—United States. I. Title.

HQ73.3.U6H86 2007
306.760973—dc22
                                                                                    2006038188

This book is dedicated to Andrea who is central to my life.
She supported me throughout the writing of this book.
Writing is a solitary process, and I deeply appreciate
that she was present and helpful in so many ways.

ABOUT THE AUTHOR

Ski Hunter, PhD, MSW, is a professor at the School of Social Work, University of Texas at Arlington. Among the courses she teaches is a course on LGBT issues. She has presented numerous workshops on this topic. Dr. Hunter has authored two books on midlife, including *Midlife and Older LGBT Adults: Knowledge and Affirmative Practice for the Social Services*. She was also the lead author of *Lesbian, Gay, and Bisexual Youths and Adults* published in 1998, co-author of *Lesbian, Gay, Bisexual, and Transgender Issues in Social Work* published in 2001, and lead author of *Affirmative Practice: Understanding and Working with Gay, Bisexual, and Transgender Persons*.

CONTENTS

Acknowledgments

I express gratitude to all LGBT persons who helped pave the way for many others to come out and make disclosures.

Coming Out and Disclosures
© 2007 by The Haworth Press, Inc. All rights reserved.
doi:10.1300/5423_a

Introduction

"Lesbian," "gay," and "bisexual" are terms applied to sexual identities and infer sexual orientations. "Transgender" and "intersex" are terms applied to identities only and do not infer sexual orientations. Yet, LGBTI persons have to contend with stigma, prejudice, discrimination, harassment, and violence. LGBT persons also want legal protections and civil rights as well as sexual freedom and freedom for sex-gender expression. A major goal for "intersex" persons is freedom from surgical decisions about gender soon after birth, as they could turn out to be the wrong decisions. All these persons also have in common coming out to themselves and disclosing information to others about their identities. Literature on these processes, however, is mostly focused on lesbian and gay persons.

The study of lesbian and gay persons increased during the past thirty years or so (Herdt, 1997; Hostetler & Herdt, 1998), and much of it addressed coming out and making disclosures. Typically coming out happens during adolescence and disclosures in late adolescence or early adulthood. Hence, much of the literature focuses on the coming-out experiences of youths and disclosures particularly to parents. Less study has been devoted to these topics across the middle and later years of adulthood (Cohler & Boxer, 1984).

Much of the material on coming out and disclosures was published in the 1970s and 1980s in a mixture of trade books and academic books and journals. Examples of the books include those that provide personal stories of coming out (e.g., Stanley & Wolfe, 1980) and coming out during adolescence and making disclosures to parents (e.g., Herdt & Boxer, 1993; Sauerman, 1984; Savin-Williams, 1990a; 2001). Other books focus on a variety of contexts where disclosures might occur such as college, work, and church (e.g., Burke, 1993). More books are available on the experiences of men (e.g., Outland, 2000; Vargo, 1998) than those of women (e.g., K.L. Jensen, 1999).

Coming Out and Disclosures
© 2007 by The Haworth Press, Inc. All rights reserved.
doi:10.1300/5423_01

The remainder of this introduction addresses terminology in more detail and the context of heterosexism in which coming out and disclosures take place. The movement of human services from being oppressive and heterosexist to being more affirmative is also addressed. Many lesbian and gay persons use these services because of the stress involved in coming out and making disclosures, as well as other issues.

TERMS

Initials such as "LGB" and "LGBT" are used in this book. Sometimes the plural LGBT "populations" or "communities" are used to indicate the diversity among these groups and within them (L.M. Woolf, 2002). Terms also vary over time and in different geographical areas, cultures, regions, and because of age or philosophies (American Psychological Association, 1991; Donovan, 1992; Martinez, 1998). The terms, "lesbian" and "gay," began to appear after the rebellion that was instigated in 1969 by LGBT patrons at the Stonewall Bar in Greenwich Village, New York. They fought police who routinely raided the bar and harassed and arrested the patrons (Cohler, Galatzer-Levy, Boxer, & Irvin, 2000). After this event, or turning point in lesbian and gay history in the United States, the term "homosexual" was dismissed because of its association with negative stereotypes as well as its use as a pathological diagnosis (M.A. Jacobs & Brown, 1997). This sin or sickness identification was replaced with a social status identification ("gay") (Herdt & Boxer, 1992). Eventually, women chose the term "lesbian" for themselves as "gay" was a term mostly used for men (Jeffreys, 1994; T.S. Stein, 1993).

The terms "homosexual" and "homosexuality" are used in this book primarily in discussions of history, because alternative terms were not used at the time. But, these clinical terms are now unacceptable to most lesbian and gay persons and appear with quotation marks to indicate this. "Intersex" is also a clinical term applied to persons born with varying degrees of both female and male sexual reproductive organs (Feinberg, 1996). The medical establishment also imposed clinical terms, implying pathology, on transgender persons such as "transvestite," "transsexual," and "sexual dysphoria." The term "transgender," which came into widespread use in the early 1990s, is the preferred term. It has broad application as it includes anyone who resists gender stereotypes or who transgresses gender norms through sexual orientation (lesbian, gay, and bisexual persons) and sex-gender (women who are not strongly feminine or men who are not strongly masculine) (Denny, 1999). Others in the transgender community prefer alternative terms such as "two-spirit" (from Native American traditions), "gender blender," "androgyne," "drag king," and "drag queen" (Cole, Denny, Eyler, & Samons, 2000; Maurer, 1999). As with "homosexual," quotation marks are used with all clinical terms to indicate decreased acceptance of them. We must not contribute to perpetuating old stereotypes by using clinical terms unless someone indicates a preference for them (G. S. Bernstein, 1992).

Though not a term chosen by them, "bisexual" seems to be acceptable to contemporary bisexual women and men, although it is not the only term used. Some women may prefer alternate terms such as "lesbian-identified bisexual" and "bisexual lesbian" or "bi dyke" and "byke." The term lesbian may be included because of a previous lesbian identification or a political commitment to women or to the lesbian community (Rust, 1995). Some women identify as "bisexual lesbians" because although they might have sexual involvements with women and identify as lesbians; they might also experience sexual desires for men. Other women identify as "transient lesbians" because, although at some point they identified as lesbians and were sexually involved with women, they later became sexually involved with men (Golden, 1996). "Gay bisexual" is a recent identification among men. Other identifications among both women and men include "bisensual" (indicating a sensuality that expresses human connections more accurately than genital sex does), "polysexual" or "polyamorous" (indicating separation of one's sexuality from sex and sexual dichotomies), and "polyfideltious" (indicating fidelity to a group of three or more persons) (Rust, 2003). On average bisexual persons use 2.6 terms and some 10 or more terms (Rodriquez Rust, 2001). Youths also use a greater range of terms including "boidyke," "trysexual," and "stem" (Savin-Williams, 2005).

Although many Native American persons use terms such as lesbian, gay, bisexual, or transgender (Tofoya, 1996), others prefer one of the terms that exist among Native Americans such as "not-men" (biological women who perform some male roles) or "not-women" (biological men who perform some female roles) (L.B. Brown, 1997).

The label "two-spirit" is also used among some Native Americans. It represents a spiritual/social identity or an integration of alternative sexuality, alternative sex-gender and Native spirituality (Tofoya, 1996, 1997).

Some people use the term "queer," but this is a controversial term. It has been used as a taunt by heterosexuals (Jeffreys, 1994) and has particularly derogatory definitions such as something unusual, abnormal, worthless, or counterfeit (Bryant & Demian, 1998). And, it has been used by radical groups such as Queer Nation. It is applied to both males and females, which means that it could eventually be a mostly a male term (Jeffreys, 1994). This term, however, has not reached a high level of popularity as an identity label since its main application is to a philosophy or political agenda (Savin-Williams, 2005).

The terms "gender" and "sex" also require clarification because they may be mistakenly seen as the same in definition. Sex generally distinguishes males and females through biological characteristics such as genitalia and reproductive organs (Rutter & Schwartz, 2000). Gender is imposed from the outside (Bohan & Russell, 1999; McKenna & Kessler, 2000). Society expects us to be a certain gender (masculine or feminine) consistent with our sex (male or female) (Maurer, 1999). But, it is not always easy to classify persons as female or male (Coombs, 1998). "Intersex" persons, for example, are not classifiable at birth as female or male. They are born with different combinations of genitals, chromosomes, and secondary sex characteristics (e.g., body hair, breasts) (E. Stein, 1999; Weston, 1999).

Some transgender persons may also embody an "intersex" identity as, for example, FM persons who say being FM does not mean one has to deny the years of living as a woman. Some MF persons view themselves as separate from genetic women. They claim they are neither women nor men (Broad, 2002). The sex assignment for others may also come into question such as an XY (chromosomal) baby born with external female genitals but who never fully develops internal female sexual organs (Maurer, 1999). And, in some cultures more than two sexes are recognized (Blackwood, 1984). Due to unsettled issues surrounding sex and gender, and following the suggestion of E. Stein (1999), the phrase "sex-gender" is used in this text instead of using the two terms separately.

HETEROSEXISM

Heterosexism is the backdrop in the lives of LGB persons and is ever present. Defined by Herek (1995), this is "the ideological system that denies, denigrates, and stigmatizes any nonheterosexual form of behavior, identity, relationship, or community" (p. 321). This system results in all LGB persons having to contend with the oppression of stigma and discrimination ("Homosexuals said to face," 1994). It creates dilemmas in everyday life ranging from whether to hold hands in public with one's partner to having children or not or what kind of careers can be had (Adelman, 2000). It is also the reason that LGB persons go through a coming-out process and usually carefully weigh whether to make disclosures of their sexual identities to others.

Heterosexism operates at both cultural and individual levels. One way it manifests itself at the cultural level is in the belief that the only acceptable affectional and sexual expression is between women and men. Since social customs and institutions regularly reinforce this belief, we take it for granted or rarely notice its existence (Herek, 1995). Yet, it has surfaced in the controversies about gay marriage and the many state laws that claim that legal marriage exists only between a woman and a man. The purpose of such laws it to prevent lesbian and gay marriages.

Another example of cultural heterosexism is how lesbian and gay persons are portrayed in the media. Stories in early films were primarily of lesbians who were lonely, emotionally unstable, or sex-crazed. By the 1990s, films began to have more positive lesbian and gay characters, and fairly neutral lesbian and gay characters now appear in TV shows. Not all media portrayals of LGBT persons are positive, however. For example, jokes on TV game shows include denigrating words when referring to gay persons such as "fruit," "queen," and "fairy" (K.L. Jensen, 1999).

Individual heterosexism is the feelings and behaviors directed at LGB persons (Herek, 1995). Feelings include disgust and indignation (Berrill, 1990; Herek, 1993), whereas behaviors include jokes or derogatory terms mocking LGB persons. Behaviors can also take the form of physical attacks, including those that result in serious injuries or death (McDougall, 1993; Neisen, 1990).

Factors Contributing to Individual Heterosexism

The core factors contributing to heterosexism at the individual level are prejudice and stereotypes. Prejudice occurs when one makes a pre-judgment, or has a negative bias about a target group, but has limited or no experience with anyone in the group (DiAngelo, 1997; Johansson, 1990). Stereotypes reinforce prejudice (Herek, 1995) by over-emphasizing certain characteristics thought to predominate in a target group (Yarhouse, 1999). Stereotypes can be general and reflect cultural ideologies about members of all subordinated groups, such as their being inferior or threatening. Or stereotypes can focus on a specific group such as all lesbians are masculine, all gay persons are feminine, or lesbian and gay persons can influence the sexual orientation of children (Herek, 1995). However, no evidence supports this stereotype or another common stereotype specifically about gay persons, that they sexually abuse children. Most child sexual abusers are heterosexual men (Birch, 2002; Elias, 2002). Whatever the stereotypes are, this is the information about a target group that is focused on, and information that is inconsistent with the stereotypes is ignored (Gross et al., 1980; Gurwitz & Marcus, 1978; Snyder & Uranowitz, 1978). In addition, as most heterosexual women and men say they do not know any LGB persons, they probably view them as symbolic. They generally represent the type of person one is not, does not want to be, and does not want in one's family. The negative symbol of LGB persons often results in heterosexual women and men distancing themselves from LGB persons or attacking them (Herek, 1995).

Children do not have negative stereotypes (Johansson, 1990), but they will develop them after reaching adolescence (Bozett, 1987). Other than moving beyond childhood, various other factors (most likely an interaction of several of them) have been associated with holding negative stereotypes about LGBT persons (Eliason, 1997). These factors include the following:

Being male. Heterosexual men, most often white men, hold more heterosexist beliefs and attitudes than do heterosexual women (Burn, 2000; Herek, 2002; LaMar & Kite, 1998; Liang & Alimo, 2005; Ragins, Cornwell, & Miller, 2003). These men include fathers, brothers, sons, and male college students (D'Augelli & Rose, 1990; Herek, 1988; Kite, 1984).

Conservatism, authoritarianism, traditionalism, and religiosity. Included here are women and men from conservative families, those with conservative political views (Seltzer, 1992; Waldo, 1998), and those characterized by sexual conservatism (Ficarrotto, 1990). In addition, these persons may exhibit authoritarian thinking (e.g., "I'm right, you're wrong"), intolerance for ambiguity (Herek, 1988; Obear, 1991), and traditionalism or holding to traditional sex-gender roles (Schope & Eliason, 2000; Stark, 1991). Those who hold rigid sex role expectations for women and men are likely to react negatively to same sex-gender sexual orientation. Newman (1989) studied the relationship between several variables and attitudes toward lesbians (e.g., religious orthodoxy, contact with lesbian and gay persons, authoritarianism, and sex-gender role attitudes). Only sex-gender role attitudes correlated with negative attitudes for both female and male respondents. Beliefs in a conservative or fundamentalist religious ideology may also be a factor (Herek, 1988; Schope & Eliason, 2000; Seltzer, 1992). For example, in one study the more parents used religious teachings to guide their views on morality, the more negative and severe their reactions were to a lesbian or gay family member (L.E. Collins & Zimmerman, 1983). Other researchers, however, did not find religiosity significantly related to attitude or acceptance (Serovich, Skeen, Walters, & Robinson, 1993). And, some denominations are more tolerant now, thus modifying negative attitudes of parents (C. Griffin, Wirth, & Wirth, 1986). Gay sons were studied by Cramer and Roach (1988). Their mothers had traditional sex role attitudes and their fathers rated high on religious orthodoxy. However, the sons perceived that their parents were more accepting of them than not. The parent's emphasis on family unity might have played a role in this finding.

Limited education. The more extensive one's education, the more tolerant of alternative beliefs and ways of life including same sex-gender sexual orientation (L. Jensen, Gambles, & Olsen, 1988). The higher their education and income, the more accepting parents' attitudes are toward lesbian and gay children (Serovich et al., 1993). Few nonaccepting mothers in one study had a college education or friends other than extended family. These mothers often retained dogmatic stereotypes, misconceptions, and conservative values (Pearlman, 1992). Persons with more negative attitudes and beliefs and who have less education also tend to be older (Eliason, 1995; Serovich et al., 1993; Simoni, 1996).

Low empathy. Being low on empathy or unable to understand another's viewpoint is associated with lower levels of comfort when around lesbian and gay persons, compared to persons with high empathy (Johnson, Brems, & Alford-Keating, 1997).

Coping styles. Persons who tend to use the coping styles of denial, who look for blame outside themselves, or who isolate or turn from others are more likely to respond to lesbian and gay persons in prejudicial and discriminatory ways (Johnson et al., 1997).

Poor crisis management. Negative outcomes have been found to relate partly to parents' poor management of crisis. They use ineffective strategies such as scapegoating and avoidance (L.E. Collins & Zimmerman, 1983; DeVine, 1983-1984).

Bigoted peers and residential areas. The peers of persons with negative attitudes tend to oppose lesbian and gay persons (Franklin, 2000). Those who are bigoted also tend to live in geographical and residential areas where negative attitudes about same sex-gender sexual orientations are the norm (including midwest and southern locations in the United States, rural areas, and small towns) (Hong, 1984).

No contact with lesbian and gay persons. Many studies have reported that heterosexuals who have experienced no personal contact with lesbian or gay persons tend to hold negative attitudes and beliefs about them (Cotten-Huston & Waite, 2000; Herek & Glunt, 1993).

Heterosexism in Social, Political, and Legal Arenas

Generally, the social, political, and legal arenas reinforce heterosexism and discrimination at the individual level. Since lesbian and gay persons are not a protected class in the U.S. Constitution, they generally cannot rely on the Constitution or the courts to shield them from discrimination (Byrne, 1993). Even if they were a protected class, they would not be protected in private circles including private businesses and colleges. The Equal Protection Clause of the Fourteenth Amendment of the U.S. Constitution requires that states provide equal protection for all residents, but courts determine what this means for LGB persons. Two positive rulings, however, have come from the U.S. Supreme Court. First, in 1996, the Court ruled that lesbian and gay persons could not be singled out for official discrimination because of their sexual orientation (Savage, 1996). This was a momentous decision as was the ruling in June 2003 that struck down sodomy laws in every state where they remained. These laws criminalized sex between persons of the same sex-gender (Pusey, 2003).

While some strides have been made, there is a long way to go for protection of LGB persons from all discrimination. It is still legal in most states to deny housing, jobs, services, and access to public accommodations because of sexual orientation (D'Aguelli & Garnets, 1995; Hartman, 1996; Herek, 1995; E. Stein, 1999). Only a handful of state laws and municipal laws provide LGB persons with legal protection from overt discrimination in these areas (D'Augelli & Garnets, 1995; Herek, 1995).

No federal law bans discrimination against lesbian and gay persons (Jost, 2000). The proposed Employment Non-Discrimination Act, first drafted in 1994, could shift federal policy on sexual orientation in the work arena, but it has never been passed by Congress. So anti-discrimination at work is left to be dealt by state and local governments.

Only seventeen states and the District of Columbia prohibit discrimination; six states prohibit discrimination for public employees only. (Available at www.lambalegal.org/cgi-bin/iowa/s.) See the Lambda Legal Web site for an up-to-date summary of states, cities, and counties that prohibit discrimination based on sexual orientation (available at www.lambdalegal.org/cgibin/iowa/documents/record? record=217). Transgender persons experience discrimination in medical treatment as well as in employment, housing, social services, the military, and sports competitions (J. Green & Brinkin, 1994). Increasingly, however, discrimination against transgender employees is banned in companies including Microsoft, Merrill Lynch, and U.S. Airways. For a full list of these companies see Armour (2005). A progressive city ordinance in San Francisco prohibits discrimination because of sex-gender expression. This city also has a range of programs that address the health and treatment needs of transgender persons. Recently $50,000 in health benefits was approved to cover some of the costs of hormone treatment and sexual reconstruction surgery for transgender city workers (Tarver, 2002).

VICTIMIZATION

Hate crimes, or bias crimes, target persons because of their sexual orientation or sex-gender expression. Most (95 percent) of the sampled lesbian and gay respondents report having experienced some degree of violence. These persons are one of the most frequent targets of bias violence (Dean, Wu, & Martin, 1992; Von Schulthess, 1992). Many transgender persons (80 percent) have also reported experiencing physical assaults because of their sex-gender expression (Gender-PAC, 1998).

In a study of LGB victims of hate crimes, Herek, Cogan, and Gillis (2002) found that they could easily recognize when a crime was based on their sexual orientation. The perpetrators knew what it was through means such as gay-identified symbols or locations such as a gay bar. In addition, the perpetrators made anti-LGB statements while committing the crimes. Berrill (1992) reported from twenty-four local, regional, and national samples of LGB persons the proportion of different types of harassment and violence that they have experienced: assault with weapons (9 percent), physical assault (17 percent), vandalization of property (19 percent), threats of violence (44 percent), objects thrown at them (25 percent), being spit at (13 percent), and verbal harassment (80 percent).

Youths As Targets

Youths thought to be lesbian or gay face verbal harassment and physical attacks at home, in school, and in their local communities. A significant number of these youths report verbal and physical assaults, robbery, rape, or sexual abuse by family members and peers (J. Hunter, 1990; Rotheram-Borus, Rosario, & Koopman, 1991). Findings from one of the largest studies of victimization among LGB persons, covering the life span, were reported by Balsam, Rothblum, and Beauchaine (2005). The study compared the violence experienced by 557 LGB and 525 heterosexual adults. LGB respondents experienced more psychological, physical, and sexual violence in childhood and adulthood than heterosexual respondents. Within the same family, LGB siblings were at greater risk for victimization by their parents. Compared to heterosexual men (12.8 percent), bisexual men (44.1 percent) and gay men (31.8 percent) reported greater rates of childhood sexual abuse.

Half of the ethnic and racial youths seeking the services of the Hetrick-Martin Institute in New York City reported teasing and humiliation because of sexual identity (Rosario, Rotheram-Borus, & Reid, 1992), and close to half experienced violent physical attacks (J. Hunter & Schaecher, 1990). Most (80 percent) of the LGB youths studied by Pilkington and D'Augelli (1995) reported experiencing verbal abuse because of their sexual orientation. This type of abuse happened more than twice for 48 percent of gay youths. Rates for other bias crimes included the threat of physical violence (44 percent—19 percent more than two times); damage of personal property (23 percent); objects thrown at them (33 percent); chased (30 percent—16 percent more than one time); spit at (13 percent); physically assaulted (punched, kicked, or beaten) (17 percent); assaulted with a weapon (10 percent); and sexually assaulted (22 percent).

Adolescents (758) who participated in a mental health intake made up the sample studied by Ciro et al. (2005). Of the males, 5.3 percent identified as LGB or questioning; 13.3 percent of the females identified in the same way. The age range was eleven to seventeen. Lesbian and gay adolescents ranked highest on feeling unsafe (61.5 percent) compared to questioning (59.5 percent), bisexual (56 percent), and heterosexual (39.3 percent) adolescents. Bisexual adolescents were the most frequent victims of violence (80 percent) compared to heterosexual (44.1 percent), questioning (32.4 percent), and lesbian and gay (30. 8 percent) adolescents. LGB females were most likely to have witnessed violence (87.5 percent) compared to heterosexual (68.1 percent) and questioning (46.4 percent) females. Females were also most often the victims of violence (68.8 percent), to have been touched uncomfortably (59.4 percent), and to have experienced forced sex (30 percent).

Most public schools are unfriendly places for LGBT youths. Almost all (97 percent) of a sample of LGB youths in high school recalled negative attitudes displayed by classmates, and more than half feared harassment, especially if they made disclosures (Sears, 1991).

Between 33 percent and 49 percent of lesbian and gay youths responding to community surveys reported being victimized in public schools (Berrill, 1990). Close to three-quarters of females (71 percent) and males (73 percent) studied by Telljohann and Price (1993) reported harassment at school because of their sexual orientation. This included rude comments and jokes, profanities written on their lockers, threats of violence, and physical abuse. In Remafedi's (1987) study of twenty-nine gay youths, 30 percent reported that they were victims of physical assaults; half of these assaults occurred on school property. Most gay youths in this study reported regular verbal abuse from classmates, and almost 40 percent lost friends at school because of their sexual orientation. Although some of the LGB youths studied by Pilkington and D'Augelli (1995) reported fear of verbal (22 percent) or physical (7 percent) abuse at home, more of them reported fear of verbal (31 percent) or physical (26 percent) abuse at school.

The Safe Schools Anti-Violence Documentation Project in the State of Washington reports antigay sexual harassment and violence in the public schools from kindergarten through high school. Reis (1998) summed up the range of violence perpetrated on lesbian and gay students while at school:

> *Gang rape*—multiple assailants; some assailants also urinated on lesbian and gay youths, ejaculated on them, vomited on them, or broke their hands.
>
> *Physical assault*—kicking, punching, and injuring lesbian and gay students with weapons, resulting in cuts, contusions, and broken bones.
>
> *Physical harassment or sexual assault, excluding rape*—pushing, pulling, or brushing one's body against lesbian and gay students; spitting on them; hitting them with flying objects; and pulling their clothes up, down, or off.
>
> *Verbal and other harassment*—repeated public humiliation of lesbian and gay students, vandalizing their property, spreading rumors about them, and making death threats toward them.
>
> *One-time, climate-setting incidents*—name calling and offensive language directed at lesbian and gay students.

Transgender youths are often scapegoats and are verbally abused in schools because they do not conform to expectations of feminine or masculine behavior. Sometimes the harassment takes the form of physical violence (Mallon, 1997).

Other students, as well as teachers, are the perpetrators. Classmates in the Los Angeles County school system were found to perpetrate much of the abuse against LGB students, and the incidence rates of this abuse were escalating dramatically (J.W. Peterson, 1989). Pilkington and D'Augelli (1995) found that 19 percent of racial and ethnic lesbian and gay youths reported being emotionally hurt by another student because of their sexual orientation and 10 percent reported that this resulted from a teacher. Over a quarter (28 percent) of these students reported that they feared being physically hurt by students or teachers if they disclosed their sexual orientation.

The situation for lesbian and gay college students is not only similar in who perpetrates abuse but is similar in most other ways to what happens in public schools. About two-thirds (64 percent) of college students studied by D'Augelli (1989a) felt their safety on campus was in jeopardy because of threats, verbal abuse, or property damage. Data collected by the National Gay and Lesbian Task Force (1991) on the campus climate at 40 colleges and universities showed that between 40 percent and 54 percent of the LGB respondents experienced verbal harassment or threats. LGB students hear demeaning remarks such as "fagot" or "bash them back into the closet" (G. Lopez & Chism, 1993), and they are targets of jokes, jeers, and threatening signs and phone calls (Slater, 1993). Negative attitudes about LGB students also happen in university housing where the resident assistants (especially if male) are likely to make negative comments about lesbian and gay students (D'Augelli, 1989b). Some instructors on college campuses also make depreciating remarks about lesbian and gay persons in the classroom (G. Lopez & Chism, 1993).

Most of the 226 college students (95 percent) surveyed by D'Augelli and Rose (1990) reported that they participated in discriminatory behavior directed at LGB students. This included laughing at jokes or agreeing with derogatory statements, and making jokes or derogatory statements. Most (nine-tenths) of 129 college students studied by Schope and Eliason (2000) reported having witnessed heterosexist acts in the last year, including verbal and written assaults and threats against lesbian and gay persons. Over 90 percent of the respondents had laughed at an antigay joke or remark. Slightly more than one-half had made an antigay joke, laughed at a lesbian or gay person, or called one of these persons a derogatory term. Even on liberal campuses such as at Oberlin College, Norris (1992) reported widespread harassment toward LGB students including hostile graffiti and verbal insults.

Older Persons As Targets

Older LGBT persons report less verbal abuse, fewer threats of violence, and fewer objects thrown at them during their lifetimes than do younger LGBT persons. But, these differences are not statistically significant. In a national and geographically diverse sample of 416 LGB persons 60 years of age or older (age range: 60-91, mean = 68.5), many reported that they had been victimized during their lives. Two thirds (63 percent) were verbally abused, more than one-quarter (29 percent) was threatened with violence; 16 percent were punched, kicked, or beaten; 11 percent had objects thrown at them; 12 percent were assaulted with a weapon; and 29 percent were threatened with disclosure of their sexual orientation. Some (20 percent) also reported employment discrimination based on their sexual orientation, and 7 percent reported housing discrimination. Older gay and bisexual men were more likely to report victimization than older lesbian and bisexual women (D'Augelli & Grossman, 2001; Grossman, D'Augelli, & O'Connell, 2001). These findings are consistent with the results of other studies on older LGB persons (Herek, Gillis, & Cogan, 1999; Otis & Skinner, 1996).

Victimization increases with greater visibility. The earlier older persons had self-identified as LGB and made disclosures to others, the more victimization they recalled experiencing. Those who were members of LGB organizations and attended them regularly reported more victimization. If they were out in less supportive times, physical victimization might have also been more brutal (D'Augelli & Grossman, 2001; Grossman et al., 2001).

Effects of Victimization

Despite the stigma and intense stressors, most lesbian and gay persons function well. Like members of other stigmatized groups, they develop strategies to cope with their status. This helps minimize the psychological consequences (Crocker & Major, 1989; Freedman, 1971). Youths actively seek the support of their families when they experience victimization. Families appear to buffer them against the harmful effects of victimization, if family support is high and victimization low (Hershberger & D'Augelli, 1995). But, assault and other victimization can still create considerable distress. Attacks directed toward persons because of their sexual orientation have a more powerful negative impact than other crimes. Even a minor incident of harassment can be frightening because one never knows what it will lead to. There are also consequences for LGB communities as these crimes give a message that LGB persons are not safe (Herek et al., 2002).

Some families are not a buffer for their lesbian and gay children but instead victimize them, which has effects on their mental health. D'Augelli (2002) studied the mental health of 206 lesbian and bisexual youths, ages 14 to 21, and drawn from social and recreational settings. Their mental health was affected when they experienced or feared victimization whether verbal or physical. Having hostile families and being victimized because of one's sexual orientation can produce stress, fear, and mental health problems. Youths who lost friends specifically because of their sexual orientation had lower self-esteem and more mental health problems. The combination of unsupportive parents and the loss of friends was particularly difficult. Some youths made suicide attempts. The most important factor affecting mental health was a fear of future victimization both at school and at home. The fear was less at home, although one-third feared verbal abuse there. Half of these youths reported verbal abuse in high school and 11 percent reported physical assaults. Worry about being verbally abused or physically attacked can be a chronic stressor lasting for years, given the time youths spend in school and at home (D'Augelli, 2003; D'Augelli, Pilkington, & Hershberger, 2002).

Being victimized also affects the mental health of older LGB persons. Herek et al. (2002) found, from a convenience sample of 450 LGB adults who had experienced bias crimes, greater and prolonged psychological distress compared to the results of other types of crimes. Otis and Skinner (1996) found that depression was associated with being victimized because of sexual orientation. In another study of older LGB persons, being physically attacked because of one's sexual orientation was especially associated with negative outcomes. Current mental health was worse for those who were physically attacked. Those who had experienced no sexual orientation victimization or only verbal attacks had higher self-esteem. Of those who made a suicide attempt, more had been physically attacked than had been verbally attacked or not attacked at all. They also had more internalized oppression leading to suicidal thoughts, compared to those who had not experienced physical attacks (D'Augelli & Grossman, 2001; Grossman et al., 2001).

ESCALATING VIOLENCE

Violence against LGBT persons is escalating in cities across the United States. The National Coalition of Anti-Violence Programs (2000) reported violent incidents directed at LGBT persons in 1999 for thirteen cities, states, and regions across the United States. Although, compared to 1998, the total number of reported anti-LGBT incidents of violence in 1999 declined slightly (3 percent) (2,017 versus 1,965), this was true for only 4 of the 13 reporting regions. Incidents in the other nine regions increased at a mean rate of 40 percent with a range from 7 percent in Columbus, Ohio, to 116 percent in Chicago. Cities and states with increased incidents in 2004 included Chicago (16 percent), Colorado (3 percent), Columbus (3 percent), Massachusetts (30 percent), Michigan (4 percent), Minnesota (71 percent), and San Francisco (7 percent). Declines were reported in Cleveland (71 percent), New York (2 percent), and Pennsylvania (13 percent). The average rate in cities experiencing increases in violence in 2004 was 19 percent. The rate of violent incidents attributable to organized hate groups increased 273 percent. Assaults decreased overall (18 percent), but assaults with weapons increased 14 percent. The weapons with the highest increased use included vehicles (60 percent), ropes and restraints (29 percent), and bats, clubs, and blunt objects (21 percent) (National Coalition of Anti-Violence Programs, 2004).

Even where data are collected on bias crimes, the estimates are lower than actual occurrences. Unreported cases are estimated to be as high as 85 percent (Berrill, 1992). Many victims of bias crimes do not report them because of the stigma of their sexual orientation (Waldo, Hesson-Mcinnis, & D'Augelli, 1998). Authorities often blame the crime victims themselves for their attacks and rationalize or excuse the violent behavior of the perpetrators (A.D. Martin & Hetrick, 1988; Uribe & Harbeck, 1992).

The victims of bias crimes fear losing control of the privacy of their identities or being "outed" (Tewksbury, Grossi, Suresh, & Helms, 1999). They also fear further harassment at the hands of police or others (Herek, 1995; Murphy, 1994). Instances of verbal harassment and abuse by police officers perpetrated on these crime victims increased by 155 percent and reports of physical abuse by police grew by 866 percent between 1977 and 1998 (National Coalition of Anti-Violence Programs, 1998).

The most extreme result of bias crimes, death, occurs with some regularity among LGBT persons. This includes the death of Allen Schindler who was beaten and stomped on a U.S. naval ship in 1992 because he was gay (Service Members Legal Defense Network, 1999). In October 1998, two men murdered twenty-one-year-old Matthew Shepard in Wyoming ("Gay Victim of Beating," 1998). Another gay man in the military, Barry Mitchell, was murdered in 1999 with a baseball bat that shattered his skull (Jost, 2000). Also in 1999, Billy Jack Gaither was murdered in a small town in Alabama because he was gay (Herek, 2000). In July 2000, two teenagers murdered Arthur "J. R." Warren, Jr., a gay African American, in West Virginia. In September 2000, a gay student, Eric Plunkett, was murdered at Gallaudet University in Washington, DC ("Year in Review," 2001). On September 22, 2000, an assailant shot seven patrons in a gay bar in Roanoke, Virginia. One of them died (Laris, 2000). A Latino lesbian activist in Milwaukee, Juama Vega, was shot repeatedly in the chest and face in November 2001 and died a few days later (National Gay and Lesbian Task Force, 2001).

Transgender persons are also murdered, including the brutal rape and killing of Brandon Teena at age twenty-one. Biologically female, she wanted to be a man and was living as one in Nebraska before being discovered and murdered on New Year's Eve in 1993 (Kirp,

1999; Thomas, 1999). Another transgender person, Ana Melisa Cortez, was stabbed to death in Nashville, Tennessee, in October, 2000. In 2002, two transgender teenagers were murdered in southeast Washington. Each of these youths had at least ten bullet wounds. (Available at www.ngltf.org/news/release.cfm?releaseID=474.)

ADVANCES IN AFFIRMATIVE PRACTICE

Given the heterosexism at the cultural and individual levels, it may seem surprising that practice with LGBT persons has become more affirmative in recent years. Lesbian and gay persons were thought to be mentally ill for many years and treatment was focused on changing their sexual orientation to heterosexual. But, on December 15, 1973, the American Psychiatric Association (APA) Board of Trustees unanimously voted to remove "homosexuality" from its official list of psychiatric disorders (Adam, 1987). This result took research showing that lesbian and gay persons were no more likely to be mentally ill than were heterosexual persons, two decades of struggle, and three years of intense activism by the Gay Liberation Movement and allies in the American Psychiatric Association (APA) (Barr & Catts, 1974; R. Green, 1972; Marmor, 1972). In the 1987 revised edition of the *Diagnostic Statistical Manual of the American Psychiatric Association* (DSM-III), the last diagnostic category related to lesbian and gay persons, "sexual orientation disturbance" (later called "ego-dystonic" "homosexuality"), was removed (Morin & Rothblum, 1991; T.S. Stein, 1993).

Transgender persons are still fighting DSM battles (Gagné, Tewksbury, & McGaughey, 1997). In the 1994 DSM-IV there is no mention of transgender or transsexual, but the diagnostic category "sex-identity disorder" (GID) does appear (Denny, 1999). In some areas of the country, transgender youths have been forced into psychiatric hospitals to "correct" their GID condition. Cross-dressing (by heterosexual or bisexual males who obtain erotic gratification from this activity) also remains in the category of "transvestic fetishism." But, a growing body of evidence shows that cross-dressing is not a mental disorder (Cole et al., 2000; Denny, 1997, 1999).

Aside from the issue of inappropriate diagnostic categories were the prescribed treatments to cure persons classified as "homosexual."

Treatments were often punitive, coercive, and involuntary. They included various biological therapies such as induced seizures, nausea-inducing drugs, electric shock, covert sensitization, masturbation while viewing pictures of a nude woman, lobotomy, castration, implantation of "normal" testes, and supplementation of various hormones. Although psychotherapy was more humane, the goal was the same—to cure "homosexuality" whether through psychoanalysis or behavior modification (Haldeman, 1994; Silverstein, 1991, 1996). However, despite such attempts at cure, a predominantly or exclusively same sex-gender sexual orientation rarely if ever changes in adulthood (Hammersmith, 1987). Even if the behaviors are stopped, same sex-gender dreams, fantasies, and attractions continue (Bell & Weinberg, 1978; Pattison & Pattison, 1980). Eventually, attempts to convert a person from a same sex-gender sexual orientation to a heterosexual sexual orientation diminished (Dynes & Donaldson, 1992). This resulted from adverse publicity about the treatments, and the research showing that same sex-gender sexual orientation is not pathological.

From the early 1970s, considerable improvement in human services surfaced. New "affirmative" approaches to treatment developed with the goal of supporting lesbian and gay persons to accept and value their sexual identities and their sexual attractions. An affirmative focus also developed for bisexual persons (Matteson, 1996a; Nichols, 1988) and is evolving for transgender persons (Carroll, Gilroy, & Ryan, 2002; Emerson & Rosenfeld, 1996; C. Rosenfeld & Emerson, 1998). Affirmative practitioners reinforce the naturalness of living with the sexual orientation or sex-gender expression that clients identify as their own (Matteson, 1996b).

Services for lesbian and gay clients have greatly improved over recent years (Little, 1999) and satisfaction with services began to rise in the late 1980s (Adam, 1987; Morin & Rothblum, 1991). Most lesbian and gay clients (86 percent) studied by M.A. Jones and Gabriel (1999) reported that therapy has had a positive effect on their lives; half (50 percent) felt "very positive" about therapy; and a third (33 percent) felt that therapy had "saved their lives." Lesbians studied by Little (1997) held more positive attitudes about seeking professional help than did heterosexual persons. In a study of the experiences of transgender persons in therapy, Rachlin (2001) discovered that more than 87 percent of the respondents reported that positive changes in their lives resulted from therapy. When asked what was most helpful, four things stood out: acceptance, respect for their sex-gender expression, flexibility in interventions, and providing a connection to the transgender community. They also appreciated the therapist's knowledge of sex-gender expression issues. However, Saulnier (2002), who studied the experiences of lesbians with mental health and health providers, suggested that new cohorts of providers may not have sufficient training. They need to be upgraded in affirmative services delivery and exposed to new knowledge. This suggestion applies to those working with gay, bisexual, and transgender persons as well.

Although there have been improvements in human services, institutional denial of the specific needs of LGBT clients still occurs. Also, not all human services practitioners are affirmative. Many social services agencies fail to recognize that LGBT clients have specific needs, and administrators often resist developing affirmative programs for them (Ball, 1994; Hancock, 1995). Most LGB clients are well aware of institutional denials of their needs and the negative attitudes held by some health and mental health professionals, as well as those of the general public (Rothblum, 1994). These clients assess environments all their lives for signs of prejudice, rejection, hatred, or violence. The cues come through voice or physical mannerisms displaying awkwardness, defensiveness, hesitancy, hostility, distance, disapproval, and contempt (L.S. Brown, 1989b; M. Pope, 1997).

When lesbian and gay clients perceive that practitioners hold negative views of them, they can experience greater psychological distress following services than they experienced before services began (Fassinger, 1991). Openness and trust of LGBT clients in their practitioners will likely diminish, a situation that is difficult to correct later (Messing, Schoenberg, & Stephens, 1983-1984; M. Pope, 1997). Some lesbian and gay clients in traditional social services agencies anticipate outright rejection. Some prematurely terminate because they think that the practitioner will terminate services with them (Alexander, 1998). Others terminate after one session because of unhelpful behaviors by the practitioner (Little, 1996).

Unfortunately, practitioners in all disciplines receive little or no education about issues pertinent to LGBT populations (Buhrke &

Douce, 1991; Mackelprang, Ray, & Hernandez-Peck, 1996), much less assistance in changing their attitudes. This is often the case although codes of ethics of human services professions now endorse affirmative training. If practitioners in human services agencies adhere to a professional code of ethics, they must be affirmative, not oppressive, with LGBT clients. They must serve all clients equitably. As human services organizations provide most of the counseling, case management, and other services for LGB persons, it is crucial that these organizations insist on nonjudgmental, affirmative attitudes by their staffs. Social services agencies should create a nonjudgmental atmosphere for staff to talk about differences, biases, and lack of knowledge about LGBT persons. It should be clear to the staff that their agencies will not tolerate negative attitudes or discrimination based on sexual orientation or sex-gender expression (N.A. Humphreys & Quam, 1998). Novices need to seek regular consultation from a practitioner who has the necessary experience and can point out subtle expressions of bias (L.S. Brown, 1995). It would help all practitioners to seek supervision from any educated, enlightened affirmative practitioner. Procuring supervision from an openly LGB or T practitioner, however, may be the most beneficial educational experience. This is especially the case if the student or professional has not been acquainted with a lesbian, gay, bisexual, or transgender person (Buhrke, 1989). See S. Hunter and Hickerson (2003) for additional information on the competencies needed to work with LGBT clients and how to create an affirmative environment. This includes, among a number of modifications, how intake forms are worded, what language is used with LGBT clients, and the types of questions asked.

The focus of this book, coming out and making disclosures, happens in the context of heterosexism. If not in the foreground, it is always in the background for every LGB person. Although these persons live more openly now, discrimination against them continues to exist and to be condoned. These are the reasons why heterosexism was discussed in this introduction and throughout the book.

The chapters in this book include "Sexual Orientation and Sexual Identities" (Chapter 1), "Coming Out: Overview" (Chapter 2), "Critique of Coming-Out Models" (Chapter 3), "Coming Out Across the Life Span" (Chapter 4), "Disclosures: Overview" (Chapter 5), "Disclosures to Parents" (Chapter 6), "Disclosures to Others Inside and

Outside the Family" (Chapter 7), "Working with Clients Who Are Coming Out" (Chapter 8), "Working with Clients Who Want to Make Disclosures" (Chapter 9), and "Working in Larger Arenas to Facilitate Disclosures" (Chapter 10).

This book is intended to be a supplemental textbook, a guide to practice for professionals, and can be used for in-service training, and workshops. The primary audiences include undergraduate- and graduate-level college students in courses on diversity, adolescent and adult development, and practice in the fields of social work, counseling, mental health, nursing, psychology, sociology, and education. LGBT persons themselves can also benefit from this book through learning about the experiences of others and understanding what is happening to them when coming out and how to prepare to make disclosures to others.

PART I:
FIGURING OUT WHO ONE IS
AND COMING OUT

Chapter 1

Sexual Orientation
and Sexual Identity

SEXUAL ORIENTATION

Sexual orientation is not easy to define. Often, it has been associated with whom one has sex with, as done in the Kinsey studies (Kinsey, Pomeroy, & Martin, 1948; Kinsey, Pomeroy, Martin, & Gebbard, 1953). The Kinsey group developed a 7-point bipolar scale to identify sexual orientation, with heterosexual on one end and "homosexual" on the other end. Positioning on this continuum depended upon the proportion of a person's sexual behavior that was oriented to one or the other sex-gender. This proportion resulted in a score that ranged from 0 (exclusive heterosexual behavior), to the midpoint of 3 (equal heterosexual and "homosexual" behavior), to 6 (exclusive "homosexual" behavior).

The Kinsey work was revolutionary (V.L. Bullough, 1994), yet it had notable shortcomings. For example, sexual orientation was reduced to numerical categories leading to the presumption that all persons who attain the same number are the same sexual type (V.L. Bullough, 1998; Laumann, Gagnon, Michael, & Michaels, 1994; Sell, 1996). The seven-point scale also essentially divided persons into exclusive heterosexual or "homosexual" categories. This made the scale problematic for respondents who reported that they could potentially become sexually involved with either women or men or that they experienced former sexual relations with both women and men (E. Stein, 1999). Since "homosexual" experiences were of more

Coming Out and Disclosures
© 2007 by The Haworth Press, Inc. All rights reserved.
doi:10.1300/5423_02

interest to the Kinsey group, "bisexual" was a default category (Guidry, 1999).

Kinsey's work began to be challenged in the 1970s. Factors other than sex were added to scales such as love and affection. And the intensity level of emotional and sexual attraction was assessed. In addition, separate scales have been developed to measure same sex-gender orientation and other sex-gender orientation (Kinsey had one scale). With this development, one of the findings was that same sex-gender and other sex-gender behaviors were independent; persons showed high levels of both same sex-gender and other sex-gender sexual behavior, low levels of both, or levels of each that varied in strength (Klein, Sepekoff, & Wolf, 1985; Shively & De Cecco, 1977; Storms, 1980).

One of the more influential advances in the measurement of sexual orientation was the Klein Sexual Orientation Grid (KSOG) (Klein et al., 1985). This scale assumes that sexual orientation is multivariate and dynamic. Seven components are measured:

1. sexual attraction;
2. sexual behavior;
3. sexual fantasies;
4. emotional preference;
5. social preference;
6. self-identification; and
7. living as a lesbian woman or gay man, heterosexual woman or man, or bisexual woman or man.

Each component is represented on a 7-point scale with a range from same sex-gender only to other sex-gender only. One can be at different places on the scale for each component so that the positions can be congruent or incongruent with each other. Positions may also be different across time periods: present, past, and ideal future. While this scale is an advancement, it also made the same binary assumption of sexuality as did the Kinsey group.

Other researchers included even more components (e.g., Coleman, 1978; Sell, 1996). A scale developed by Berkey, Perelman-Hall, and Kurdek (1990) was a more sophisticated version of the Klein scale and not binary (E. Stein, 1999). But, all the scales have limitations, and no thorough factor analysis of the components has been done. The scales also do not accommodate other possibilities. For example, do transgender or "intersex" persons constitute a second sex-gender or a third or a fourth? If so, where do we locate them on scales? And where do we locate women and men who experience attractions to "intersex" or transgender persons but are not "intersex" or transgender themselves (E. Stein, 1999)? Or, as posed by Bockting (1999), where do we locate transgender persons who experience attractions to women, men, or other transgender persons, and who may sexually interact with lesbian, gay, bisexual, or heterosexual identified others? As suggested by Tarver (2002), some persons may adopt a political sex-gender of female or male, although they are not that sex-gender biologically or psychologically.

Persons can be sorted into various groups by virtue of their sexual interests, including body type, hair color, personality, profession, sex-gender, types of sexual acts, locations for engaging in sexual acts, and entities engaged (e.g., humans, animals, inanimate objects) (E. Stein, 1999). Furthermore, Savin-Williams (2005) noted that what sex means to any particular person varies. Youths, for example, are likely to think of a large variety of behaviors as sex; intercourse is only one form. Romance may be more important to lesbians than genital sex.

Where do these developments and questions leave sexual orientation? Although there have been advancements post-Kinsey, many questions about sexual orientation remain unanswered. A paradigm is emerging that conceptualizes sexual orientations still on a continuum, but acknowledges a highly individualized process of arriving at a sexual orientation (Garnets, 2001). And most likely there are a number of categories of sexual orientations beyond the current narrow group (E. Stein, 1999).

SEXUAL IDENTITY

Whereas sexual orientation has to do with sexual dispositions, sexual fantasies, sexual desires, and sexual behaviors, sexual identity has to do with what one identifies oneself to be. We choose a sexual identity from a given pool of potentialities, and the cultural and historical contexts of our lives provide meaning to the selected sexual identity (A.L. Ellis & Mitchell, 2000). In addition, in contrast to sexual orientation, which is stable and resistant to self-control or control by others, sexual identity is fluid. It can change or take on new meanings (Savin-Williams, 2005). For example, Diamond (2005) found that over an eight-year period 60 percent of young women changed their sexual identity at least once and nearly 50 percent gave up a lesbian or bisexual label. Others may not link their sexual orientation to a sexual identity. Over half (53 percent) of lesbians studied by S.C. Anderson and Holliday (2005) did not view their sexual orientation as central to their identity whereas others (47 percent) did view being lesbian as central to their identity. However, the centrality of sexual identity decreased with age; these women more likely saw their sexual identity as just one of multiple identities they claimed.

We typically expect that a person's selected sexual identity is concordant with certain components such as sexual desire, affectional desire, sexual behavior, and community participation (Firestein, 1996; Golden, 1987; Laumann et al., 1994; Rothblum, 1994; Shively, Jones, & De Cecco, 1983-1984; E. Stein, 1999). Lesbian and gay persons may have a more congruent sexual orientation/sexual identity than heterosexual or bisexual persons. If they think of themselves as lesbian or gay they tend to have behaviors, fantasies, attractions, and preferences that correspond with this self-view. Some bisexual and heterosexual persons, however, label their sexual orientation in ways that are inconsistent with their behavior, fantasies, attractions, and preferences (Moore & Norris, 2005). Yet, nothing is definite about the links between these components for any group as they are independent of one another (see S. Hunter, Shannon, Knox, & Martin, 1998; S. Hunter & Hickerson, 2003). They also mix in different ways, as exemplified in the following list:

Sexual desire incongruent with sexual identity: Some persons who claim sexual desire for others of the same sex-gender do not claim a lesbian, gay, or bisexual identity. In a national sample of adults, more had same sex-gender attractions (8 percent) than identified as lesbian, gay, or bisexual (2 percent) (Laumann et al., 1994). Yet, certain psychological literature would say that if one has sexual desires for others of the same sex-gender, one is lesbian, gay, or bisexual, as sexual desire is seen as a basic indicator of sexual orientation (Marmor, 1980). Other persons can experience the reverse incongruency: they self-identify as lesbian, gay, or bisexual but experience no sexual desire for a same sex-gender partner. Or, sexual desire that was once present disappeared (Esterberg, 1997; Peplau & Cochran, 1990).

Sexual desire and sexual behavior incongruent with sexual identity: Not all women and men who experience sexual desires for and sexual behavior with persons of the same sex-gender self-identify as lesbian, gay, or bisexual (Massey & Ouellette, 1996; Radonsky & Borders, 1995). In surveys on sexual behavior and mental (cognitive/affective) states, about one-third of women and men who in the past year desired same sex-gender partners and had sex with them did not identify themselves as lesbian, gay, or bisexual (Davis & Smith, 1993; Laumann et al., 1994). This circumstance also happens among persons in sex-gender segregated institutions such as prisons (Wooden & Parker, 1982).

Affectional desire incongruent with sexual desire and sexual identity: This arrangement has been called "romantic friendships" or "Boston marriages." Some women are psychologically or emotionally passionate about each other but do not sexually desire each other and do not self-identify as lesbian (Faderman, 1981; Rothblum & Brehony, 1993; Rupp, 1997).

Affectional and sexual desire congruent with self-identity but not behavior: Some women and men identify as lesbian, gay, or bisexual and experience both affectional and sexual desire for others of the same sex-gender but currently have no sexual partner. This could be a desired or undesired state (Davis & Smith, 1993; Esterberg, 1997; Laumann et al., 1994; Peplau & Cochran, 1990).

Sexual desire and sexual identity incongruent with community participation: Some persons who self-identify as lesbian or gay, and desire sex with persons of the same sex-gender, or who self-identify as bisexual and desire sex with persons of both sex-genders, do not participate in LGB social or political events. They may lack interest or time, or they may choose not to make their sexual identity public (Herek, 1991).

Sexual desire incongruent with sexual identity and community participation: Some persons who have no desire to participate in same sex-gender sexual behavior, self-identify as lesbian, gay, or bisexual and participate in LGB communities. They do this for social or political purposes (Rothblum, 1994). Women are more likely to do this as they base their identities more on social and political factors compared to men who base their identities more directly on their sexual attractions and experiences (Rust, 2000). An example is a woman who prefers sex with men but adopts a lesbian identity to express emotional and political solidarity with the lesbian feminist community (Faderman, 1984-1985; Golden, 1994). Women who adopt lesbian or bisexual identities for political or ideological reasons, however, are not always uninvolved sexually with women. The political pursuit of some women studied by Golden seemed to be an erotic as well as a political choice. Elective or political lesbians studied by Diamond (1998) also did not report fewer sexual attractions to women than those who did not identify as political.

Given the variations here, each person experiences a unique combination of erotic and affectional desires, fantasies, emotional attachments, behaviors, sexual identities, and community involvement. When there are only a few categories, people try to fit into one of them, but it may not accurately represent their experiences.

RACIAL AND ETHNIC PERSONS AND IDENTITY

Sexual identifications can also be influenced by one's racial and ethnic culture. Persons in these cultures who have same sex-gender sexual relations may not identify as lesbian, gay, or bisexual. No sexual identities in East Asian cultures are analogous to the modern Western constructs of lesbian and gay identities (Chan, 1997). Some African American women reject the term lesbian because it is Eurocentric (Mason-John & Khambatta, 1993).

In some cultures, it is not uncommon for men to engage in sex with other men without labeling themselves as gay. In Latino cultures, this is especially common with men who take the masculine active sexual role of inserter (Carballo-Diéguez, 1989; Espin, 1984). These men may also not identify as gay because they view this identity as part of the white gay political movement (Morales, 1990). They more easily view themselves as experiencing bisexual sexual experiences (but not the identity). Bisexual sexual practices are partly extensions of heterosexual machismo or masculine heterosexuality. For some Latino men, however, these practices hide a gay sexual orientation (Manalansan, 1996). In some Native American communities, a masculine male who engages in the active role of inserter in sex with another male is also not labeled as gay. If a male is masculine, the sex-gender of a sexual partner is irrelevant. However, a male who takes the role of a passive, receptive partner while experiencing sex with another male gets labeled as gay (Tofoya, 1996).

YOUTHS AND IDENTITY

Most youths who identify, or who eventually identify, as lesbian, gay, or bisexual may engage in heterosexual sex during adolescence (D'Augelli, 1991; Golden, 1997). In Savin-Williams's (1995a, 1998a) studies of boys, some did not recognize or acknowledge a gay or bisexual sexual identity but still desired sex with other boys exclusively, or engaged in sex with both boys and girls. Other boys self-identified as gay but were celibate. Some youths experienced substantial and persistent sexual attractions for and fantasies about persons of the same sex-gender but were unprepared to identify with a culturally defined sexual identity category because of developmental or political reasons (Savin-Williams, 2001).

One study found that over 80 percent of youths in an urban community-based social and recreational agency considered at some point in their development that they might be lesbian, gay, or bisexual. This indicated that they were in a process of sexual questioning (Rosario et al., 1996). Some youths realize the obvious and inevitable and go ahead and claim a nonheterosexual identity. Others, however, do not link sexual questioning during adolescence to sexual identity; most wait until their high school years to make this link (Savin-Williams, 2005). For boys, sex may be the main event moving this transition along (Dubé, 2000; Herdt & Boxer, 1993). But for girls, sex is not central. Instead, it is an emotional attachment or crush that moves them along, or it could be a book, college course, or movie that is the motivator (Savin-Williams, 2005).

WOMEN AND IDENTITY

Women show striking variability in their combinations of sexual identity, sexual attractions, and sexual behaviors. This variability was demonstrated in Golden's (1996, 1997) sample of over 100 women in their twenties, thirties, and forties (primarily white, but of varying sexual orientations and social classes). The identifications of these women included the following:

1. Identifying as lesbian but experiencing sex only with men
2. Identifying as heterosexual or bisexual but currently experiencing sex only with women
3. Identifying as lesbian or heterosexual, but experiencing sex with both women and men
4. Identifying as bisexual but only experiencing sex with men

Some bisexual women studied by Golden (1997) reported that although they did not fall in love with other women, they were sexually attracted to women. Some heterosexual women reported they were in love with their girlfriends but not sexually aroused by them. Some lesbians reported that their relationships with other women, though loving, were asexual. Some women experienced same sex-gender attractions but never acted on them sexually, whereas other women made a conscious determination to pursue and act on the sexual part of their attractions to other women.

As noted earlier, sexual identity can be fluid; women are more fluid in sexual identity than are men. Women may change their identities or alternate between heterosexual and lesbian identities (Kinnish, Strassberg, & Turner, 2005). Rust (2003) reported that less than 4 percent of lesbians had been at the same point on an 11-point scale of sexual attraction all their lives. Over half (58 percent) had moved 5 scale points or more. This could reflect movement from exclusive attraction to one sex-gender to 50-50 attraction to both sex-genders, or from predominant attraction to one sex-gender to predominant attraction to the other sex-gender.

In a sample of young nonheterosexual women, Diamond (2003) did three interviews over a five-year period. Lesbian/bisexual identities were relinquished by over a quarter of this sample. Half reclaimed heterosexual identities, and half gave up all identity labels. So, not all women who claim sexual minority identities during adolescence and young adulthood continue to do so indefinitely. Since experimentation is more socially tolerated during adolescence and young adulthood, situational same sex-gender sexuality may be particularly likely during this time. However, those who changed identities did not differ from those who maintained lesbian/bisexual identities in the following respects: the age at which they underwent sexual identity milestones, the factors that precipitated their sexual questioning, or their recollection of childhood "indicators" of same sex-gender activity. And, although these women had been pursuing less and less same sex-gender behavior over the five years, their same sex-gender attractions did not show similar declines. So, identity relinquishment does not represent a fundamental change in sexual orientation but in how one interprets and acts on one's sexual orientation. All these women acknowledged the possibility of future same sex-gender attractions and/or behaviors, and they were not admitting that their previous sexual minority identity was "wrong." Diamond (2005) reported that over an eight-year period, the physical and emotional attractions and sexual and romantic behavior of fluid lesbians were primarily oriented to women. However, they were less likely than stable lesbians to maintain a lesbian identity over time. They tended to change identity labels and to adopt nonlesbian labels. Stable lesbians reported more consistent identities and exclusive same sex-gender attraction and behavior. Hence, according to Diamond, it is useful to study women both pre– and post–coming out because early sexual identity development may be different from long-term identity development. It may also be useful to explore a range of typologies in terms of women's same sex-gender experiences over their lives.

BISEXUAL PERSONS AND IDENTITY

The Kinsey studies (Kinsey et al., 1948, 1953) established that more women and men display bisexual rather than exclusively same sex-gender attractions or sexual behaviors. More recent studies reported similar findings (Laumann et al., 1994; Rogers & Turner, 1991). Yet, because of the prevailing assumption of sexual dualism, persons who claim a bisexual identity confront a number of myths about their identity, including the pronouncement that "there is no such thing as a bisexual sexual identity" (Guidry, 1999; Rust, 1996). These persons often seem to others as refusing to admit their real sexual orientation (heterosexual, lesbian, or gay); they are viewed as indecisive or covering up what they really are (Firestein, 1996; R.L. Pope & Reynolds, 1991). Or, they are in a temporary phase adopted when either coming out as lesbian or gay or returning to a heterosexual sexual orientation (Udis-Kessler, 1996). When they accomplish coming out or when they choose a partner, it is assumed that their real sexual orientation will show itself, and they will no longer identify as bisexual (Rust, 1996; Udis-Kessler, 1996). Due to these myths, persons who want to claim a bisexual identity may think that their dual attractions are temporary. Or, they may feel forced to choose some other identity (Rust, 1996). Bisexual persons were found by Rodriquez Rust (2000, 2002) to maintain a stable identity less often than lesbian and gay persons, perhaps because of the myths about them and because they have few supports to help them achieve developmental milestones in coming out as bisexual.

TRANSGENDER PERSONS AND IDENTITY

For transgender persons, their internal sex-gender identity does not match their genital sex (Maurer, 1999). For example, some persons who have XY chromosomes and male-typical internal and external genitalia feel that they are female (E. Stein, 1999). Others do not share the feeling that they are the other sex-gender but may cross-dress for sexual gratification. Cross-dressers are usually heterosexual men (bisexual in a few instances). Their sex-gender identity during childhood was masculine (Bailey, 1996; Talamini, 1982), and in adulthood, they usually marry and become fathers (Bailey, 1996). Hence, not all cross-dressers are uncomfortable with their sex-gender. Most of these men reported that they were happy with being male. They could usually conceal cross-dressing or segment it from the rest of their lives. The situation was different for cross-dressers who expressed and presented themselves in feminine ways beyond the cross-dressing, and who wanted to be girls (Gagné et al., 1997).

In their sample of men who wished for their biological sex to match their sex-gender, Gagné et al. (1997) found that most of the respondents began to cross-dress in childhood, while a few (four) began this behavior in adolescence. These men wore women's clothing to relax and to express their "feminine" selves. While the motivation for cross-dressing for many of these men was erotic, for others, this was not the case, or the erotic aspect had dissipated over time. Far more crucial than cross-dressing was the discrepancy they felt between their sex-gender and their biological sex (R. Green, 1987; Zuger, 1984).

Adults who wish for a match in sex-gender and biological sex report that they always felt that nature assigned them the wrong body (Seil, 1996). From as early as age three to about age ten, they reported strong feelings that they belonged to the other sex-gender and felt comfortable with the corresponding behavioral manifestations (Gagné et al., 1997; Seil, 1996). In the Gagné et al. sample of men, about a third (sixteen) felt a strong desire to become a girl, or they felt that they were female during childhood (before age ten). About the same number (fifteen) first felt this way in adolescence, and fewer first felt this way in adulthood (ten).

Although the feeling that one's sex-gender does not match one's biological sex is agonizing, the situation is usually more stressful for feminine males because they are often the targets of teasing and rejection by families and peers. Without understanding and support in the family, feminine adolescent males tend to drop out of school and run away from home. On the streets, they are vulnerable to involvement with drugs and prostitution, and to HIV/AIDS. Usually, they live in poverty and, therefore, cannot attain treatment, including sexual reassignment surgery (SRS) (Seil, 1996). Some of these persons mutilate their genitals in a futile effort to reconcile their sex-gender and biological sex (B.F. Anderson, 1998).

Sexual Reassignment Surgery

The first known sexual reassignment surgery occurred in 1930, a reassignment from male to female (Tarver, 2002). This surgical procedure cannot change a person's chromosomal sex, but it can remove internal genital structures, alter external genitalia, and, combined with hormone treatments, dramatically affect a person's secondary sex characteristics. A person who has undergone successful SRS will seem to most persons to be a member of the sex-gender this person wants to be. "Intersex" persons who have ambiguous genitals at birth also often undergo surgical reconstruction, usually in infancy. However, later in life they may discover that the surgically assigned sex-gender does not match what they feel it is (Mauer, 1999; E. Stein, 1999).

Persons reassigned from male to female (MF) were usually feminine boys in childhood. Those reassigned from female to male (FM) were usually masculine girls (Bailey, 1996) and expressed their sex-gender desires through tomboy behavior and/or wishes and fantasies of being boys (Devor, 1997). Rehman, Lazer, Benet, Schaefer, and Melman (1999) and M. Stein, Tiefer, and Melman (1990) reported on three years of follow-up studies for twenty-eight persons who experienced MF surgery. All the respondents were at least twenty-one years of age at the time of surgery. All underwent one to two years of preparatory psychotherapy. Following surgery, the study respondents felt generally satisfied with the results both cosmetically (normal-appearing genitalia) and functionally (ability to experience orgasms). Most returned to their jobs and lived satisfactory social and personal lives. Support from friends and family was strong, and intimate relationships were stable. In addition, they reported a marked decrease in suicide attempts, criminal activity, and drug use.

No MF person studied by Rehman et al. (1999) and M. Stein et al. (1990) regretted SRS, but some respondents reported that the surgery did not solve everything. They experienced difficulties in assuming their new sex-gender role and functioning as women. They felt unpracticed in how to act as women—ranging from how to shop for women's clothes to how to respond sexually as a woman. It was not easy to form interpersonal and intimate sexual relations with men. Some worried that intercourse would damage their new vaginal entrance. Although these respondents received some emotional and mental preparation, they had not tried to live as women before surgery. For those experiencing difficulties after surgery, more counseling was necessary.

Five years after SRS about 70 percent of Swedish adult respondents studied by Bodlund and Kullgren (1996) improved in social, psychological, and psychiatric areas. Yet, about a third or more (30 to 40 percent) did not seem to benefit from SRS, and 16 percent experienced an unsatisfactory result. MF adults experienced a slightly better result than did FM adults. The discrepancy between these two groups was especially notable in establishing and maintaining partnerships and improving socioeconomic status. In another study, 162 adults who went through SRS were observed by Y.L.S. Smith, Van Goozen, Kuiper, and Cohen-Kettenis (2005). After the surgery, most did well psychologically, socially, and sexually. They were content with how things turned out, including their sex lives. Only two persons (MF, not gay) expressed regrets; FM (gay) persons functioned better than MF (not gay) persons.

Adolescents Who Experience SRS

Persons who undergo SRS usually do this in young adulthood when they are young enough but also mature enough to cope with new life stressors (Rehman et al., 1999; M. Stein et al., 1990). Professionals are reluctant to recommend SRS to persons younger than eighteen to twenty-one years of age, and parents may not grant consent for minor children to go through this procedure. Yet, researchers have reported advantages to beginning hormone treatment and doing the SRS procedure earlier than adulthood. Adolescents who show an extreme pattern of cross sex-gender identification from their earliest years and suffer from the inability to be open about their feelings or self-concept are good candidates for early intervention. Waiting many years for treatment can evoke a sense of hopelessness in these youths. Another advantage to early intervention concerns physical appearance. Especially, those experiencing MF transitions do not have to live the rest of their lives with a deep voice and facial scaring from electrical epilation. Hence, they can more easily pass as female (Cohen-Kettenis & Van Goozen, 1997).

The outcomes for twenty-two adolescents who underwent SRS (not less than one year before the study) were evaluated in a sex clinic in Amsterdam. Twelve of these youths began hormone treatment between the ages of sixteen and eighteen. They were all functioning quite well socially and did not express feelings of regret about their sex-gender reassignment. From one to five years after SRS, they rated their reassignment as "therapeutic" and beneficial. They had resolved issues with sex-gender identity and were living inconspicuously in their new sex-gender roles. Socially and psychologically, they did not function differently from peers who never questioned their sex-gender identity (Cohen-Kettenis & Van Goozen, 1997).

In a study of Dutch adults and adolescents undergoing SRS (Kuiper, 1991; Kuiper & Cohen-Kettenis, 1988), sex-gender reassignment was an effective treatment for adults, but not as effective as it was for adolescents. Adults experienced more social issues and received less support from their families and friends. The adults also did not experience as much of a realistic appearance after surgery, which made passing in the desired sex-gender role more difficult. The voices of all except one MF adolescent were not noticeably male sounding, and beard growth on all adolescent MFs was only sparse at the time of hormonal treatment.

The positive results of SRS for adolescents may also be associated with the criteria for treatment eligibility. A careful assessment by a specialized team is made to determine whether an early start is warranted. Strong determination from these youths is essential. They have to also be psychologically stable, except for the depression that is often a consequence of living in the unwanted sex-gender role. They must also be functioning well socially, have a supportive family, and be performing well at school. Youths who meet the criteria for surgery underwent partial hormone treatment while also experiencing a real-life diagnostic test where they lived full time in the desired sex-gender role. They encountered the advantages and disadvantages of the new situation and discovered whether they could pass as someone of the other sex-gender. The minimal duration of the real-life test was one year for FMs and one-and-a-half years for MFs. MFs required more time because this sex-gender change seemed to affect their lives more than the lives of FMs, and they needed more time to adjust to the new situation (Cohen-Kettenis & Van Goozen, 1997).

In another follow-up study of carefully selected adolescents who underwent SRS (one to four years prior to follow-up), Y.L.S. Smith, Van Goozen, and Cohen-Kettenis (2005) reported that no one felt any regrets about electing SRS and all were functioning well socially and psychologically. Adolescents who experienced SRS also expressed fewer regrets following surgery than persons who experienced a much longer and more inconsistent history of untreated sex-gender issues. In addition, a longer history prior to SRS resulted in stronger ties to the original role (as a partner, a parent, or a colleague) (Kuiper

& Cohen-Kettenis, 1988). And, some adults (in their thirties) were found to be so successful in performing their expected sex-gender role that the announcement of their desired sex-gender identity astounded their family and friends. Many lost marriages and jobs, and they experienced rejection from their children. These outcomes often resulted in isolation and loneliness (Seil, 1996).

Though sex-gender reassignment for adolescents is a matter of debate, it seems reasonable to conclude that youths treated during late adolescence, or shortly after, may function as well or better following surgery compared to persons treated when they are older. This is especially the case if they have been properly screened and counseled and if they have family support.

The Evolving Transgender Umbrella

The transgender "umbrella" increasingly includes more diversity. SRS is less inevitable. Biological changes may not be the desired goal (B. Bullough & Bullough, 1997), although some persons may elect selected medical and cosmetic procedures such as breast implants and electrolysis (Coombs, 1998; Tewksbury & Gagné 1996).

More and more persons realize that they can live as transgender women or men without altering their genitals (Bockting, 1999; Denny, 1997). The goal most commonly discussed now is the ability to "pass" as the other sex-gender (Gagné & Tewksbury, 1999). Even without surgery, transgender persons can view themselves as the other sex-gender and publicly present themselves as such (Coombs, 1998). Cross-dressers also often dress in whatever way they want, with no desire to pass as women or men (Denny, 1997).

Many others are now under the transgender umbrella, including bigender persons (who identify as both man and woman); drag queens and kings (usually lesbian and gay persons who "do drag" and dress, respectively, in women's and men's clothes); and female and male impersonators (who impersonate women or men, usually for entertainment). The latest groups of transgender persons include those called gender blender, gender bender, gender outlaw, and gender free (Bockting, 1999). Others who identify as radical transgender, ambigenderist, and third sex are viewed as sex radicals because they challenge not just their own sex-gender but the existing sex-gender system (Gagné et al., 1997).

Chapter 2

Coming Out: Overview

Coming out is a shortened term for "coming out of the closet." "Identity development" is another term used as is "sexual questioning" which indicates that the process has started but will not necessarily go further. Coming out of the closet infers disclosure of one's same sex-gender sexual identity to others, but not everyone engages in this activity. Hence, in this book, as coming out does not automatically imply disclosure, this term will only indicate internal identity development. The term "disclosure" will indicate the revelation of one's identity to others.

Everyone is raised with a default heterosexual identity. So the psychological processes involved in coming out also involve resocialization into LGB culture. To be resocialized, one must unlearn one's socialization as heterosexual or separate one's self from a heterosexual sexual identity. One also separates from the norms, values, and traditions of the heterosexual culture. The resocialization process also includes rejecting the stereotypes associated with being lesbian, gay, or bisexual and the ideology that heterosexuality is the only acceptable and normal sexual orientation. One declares a sexual identity in defiance of heterosexism and reconstructs stigmatized parts of one's self. However, stigma is always attached to a lesbian, gay, or bisexual identity via heterosexism; so one also learns how to manage the stigma (Herdt & Boxer, 1993). Coming out is the process in which much of one's resocialization takes place.

Coming Out and Disclosures
© 2007 by The Haworth Press, Inc. All rights reserved.
doi:10.1300/5423_03

41

DEVELOPMENTAL MODELS OF COMING OUT

Early researchers and theorists typically defined coming out not as a process but as a single or discrete event. Usually, this was the first acknowledgment of one's self as lesbian or gay or recognition of one's true self (e.g., Cronin, 1974; Dank, 1971; Gagnon & Simon, 1968; Hooker, 1967; Simon & Gagnon, 1967). This discrete event notion appeared in early psychoanalytic views of "homosexuality." Becoming a nonheterosexual person was thought to result from a single traumatic event or pattern of family interaction (Bieber et al., 1962; Socarides, 1978).

In contrast to the single event notion, coming out is more typically viewed as a developmental process with stages. Many stage models of coming out have been developed (e.g., Cass, 1979; Coleman, 1981-1982b; Dank, 1971; de Monteflores & Schultz, 1978; DuBay, 1987; Fassinger & Miller, 1996; Gonsiorek, 1993, 1995; Grace, 1992; Hanley-Hackenbruck, 1989; Hencken & O'Dowd, 1977; L. Humphreys, 1972; Lee, 1977; A.D. Martin, 1982; McCarn & Fassinger, 1996; McDonald, 1982, 1983-1984; Minton & McDonald, 1983-1984; Plummer, 1975; Troiden, 1979, 1988, 1989; Troiden & Goode, 1980; Warren, 1974). Whereas some scholars addressed more psychological factors and others more social factors, a few incorporated both factors.

The first investigations of the coming-out process were on samples of gay men in the 1970s. The subjects typically described their experiences as a linear developmental process of self-discovery. They emphasized milestone events that marked turning points or progress in coming out such as their first feelings of same sex-gender attractions or the first time they labeled themselves as lesbian or gay (Rust, 2003).

Differences in the models include the number of stages (three to seven), developmental tasks within stages, how one gets from one stage to another, and the language that describes the process. However, all theorists described a similar overall process. And, they all included a series of linear, invariant, universal, and predictable steps or stages (Marszalek, Cashwell, Dunn, & Jones, 2004; K.M. Cohen & Savin-Williams, 1996). Four of the most common coming-out stages include (1) increasing acceptance of a lesbian or gay label as applying to one's self; (2) increasing change in feelings from negative to positive about this self identity; (3) increasing desire to inform lesbian, gay, and heterosexual persons of one's self identity; (4) increasing involvement with the lesbian and gay community (K.L. Jensen, 1999). Theorists also agreed that integration of same sex-gender sexual orientation into one's identity is an outcome of the process (Adelman, 1991). This last stage is a "goal" toward which movement through the other stages is directed. When one reaches the last stage one has attained advanced status or maturity (Rust, 2003).

These coming-out models have become reified or master models (Savin-Williams, 2001). Only a few of them, however, have been subjected to empirical investigation. This includes the Sexual Identity Formation Model (SIF) (Cass, 1979, 1984, 1996) and the inclusive model of sexual minority identity development (Fassinger & Miller, 1996; McCarn & Fassinger, 1996). As these two models have some research to back them up, they are presented in detail here.

Sexual Identity Formation Model

The Sexual Identity Formation model developed by Cass (1979, 1984, 1996) is the most well known of the coming-out models and the most extensively studied model. SIF provides a particularly comprehensive description of lesbian and gay identity development as it addresses changes at cognitive, emotional, and behavioral levels and integrates social and psychological factors. Cass based her model on interpersonal congruence theory, which assumes that stability and change in human behavior are influenced by the congruency or incongruency that exists in a person's interpersonal environment.

Changing perceptions make up an interpersonal matrix that accompanies the stages. Perceptions include those of one's self (e.g., "I am lesbian or gay"), those of one's behavior (e.g., "My behavior may represent same sex-gender sexual orientation"), and those of the responses of others (e.g., "Others think I am lesbian or gay"). The model includes the following six stages: Identity Confusion ("Who am I?"), Identity Comparison ("I am different"), Identity Tolerance ("I am probably lesbian or gay"), Identity Acceptance ("I am lesbian or gay"), Identity Pride ("I am lesbian or gay!"), and Identity Synthesis ("My sexual orientation is a part of me"). At each stage, conflict will occur within or between perceptions. For example, at stage 1

(Confusion), self-perception of same sex-gender thoughts, feelings, or behaviors conflict with earlier perceptions of a heterosexual orientation by one's self and others. Resolution of the conflict at each stage results in advancement to a new stage, resulting in increased congruency between perceptions of one's behavior, self-identity, and other's beliefs about one's self (Cass, 1979, 1996). The goal is to integrate one's identity into one's overall perception of self. Integration means there is consistency between perceptions of one's behavior and one's self, and between one's private and public identities (Rust, 2003). When one does not advance in this way, one is said to be in identity foreclosure (Cass, 1979, 1996). This happens when one experiences cognitive conflict about one's sexual identity and cannot accommodate new information related to being lesbian or gay. One's identity development is considered stalled when one is in foreclosure (Marszalek et al., 2004).

One starts out in a *prestage* in which one views one's self as heterosexual and does not think of one's self as lesbian or gay. Once questioning of one's sexual orientation begins, one is in the first stage, *Identity Confusion*. Here, a person begins to question whether information about same sex-gender sexual orientation is relevant to one's self. This may result in confusion and emotional turmoil, because this is not a normative developmental event (Cass, 1979, 1996). One does not anticipate this kind of confusion and often faces it alone (Reid, 1995). The confusion stage can last for years with a vague sense that something is different about one's self. Several possible pathways in each stage were identified by Cass (1979, 1996). One of three pathways is taken at the confusion stage. First, one accepts the relevance of the meaning of lesbian or gay and thinks this is desirable. Second, one accepts the relevance but not the desirability of the meaning. Third, one refuses to accept that this meaning is either relevant or desirable. And, one stops behaviors that could be viewed as lesbian or gay, blocks access to information about being lesbian or gay, and avoids any provocative situations that might counter these actions. One may use irrational or magical thinking to deny that one is lesbian or gay ("I must be going through a phase; I'm not really attracted to same sex-gender persons"). Or, the person does not think concretely enough to attach thoughts and emotions to being lesbian or gay (Marszalek & Cashwell, 1998). Both the second and third pathways are examples of identity foreclosure. If one does not foreclose because one cannot suppress the applicability of the meaning of lesbian or gay to one's self, or one accepts it, one enters Stage 2.

In the second stage, *Identity Comparison,* a person tentatively accepts the possibility of being lesbian or gay but is not yet able to define one's same sex-gender feelings and thoughts, and is still experiencing confusion. Even if one can provide a concrete description of feelings, cognitions, and behavior, to accept a lesbian or gay identity, abstract thinking is required (Marszalek et al., 2004). Cass (1979, 1996) thought that the confusion could result in a sense of alienation from one's family of origin, other support networks, and society generally. One of four pathways is taken. First, one develops a positive evaluation of one's self and anticipates high rewards. Second, one develops a positive evaluation of one's self but anticipates low rewards. And one rejects the relevance of the meaning of a lesbian or gay self-image (foreclosure). If this maneuver fails, however, one is likely to conclude that one is probably lesbian or gay. Third, one develops a negative evaluation of one's self but perceives high rewards. This can lead to the desire to assess one's self as heterosexual, not lesbian or gay. Fourth, one develops a negative evaluation of self and perceives low rewards. This can also lead to devaluation of a lesbian or gay self-identification and a positive evaluation of a heterosexual self-identification. If one does not foreclose, one will probably acknowledge a lesbian or gay identity. But, if this acknowledgment is accompanied by a negative self-evaluation, this can result in self-hatred and possibly self-destructive behaviors such as self-mutilation or suicide attempts.

In the third stage, *Identity Tolerance,* a person comes closer to committing to the new identity or acknowledging that one is "probably" lesbian or gay. One might begin to associate with other lesbian or gay persons, engage in same sex-gender sex, and develop new lesbian or gay support networks (Cass, 1979, 1996). According to Marszalek et al. (2004) persons at this stage use causal, if-then logic to reason that if they have same sex-gender feelings, thoughts, or actions then they are probably lesbian and gay. They tolerate this new understanding of themselves by acknowledging same sex-gender attractions but not necessarily viewing them positively. One of six pathways is taken. First, one develops a positive view of one's self as probably lesbian or gay and experiences positive contacts with other lesbian and gay persons. Second, one develops a positive view of one's self but experiences negative contacts with other lesbian and gay persons. These persons are devalued, and contact with them reduced (identity foreclosure). The conception of one's self as lesbian or gay is reevaluated as less positive. Third, one develops a negative view of one's self but experiences positive contacts with lesbian and gay persons. The positive contacts can lessen one's negative evaluation of one's self. Fourth, one develops a negative evaluation of one's self and experiences negative contacts with lesbian and gay persons. This can lead to avoidance of contacts (identity foreclosure), but a negative evaluation of one's self is modifiable if future contacts are positive. Fifth, one develops a positive evaluation of one's self as partly lesbian or gay and experiences negative contacts with lesbian and gay persons. This can lead to a devaluation of lesbian and gay persons (identity foreclosure). Sixth, one develops a positive evaluation of one's self and experiences positive contacts with lesbian and gay persons. This can lead to greater commitment as lesbian or gay (Cass, 1979, 1996).

In the fourth stage, *Identity Acceptance,* one begins to feel that being lesbian or gay is valid and may prefer being around others who are lesbian and gay. The new identity is disclosed to more persons, decreasing the incongruence between one's self-perceptions and the perceptions of others or between one's positive evaluation of one's self and negative evaluations of others. Continued "passing" as heterosexual at this stage is seen as identity foreclosure (Cass, 1979, 1996).

In the fifth stage, *Identity Pride,* all that is heterosexual is devalued, while all that is lesbian or gay is valued. Disclosure is likely to happen in all or most areas of one's life. Negative reactions to disclosures tend to reinforce one's negative perceptions of heterosexuals. One may also attempt to resolve the incongruence between self-acceptance and the devaluation by others through disregarding negative opinions (Cass, 1979, 1996). One may experience anger when one realizes that heterosexism, which was internalized from a heterosexist society, prevented an earlier coming out. One feels pride about being part of a community of other lesbian and gay persons, and one may become an activist on behalf of the community (Cass, 1979, 1996; Marszalek et al., 2004).

In the sixth stage, *Identity Synthesis,* one gradually modifies the us-against-them stance of the previous stage. One experiences less anger about heterosexism and realizes that not all heterosexuals are heterosexist. Contact increases with supportive heterosexuals, and some of them may be in one's support network. A person at this stage experiences congruence between perceptions of one's self and one's behavior and between one's private and public identities. More psychological integration is experienced, and being lesbian or gay is consolidated with the rest of one's identity (Cass, 1979, 1996). At this stage one may also contemplate existential issues, such as what it means to one's self to be lesbian or gay or how one's sexual identity affects one's relationships with others. This also calls for abstract thinking (Marszalek et al., 2004).

SIF has both theoretical and empirical validity but some of the research findings are mixed (Brady & Busse, 1994; Degges-White, Rice, & Myers, 2000; H. Levine, 1997; Whitman, Cormier, & Boyd, 2000). Brady and Busse (1994) studied the validity of the SIF model to predict stages of coming out. They found some support for the model's predictions and an association of the predictions with stage progression. The data suggested, however, that identity formation might be a two-stage process rather than a six-stage process. The first stage would combine stages 1 through 3 and the second stage would combine stages 4 through 6. The distinction between the two stages is whether one achieves a coherent self-identity as lesbian or gay and experiences a sense of belonging in society.

Johns and Probst (2004) studied 107 lesbian and 31 gay adults from convenience samples. The average age was thirty-four. Self-reported sexual orientation was 30.1 percent gay, 58 percent lesbian, 2.8 percent bisexual, and 5.6 percent heterosexual. A small number (3.5 percent) did not identify their sexual orientation. The majority was white (84 percent) with some from racial and ethnic groups. Four stages (3, 4, 5, and 6) from the Cass model were assessed. The findings showed that the lesbian and gay respondents did not discriminate among these stages. Instead, they viewed their identity as either reaching a state of being fully integrated into their sense of self or they were still in an unintegrated state. These researchers concluded that the six discrete linear stages in the Cass model were not supported.

From her own evaluation, Cass (1984) noted that not everyone completes development through all six stages. Some might stop progress at any point in the coming-out process. Mostly, however, Cass concluded that persons display the cognitive, behavioral, and affective dimensions that are identified at the different stages in her model. And if they do not, they will experience temporary or permanent identity foreclosure.

Halpin and Allen (2004) studied 425 males who reported sexual attraction to other men. They ranged in age from twelve to sixty-four (mean = 39.2). The sample was mostly from the United States and Australia with a few from other countries. They found support for the progressive nature of the SIF model (Cass, 1979, 1984). They also found significant relationships between stages of gay identity formation and happiness/sadness, satisfaction with life, self-esteem, and loneliness. However, there was also a U-shaped phenomenon, in which greater levels of distress were associated with the middle stages of Identity Tolerance and Identity Acceptance. The initial stages of Identity Confusion and Identity Comparison were similar to the late stages of Identity Pride and Identity Synthesis with relatively low levels of distress. It is in the middle stages that one does the most testing of one's gay identity development. One begins to disclose, and there may be stigma and harassment along with a lack of confidence in one's newly developing identity. The later stages are associated with a more subtle sense of sexual identity and the presence of relationships and support. At the later stages, the respondents were also less lonely, experienced increased satisfaction with life, were relatively happy, and had a strong sense of self-esteem.

In a study of youths by Dempsey (1994), coming to terms with an increasing awareness of a gay identity was associated with isolation, poor self-esteem, depression, suicidal ideation, and substance use. In contrast to the Halpin and Allen (2004) findings, the early stages were associated with the highest level of distress, but this modified as identity formation progressed. Stage 1 (Identity Confusion) can be a difficult stage (see Chapter 8). In addition, as discussed earlier, Cass noted that when in Stage 2 (Identity Comparison), it can be distressful to acknowledge being lesbian or gay, and one can experience a negative self-evaluation. This can lead to self-hatred and possibly self-destructive behaviors. As also found by Halpin and Allen, the respondents studied by Dempsey experienced relatively little distress at the later stages. This is also an expectation of the Cass model.

Inclusive Model of Sexual Minority Identity Development

The coming-out model developed by Cass and other earlier models focused on the internal developmental tasks in the early stages of coming out and on creating a public and politicized identity in the later stages. These models were heavily influenced by the politics of the Stonewall riots, the gay rights movement, and the women's movement. The second identity model to be described here, the inclusive model of sexual minority identity development, is separated into two developmental tracks: individual sexual identity and group membership identity. Individual sexual identity focuses on the internal process of confirming same sex-gender emotional and sexual wishes and incorporating them into one's identity. Group membership identity focuses on the context in which the internal processes happen and one's attitudes and feelings about lesbian and gay persons, non-lesbian and gay persons, and one's self. Initially, empirical validation of this model was based on the experiences of lesbians, but the model has evolved to address the experiences of gay persons with greater emphasis on sexual exploration and activity.

Although persons do not progress through the two tracks simultaneously, addressing developmental tasks on one track can trigger movement on the other track. However, progress in group membership identity does not always imply simultaneous progress in individual sexual identity (Fassinger & Miller, 1996; McCarn & Fassinger, 1996). For example, as suggested in Chapter 1, a woman developing a feminist consciousness may develop a positive view of lesbians but does not yet (and may never) identify herself as a member of this group.

This model has the following four phases: awareness, exploration, deepening/commitment, and internalization/synthesis. Each of these phases occurs in both branches of the model, as described in the sections that follow.

Phase 1—Awareness

Individual Sexual Identity. One is cognizant of feeling or being different from the heterosexual norm and from what one predicted for one's self. Affective states may include confusion, bewilderment, and fear.

Group Membership Identity. One becomes aware of heterosexism and the lesbian and gay community. Falling in love with a person of the same sex-gender (an individual identity process) may trigger these realizations and produce bewilderment and confusion.

Phase 2—Exploration

Individual Sexual Identity. One experiences strong feelings, often sexual, for others of the same sex-gender or for a particular person of the same sex-gender. Despite these feelings, one may not explore sexual involvements. Affective states may include wonderment, ebullience, and longing.

Group Membership Identity. One explores knowledge about lesbian and gay persons as a group, one's attitudes about this group, and one's possible membership in this group. Clarity about one's attitudes, however, can be difficult to attain because of one's previous heterosexist attitudes or limited access to correct information. Anger, anxiety, and guilt may emerge because of one's own participation in heterosexism, but one can also experience exhilaration, curiosity, and joy in becoming acquainted with other lesbian and gay persons.

Phase 3—Deepening/Commitment

Individual Sexual Identity. One experiences a deepened commitment to self-knowledge, solidification of sexual identity, and a sense of self-fulfillment. Not every woman or man at this phase, however, will commit to only women or men as sexual partners. Instead, some may commit to both women and men. Affective states may include anger and sadness but in addition acceptance and self-assurance.

Group Membership Identity. One experiences a deepened commitment to personal involvement with the lesbian and gay community as a reference group. Awareness of oppression increases, as does the awareness of consequences of involvement in an oppressed group. Not every lesbian or gay person, however, will experience the same intensity of commitment to the lesbian or gay culture or of deprecation of heterosexist society. Yet, many will likely share some affective states such as excitement and pride as well as rage and internal conflict.

Phase 4—Internalization/Synthesis

Individual Sexual Identity. One experiences a deepened self-acceptance of sexual desire for and love of a person of the same sex-gender. This becomes part of one's identity, along with a sense of internal consistency and an unwillingness to change course. Affective states may be more consistent such as contentment and pride. Public identity and the meaning of being a lesbian or gay person in one's society are also likely to be reformulated in this phase.

Group Membership Identity. One fully internalizes one's identity as a member of an oppressed group and develops a sense of one's self as lesbian or gay across contexts. Individual lesbian and gay persons are distinguished from stereotypes about them. Though it is likely that some disclosures will happen, one may or may not become politicized or make public disclosures. Affective states of rage, anxiety, and insecurity turn into directed anger, dedication, fulfillment, comfort, security, and self-love (Fassinger & Miller, 1996; McCarn & Fassinger, 1996).

This inclusive model shares aspects of other stage models in that the four phases are progressive in nature with the final favorable outcome being integration of individual and group identities into one's total self-concept. However, how this model differs is that it does not mandate political activism and universal disclosure as necessary for an integrated identity (Horowitz & Newcomb, 2001).

The relationship of self-esteem and phases of this model was studied by Swann and Spivey (2004). The sample included 205 females aged sixteen to twenty-four. Most (61 percent) defined themselves as lesbian or questioning. Others were on a continuum of bisexual-mostly lesbian, bisexual equally lesbian and heterosexual, and bisexual-mostly heterosexual. Only phase four (internalization/synthesis), including both individual sexual identity and group membership identity, was positively correlated with self-esteem. The first three phases were negatively associated with self-esteem. Hence, those at phase four exhibited higher levels of self-esteem than those who were either just becoming aware of their lesbian identity or who were in the exploration process, still searching for a sexual identity that fit. Those who had gone through some initial exploration of their sexual identity and internalized a sense of a lesbian self demonstrated higher levels of self-esteem. However, self-esteem was highest when individual sexual identity and group membership identity were at the same levels. Those who understood themselves as lesbian but had little or no affiliation with a larger peer group emerged as the group with the lowest self-esteem.

Timing of the Coming-Out Process

Researchers have identified average chronological ages at which persons achieve milestone events in coming out (Rust, 2003). Anhalt and Morris (2003) and others have summarized some of these findings. For lesbians and bisexual women the average age of first *awareness of same sex-gender attraction* has been reported as happening between ages ten and eleven (e.g., D'Augelli & Hershberger, 1993; Herdt & Boxer, 1993; Sears, 1991). For gay and bisexual males this event occurs on average between ages nine and thirteen (D'Augelli, 1991; D'Augelli & Hershberger, 1993; Herdt & Boxer, 1993; Newman & Muzzonigro, 1993; Sears, 1991). *First sexual experiences* usually occur between ages thirteen and sixteen for gay youths (D'Augelli, 1991; Herdt & Boxer, 1993; Sears, 1991) whereas for lesbian youths they occur later, around age twenty (e.g., Bell, Weinberg, & Hammersmith, 1981; Chapman & Brannock, 1987; Coleman, 1981- 1982b; Jay & Young, 1979; Klein et al., 1985; Mays & Cochran, 1988; McDonald, 1982; Saghir & Robins, 1973; Schaefer, 1977; Troiden, 1988; M.S. Weinberg, Williams, & Pryor 1994). Other studies reported earlier ages for lesbians such as mostly in the late teens or early twenties (J. Bradford & Ryan, 1991) or between the ages of fifteen and seventeen (Herdt & Boxer, 1993; Sears, 1991). *Self-labeling* occurs between ages fourteen and seventeen for lesbian youths (D'Augelli & Hershberger, 1993; Sears, 1991) and between ages twelve and seventeen for gay youths (D'Augelli, 1991; D'Augelli & Hershberger, 1993; Newman & Muzzonigro, 1993; Sears, 1991). Age of *first disclosure* of sexual orientation happens between ages sixteen and nineteen for lesbian youths (D'Augelli & Hershberger, 1993; Sears; 1991) and between ages sixteen and twenty for gay youths (D'Augelli, 1991; D'Augelli & Hershberger, 1993; Newman & Muzzonigro, 1993; Sears, 1991).

These average ages of reaching coming-out stages, reflected in absolute time, conceal variation among individuals (Rust, 2003). Relative time tells a different story (Savin-Williams, 1990a). D'Augelli (1991) found considerable variability in the relative timing on all milestones of identity development for gay persons, or how long each step took. The time ranged from one to twenty years for awareness of same-gender feelings, five to twenty-two years for first sexual experience, eleven to twenty-one years for self-labeling as gay, fifteen to twenty-three years for first disclosure, and twelve to twenty-four years for initiating one's first intimate relationship.

COMING OUT AS BISEXUAL

Coming out as bisexual is a more ambiguous status than coming out as lesbian or gay (Matteson, 1996a). Bisexual persons are trying to come to terms with their attractions to both women and men but often do not have accurate role models for these dual attractions. For example, the media portrays bisexual women and men as experiencing sex with both genders and usually in short-term liaisons. Women and men who are coming out as bisexual may think that such a pattern is necessary to establish a bisexual identity. Or, they may feel pressure to play out the hybrid conceptualization of bisexual identity to qualify as bisexual: equal parts of same sex-gender and other sex-gender attraction. However, bisexual women and men rarely report having equal attraction to women and men (less than one in four). No typical process or pattern fits all bisexual persons (Fox, 1995; Rust, 1992, 1993). They may have relationships with both women and men, but with only one person at a time or have relationships with both during the same time period (Klein, 1990). In addition, emotional attractions and sexual attractions can differ regarding women and men. For example, one may feel emotionally closer to women and sexually more attracted to men (Rust, 2003). Books that present more realistic views of coming out as bisexual are helpful (e.g., Hutchins & Káahumanu, 1991).

In terms of a coming-out process, only a few developmental models of bisexual identity development exist. The Klein Sexual Orientation Grid (Klein 1993), discussed in Chapter 1, can be applied. Another model came from longitudinal data based on a sample of bisexual women and men in San Francisco (M.S. Weinberg et al., 1994; M.S. Weinberg, Williams, & Prior, 1998). Four broad stages of bisexual identity development were proposed based on the most common experiences of the sample:

1. *Initial Confusion.* Experiencing incomprehensible and unsettling sexual feelings for both women and men and questioning of one's heterosexual identity; uncertainty about which sexual category one fits in; feeling isolated.
2. *Finding and Applying the Label to One's Self, Discovering the Label Bisexual.* Discovering that sex with both women and men is pleasurable; realizing that one's sexual attractions are too strong to deny; lessening of confusion; learning of bisexual organizations; seeking social support.
3. *Settling into the Identity.* Complete self-labeling; greater self-acceptance; more consolidated sense of bisexual self-identification; not fully clear on the specifics of what a bisexual person does; continued seeking of support.
4. *Continued Uncertainty.* Intermittent periods of doubt and uncertainty; lack of social validation and support; absence of bisexual role models and community; relationship confusions such as not being able to turn attractions into sexual links; managing multiple relationships; settling into an exclusive sexual relationship; and weaker sexual attractions for the other sex-gender or lack of sexual relations with the other sex-gender.

The initial confusion may last for years until something leads to the second stage of application of the label of bisexual to one's attractions (M.S. Weinberg et al., 1994). Before settling on a bisexual identity, women and men may first identify as lesbian or gay and move back and forth several times between one of those identities and a heterosexual identity (Fox, 1995; Rust, 1995). Some women and men are self-identified as lesbian or gay for years before they realize that they are bisexual. The third stage, settling into the identity, may not happen for years following labeling and self-identification as bisexual and the time of the first sexual attractions to or sexual involvements with both sex-genders.

Many bisexual women and men remain in a state of uncertainty about the permanency of their bisexual identity, especially when they have no sexual involvement with both sex-genders. It appears that lack of closure may be part of what bisexual persons come to accept (M.S. Weinberg et al., 1994, 1998).

A coming-out model, developed by M. Bradford (2004), for bisexual persons came from a study of ten men and ten women, ages twenty-two to fifty-four. All self-identified as bisexual, although one-third had originally identified as lesbian or gay. The stages for coming out as bisexual included the following:

1. *Question Reality* (struggle with doubt, but experience a successful outcome
2. *Invent Reality* (search for meaning, create one's own meaning
3. *Maintain Identity* (encounter isolation and invisibility, experience a sense of community and increased self-reliance)
4. *Transform Adversity* (participate in social action, experience personal satisfaction)

Although the respondents studied by M. Bradford struggled to cope with prejudice, they expressed certainty about their bisexual identity. This is in contrast to other descriptions of bisexual identity development as continuing in transition (Ochs, 1996), or bisexuals having less certain identities (Rust, 1995; M.S. Weinberg et al., 1994).

Fifteen Japanese Americans, ages twenty to forty, were studied by J.F. Collins (2000). Based on the experiences of these respondents the researcher developed a coming-out model for persons who are bisexual and biracial:

1. *Questioning/Confusion.* They are aware of their differences and may experience feelings of alienation and the question "What am I?" This creates a period of confusion and guilt. However, some may accept only those views that result in a more positive identity and filter out those that are devaluing or marginalizing.
2. *Refusal/Suppression.* They select one identity over others and attempt to suppress or deny what they have rejected. They keep a certain reference group or look for other reference groups. The family may be the most important of these groups, but a sense of who they are and what they can become comes from subgroups, such as other sexual minorities.

3. *Infusion/Exploration.* They reach out to others so they can integrate missing parts of themselves. They move away from the dominant culture/identity and toward their new culture/identity.
4. *Resolution/Acceptance.* This is an exhilarating phase of "I am who I am," which is a multiple identity. They value all their identities and develop a secure and integrated identity.

Once women and men identify as bisexual, some of the internal and social issues they may face include feeling different from heterosexual women and men and from lesbian and gay persons, isolation and feeling a lack of community, dealing with prejudice and discrimination, and apprehension about disclosing attractions to both women and men (Coleman, 1981-1982a, 1985a,b; Fox, 1996; Nichols, 1989). Another social reality is that lesbian and gay communities often put pressure on bisexual women and men to adopt a lesbian or gay identity (M.S. Weinberg et al., 1994). If bisexual persons continue to feel confusion about themselves and are trying to figure out what they really are, they may give into this pressure. However, this is done at the cost of denying the full range of their sexual identity (Rust, 1992, 2003). Some bisexual persons choose on their own, however, to move to a same sex-gender identification. Stokes, Damon, and McKirnan (1997) studied bisexual men who made a voluntary shift to a gay identity over two time periods, separated by about a year. This included a third of their sample of 216 men. Compared to those who did not make this shift, these men reported less current and lifetime sexual partners who were women. They also had their first heterosexual sexual activity at a later age. At the first contact with these men, they also reported that they were more likely to fantasize about men during masturbation.

COMING OUT AS TRANSGENDER

Coming out for transgender persons is a process of experimenting with another sex-gender identity until they discover the most comfortable "fit." This experimentation often starts early in life. The sixty-five males studied by Gagné et al. (1997) reported early recollections of feeling that their sex or sex-gender was "wrong" for them or did not "fit." Sixteen of these males reported that they wanted to be girls or knew that they really were girls during early childhood. Of those who cross-dressed, four wished they could be girls during early childhood and two during adolescence. Whether cross-dressing began in childhood (sixteen), adolescence (twenty), or adulthood (sixteen), it allowed a way to experiment with feminine sex-gender presentation.

Male children uncomfortable with their sex-gender liked to participate in play and other activities with girls. However, most of them were labeled "sissies" at home and at school. This led to extreme stigmatization and accusations. Insults from family members affected self-esteem and self-concept more than when they came from peers and others outside of the family. Other consequences included isolation and sometimes abuse. They thought that how they felt and behaved was wrong, sick, or deviant (Gagné et al., 1997). They also experienced feelings of being different, guilt, self-loathing, confusion, and anxiety about being discovered. They also wondered how they would fit into the world.

Cross-dressing and cross sex-gender behaviors are apparently tolerable in families up to the "toddler" stage. However, at that point, adults and other children pressured male children who display these behaviors to follow traditional sex-gender norms and stereotypes of masculine behavior. Many attempt to conform to this pressure. In adulthood, some hope for a "cure" by getting married or joining the military. Others engage in masculine activities hoping to develop proper masculine identities. Some become hypermasculine, and many choose physically strenuous or high-risk jobs (Gagné et al., 1997). However, enactments of masculinity fail to create a masculine sex-gender identity (Gagné & Tewksbury, 1999).

It helps to get knowledge about transgender identity and identity symbols. These resources are available in many sources including online Web sites, TV shows, movies, magazine articles, and medical and psychological reports (Gagné et al., 1997). Exposure to these resources can raise consciousness about sex-gender alternatives and counter confusion and shame (Gagné & Tewksbury, 1999). Just learning about the possibilities of SRS encourages some transgender persons to reassess their identities and evokes a feeling that they have a place in the world. Transgender magazines and online computer services are also useful for finding role models and mentors. However, these mediums sometimes raise more issues than they resolve. One can discover, for example, that one is quite different from others who label themselves in the same way. And, some identity symbols imply that transgender persons are "freaks" (Gagné & Tewksbury, 1999; Gagné et al., 1997).

Those who opt to go further in changing sex-gender go through a coming-out process. Coming out for the persons studied by Gagné et al. (1997) and Gagné and Tewsbury (1999) was defined as "crossing over" from one sex-gender category to another. This is a complicated process because of the changes in both in sex-gender and genital composition. The process also entails other factors such as (1) dealing with the struggles between society's negative sanctions and what feels natural; (2) discovering names for one's feelings; and (3) finding others who are experiencing similar feelings, the most common factor leading to acceptance of one's identity (Gagné et al., 1997).

A process of coming out as transgender and moving toward SRS was proposed by Devor (1997). It includes fourteen stages and was based on her study of forty-five FM participants. Several stages are repeated at specific points in slightly altered forms and accomplish different tasks. The stages include the following:

1. "Abiding Anxiety." Feeling uncomfortable.
2. "Identity Confusion." Questioning the fit between one's assigned sex-gender and biological sex.
3. "Identity Comparison." Exploring female identities.
4. "Discovery." Realization of transsexualism.
5. "Identity Confusion." Doubting whether one is transsexual.
6. "Identity Comparison." Testing one's transsexualism with a transsexual group.
7. "Identity Tolerance." Identification as likely "transsexual."
8. "Delay." Attempting to confirm a "transsexual" identity or waiting for circumstances to push them through the transition.
9. "Identity Acceptance." Identifying as "transsexual."
10. "Delay." Letting go of previous female identity; "transsexual" identity taking hold; and preparing for transition such as saving money to pay for surgery and developing a support network.

11. "Transition." Experiencing sex-gender changes, and sex reassignment.
12. "Identity Acceptance" reviewed again. Establishing an identity as a "transsexual" man.
13. "Integration." Living as a man whose "transexuality" is not noticed unless revealed to selected others.
14. "Identity Pride." Publicly living as transsexual and may be participating in "transsexual" activism.

The participants in Devor's (1997) study were at various stages. Some were still living as women while others had progressed to hormonal therapy and/or surgery. All self-identified as "transsexual."

Sakai (2003) interviewed eleven "transsexual" men about their experiences and thoughts and feelings about their identities and FM transitions. The following six major themes emerged:

1. "Living Female." Adapting initially to their female sex statuses by adopting feminine social roles or identities. Trying to fit in as girls and women through dress, behavior, or romantic relationships with men. Some made efforts to live as women within lesbian communities.
2. "Developing a Male Identity." Expressing identities as men and deciding what kind of men to be. Behaviors and traits they viewed as masculine helped solidify their male identities.
3. "Developing a Transgender Identity." Recognizing or exhibiting a "transsexual" identity.
4. "Physical Transition." Experiencing feelings about their bodies before transition and the current physical transition to a masculinized body.
5. "Stigma and Privilege." Taking on new privileged social roles as male and dropping obsolete roles such as a stigmatized lesbian identity.
6. "Factors That Slowed, Delayed, or Facilitated FM Transitions." Experiencing factors that slowed or delayed FM transitions such as a lack of information or fear of loss and factors that helped move a transition along such as decision-making strategies and efforts to attain support (Sakai, 2003).

When they decided to move into public arenas, the FM transgender persons studied by Gagné et al. (1997) thought carefully about their initial public excursions. They chose safe places where disapproval was unlikely and where a quick entry and exit could be made. They often first went to gatherings specifically for transgender persons. They also went to gay community events, bars, or other locations, although they did not want to be perceived as gay. When in the gay community, they may be viewed as marginal members, but they can experiment both with sex-gender identity and sex. They can work on perfecting a feminine persona. And for the first time they may receive responses to themselves as "women" or "ladies," which they strongly desire. They may also experience opportunities for sexual exploration, some of which might occur with "punters" or men who do not want to participate in sex with either a man or a woman but who might agree to participate in sex with what they perceive is a man attired as a woman (Woodhouse, 1989).

Chapter 3

Critique of Coming-Out Models

Traditional linear models of coming out clarify the developmental processes that many persons coming out face. Many persons understand their own coming-out experiences as consisting of steps toward an end stage or goal as suggested by the models. However, these models have notable limitations that are discussed here. More detailed critiques exist in others sources (e.g., McCarn & Fassinger, 1996).

PROBLEMATIC RESEARCH METHODS AND SAMPLES

Most coming-out models evolved from clinical and anecdotal data and the stages were usually conceptualized after data collection (Gruskin, 1999). Few models were tested and the research was flawed for models that were tested (Fassinger, 1994). The samples were small and not representative, research designs were weak, and the measures unsound or undeveloped (Evans & Levine, 1990; Fassinger, 1994). The research samples were also mostly limited to white, middle-class, self-identified lesbian and gay respondents willing to participate in research studies. Few of the models addressed or explained the interaction of sexual identity development with other significant factors such as social class, culture, race and ethnicity, sex-gender, different age groups, or bisexual and transgender identities (Gonsiorek, 1995; Harry, 1993). The models are also dated. Early findings may not generalize beyond the cohorts that entered adolescence in the 1960s and 1970s (Herdt, 1992).

Coming Out and Disclosures
© 2007 by The Haworth Press, Inc. All rights reserved.
doi:10.1300/5423_04

SMOOTH STAGES OR DISORDERED PROCESS?

The expectation in linear coming-out models is that persons move one step at a time in sequence until they reach the final and most "mature" stage. All prior activity is to be directed toward this final stage (Rust, 1993). Deviations from this progression are overlooked (Horowitz & Newcomb, 2001) or no optional paths are acknowledged. Stalled progression is interpreted as regression, foreclosure, or immaturity (Rust, 2003).

Researchers and theorists typically noted that not all persons proceeded through every stage or in the predicted order (e.g., McDonald, 1982; Coleman, 1981-1982b; Cass, 1979, 1990). However, these deviations were not viewed as invalidating the underlying linear process (Rust, 1993). However, others think that the appearance of smoothness and order is hypothetical (T.S. Stein, 1993). Persons can experience stages in different orders, skip stages, repeat stages, remain in one stage indefinitely, backtrack, or abort the coming-out process altogether and retain a heterosexual identity (Gonsiorek, 1993; Rust, 1993; Savin-Williams & Diamond, 1999). Some persons may revisit stages and attain new perspectives on their coming-out process (Olson & King, 1995). And, instead of one path from which there is deviation, there are probably a variety of paths of coming out. For example, some lesbian and gay persons reported no memory of any steps of a coming-out process. They were never in doubt about who and what they were; they were always "out" to themselves and others. Some who reported a sudden revelation of their sexual orientation were comfortable with it overnight (Savin-Williams, 1990a). Yet, no matter what alternative paths are reported, the exemplar of coming out in a linear series of stages persists in the literature (Harry, 1993).

MORAL PRESCRIPTIONS

Linear models are prescriptive of what is supposed to happen during coming out (Gruskin, 1999). Movement toward the end state is progress, whereas movement in the reverse direction is regression. This conceptualization of coming out makes these models prescriptive and moral in terms of the rightness and direction of progression (Rust, 2003).

POLITICALIZATION AND MANDATORY DISCLOSURE

Activism and a politicized public identity signify developmental maturity in some coming-out models. These models presume widespread public disclosure in the final stage; a lack of disclosure or activism signals developmental arrest. However, the social realities of diverse groups or contexts (e.g., work settings, family situations, racial and ethnic heritage, geographical locations) are not taken into account nor is the fact of whether one has support systems (McCarn & Fassinger, 1996; Fassinger, 1991; Fassinger & Miller, 1996).

COMPLETED PROCESS OR CONTINUING ONE?

Linear models suggest that once one reaches the end stage, identity development ends. So once persons come out, they have discovered their true sexuality and, therefore, will not change again (Rust, 2003). However, the reality for most persons is that coming out is a lifelong process (Esterberg, 1997). Even persons who are certain about their sexual identity and feel comfortable with it may experience changes in their sexual attractions and behaviors and perhaps change back later (Rosario et al., 1996; Rust, 2003) (See Chapter 1).

SEX-GENDER

Most coming-out models are male-centric as they were based on male samples (Savin-Williams, 2001). However, only a few young lesbians and bisexual women were discovered by Diamond (1996) to follow the male-oriented "master narrative" of identity development. In a study of 164 young lesbian and gay adults (78 women, 86 men; ages 17 to 25), men reached all coming-out milestones earlier than women except for disclosure (Savin-Williams & Diamond, 2000). In addition, women's awareness of same sex-gender attraction for other women usually begins before sex, in an affectionate link with another woman (Esterberg, 1994; Gramick, 1984; Schippers, 1990; Sears, 1989). For men, this awareness more often occurs after sexual experiences (not necessarily in the context of an affectionate link). Same sex-gender attractions, once experienced by females, are less threatening for them than they are for males (de Monteflores & Schultz, 1978; Marmor, 1980). This difference may result from becoming aware of their sexual identity at later ages (Paul, 1984) and because their sexual links are less stigmatized than those between men (Marmor, 1980; Paul, 1984; Sohier, 1985-1986).

A sample of several hundred (206) lesbian and bisexual youths, aged fourteen to twenty-one, was drawn by D'Augelli (2003) from social and recreational settings. Nearly three-quarters of the females had sexual contact with a male, with heterosexual contact often preceding same sex-gender sexual contact. D'Augelli thought that this could be a reflection of greater pressures for females to engage in traditional dating, the greater fluidity of female sexual identity development, less rigid sex-gender concepts for females, and lower visibility than gay persons. Females also have greater latitude to express emotional and physical affection for other women. Savin-Williams and Diamond (2000) suggested that because expressions of affection between females are customary behaviors they may not interpret these expressions as meaning they are lesbian or bisexual. To adopt a lesbian or bisexual identity, they may need other kinds of interpersonal situations to reinterpret their feelings. Lesbian and bisexual women are more likely than gay persons to be influenced by current circumstances and choices in their same sex-gender behaviors instead of by early-life predictors or same sex-gender desires. Sexual questioning for women is more likely initially triggered by ideological factors, social reference groups, and a rejection of or commitment to particular social/political rules (Blumstein & Schwartz, 1990; Cass, 1990; Esterberg, 1994; Nichols, 1990; Whisman, 1996).

Not all males follow the master or dominant narrative. It may fit particular cohorts of males (Plummer, 1995), but there may be significant intracohort variation in the pathways taken (Cohler & Hostetler, 2002). Dubé (1997) found that although many older white gay persons followed the male-oriented "master narrative," younger cohorts of white gay and bisexual men are less likely to follow it. For example, many younger men identify themselves as gay or bisexual before engaging in same sex-gender sexual encounters. The classical ordering of developmental milestones also fit only two of the gay youths studied by Savin-Williams (1998a). Nearly 40 percent of these youths did not engage in same sex-gender sex until after they labeled their sexual identity as gay or bisexual. For 30 percent, disclosure of their sexual identity to another person happened before experiencing same sex-gender sexual encounters; 15 percent reported feeling good about their sexual identity before experiencing same sex-gender sexual encounters. Dubé (1997) noted, however, that these cohort changes are less prevalent among Latino, Asian American, and African American gay and bisexual youths.

DISABILITIES AND CHRONIC ILLNESSES

Disabilities and chronic illnesses are rarely addressed in LGBT literature. However, these factors further stigmatize LGBT persons and interfere with their identity development. Lack of or inconsistent transmission of LGBT culture creates difficulties in developing a LGBT identity, a sense of group cohesion, and a sense of culture (Linton, 1998). If persons with disabilities or chronic illnesses want to move outside their families to meet others in LGBT communities, access to these communities may be limited if one must depend on family members for mobility. Opportunities for these persons to get involved with LGBT communities or develop friendships may be hampered even more if families do not approve of their sexual orientation (Greene & Croom, 2000).

RACIAL OR ETHNIC CONTEXTS

Research on the identity development process is beginning to include samples that are more diverse in race and ethnicity including African Americans (Greene, 1986, 1994a,c; Icard, 1985-1986; Loiacano, 1989); Asian and Pacific Islander Americans (Chan, 1987, 1989, 1995; Gock, 1985, 1992; Wooden, Kawaski, & Mayeda, 1983); Native Americans (Allen, 1984); Hispanic Americans (Espin, 1987; Hidalgo, 1984); and Third World lesbians and gay persons (Morales, 1983). However, considerable diversity exists between ethnic and racial groups and within the groups according to generation, the importance of continuation of the family line, assimilation into the dominant culture, and the meanings applied to sexuality (Greene, 1994a).

Many Latino, African American, and Asian American lesbian and gay persons are in a struggle between who they are and who they feel others in their cultures want them to be (Savin-Williams, 1998a). They frequently experience the dilemma of managing conflicting allegiances (Cazenave, 1984; Gock, 1985; Mays, 1985). Most of the conflict happens following disclosures (see Chapters 5 and 6).

IMMIGRATION AND ACCULTURATION

Coming-out models do not consider the issues faced by those who immigrate from other countries to the United States. However, moving into a new culture can be central to how identity issues are negotiated. In studies of immigrant lesbians, it was observed that how one was a lesbian before migration may not transfer to the new cultural context with new social expectations. One must ascertain how to be a lesbian in the new context (Espin, 1997; González & Espin, 1996). In addition, if one is from a background other than European, one will be acculturated as a "subordinated" person (Espin, 1997).

If not acculturated, new immigrants may not have contact with lesbian and gay communities or lesbian and gay persons in their own communities. Even with these contacts there will very likely be conflict in loyalties as ties to one's homeland usually remain strong. And, if immigration is recent, there may especially be a dependence on family members and one's racial or ethnic community for emotional and possibly economic support (Espin, 1987).

SOCIAL CONTEXTS AND SOCIAL CONSTRUCTS

Linear developmental models are essentialist and usually ignore contextual factors. They assume that sexual orientation is a core trait to be discovered, acknowledged, and accepted (Gruskin, 1999). It is established early in life and represents one's true self. In a sample of older LGB adults studied by Cohler and Hosteller (2002), many presumed that sexual orientation was a fixed and essential characteristic. They believed they had always been lesbian or gay.

What is missing in the essentialist conceptualization of coming out is that the process is mediated by environmental or contextual factors

(J. Hollander & Haber, 1992). Perspectives that address the social context include symbolic interactionist (Schneider, 1986); interactionist (Plummer, 1975); life span (D'Augelli, 1994); ecological (J. Hollander & Haber, 1992); sociological (Harry, 1993); and social constructionist (Kitzinger & Wilkinson, 1995; Rust, 1993). The social constructionist perspective particularly challenges the essentialist perspective because identity is not seen as an intrinsic quality but rather as a social construction or an interpretation of personal and sociopolitical experiences. This view also notes that lesbian or gay identity can only arise in societies in which these categories are acknowledged (Cass, 1984). And even where acknowledged certain experiences may be necessary to construct one's identity such as the lesbian and gay rights movement, new romantic or sexual relationships with same sex-gender persons, or the introduction of a bisexual person into one's life (Rust, 1996).

The social constructionist perspective also emphasizes continuing exploration and fluidity of identity and does not dictate that one must lock oneself into a life script prematurely (Bohan & Russell, 1999). Sexual identity is not viewed as a static self-construct. As the identity we construct is not an underlying essence of us, both the identity and its expression may change over time and as experiences change (Horowitz & Newcomb, 2001). The constructionist perspective acknowledges the benefits provided by the essentialist perspective on coming out, but it expands our understandings of the influence of other factors on coming out (G.M. Russell & Bohan, 1999).

HISTORICAL EFFECTS

Our historical location is another aspect that can influence or play into the construction of coming out. It can open up or suppress one's awareness of and access to others like oneself. Parks (1999) interviewed lesbians born between 1917 and 1972. The internal progression from self-awareness to self-identification was linked to awareness of and access to other lesbians and lesbian-identified events. Awareness and access were hampered by generational location: the pre-Stonewall era, age forty-five and older; the gay liberation era, ages thirty to forty-four; and the gay rights era, age thirty and younger. Awareness and access were easier for women in the gay rights era because they did not experience the severe isolation and silence experienced by women in the pre-Stonewall era or the condemnation experienced by women in the liberation era. How to be a lesbian is also influenced by historical location. For example, in the "old dyke world" being a lesbian meant developing a social identity based on sex-gender roles or a butch-femme adaptation. However, in the newer lesbian-feminist culture, women tend not to adopt an identity based on sex-gender roles (T.S. Stein, 1997).

This overview of some of the limitations of the coming-out models indicates that they overlook important factors for many LGBT persons. Hence, these models do not fit everyone.

Chapter 4

Coming Out Across the Life Span

COMING OUT IN ADOLESCENCE

Youths are developing in numerous ways (Turner & Helms, 1995). Yet, most of them adjust to biological, cognitive, psychological, and social changes (Germain, 1991). And, they rarely experience a "crisis" often thought to be inevitable at this stage of life (Jackson & Sullivan, 1994). Yet, developmental tasks of this life period are transforming and often stressful (B.F. Anderson, 1998; Fontaine & Hammond, 1996). In addition, although coming out involves similar processes at all ages, unique issues accompany this life event when it happens in adolescence.

Adolescence is a time of exploration and experimentation, but LGBT youths also confront the daunting task of exiting from their heterosexual socialization and creating a new self (D'Augelli, 1996b; Mallon, 1998a). Many youths may experience confusion while trying to discover the meaning of their emotional and sexual feelings and experiences. Most of these youths will eventually end up defining themselves as heterosexual (Fontaine & Hammond, 1996), but others will experience intense and unrelenting emotional or sexual attractions to the same sex-gender. And after additional experiences discussed here, they will move on to claim a lesbian, gay, or bisexual identity, although for some this is not easy to do (Savin-Williams & Diamond, 1999).

Feeling Different

Researchers have speculated that personal awareness of same sex-gender attractions generally predates puberty (D'Augelli 1996b).

Coming Out and Disclosures
© 2007 by The Haworth Press, Inc. All rights reserved.
doi:10.1300/5423_05

Many lesbian and gay youths report during this time that they feel different from other peers and may think of themselves as outsiders (J. Hunter & Schaecher, 1987). In retrospective studies of adults, over three-quarters of lesbian and gay persons reported a feeling of being different during their childhood and adolescence (Bell et al., 1981; Troiden, 1979). In Savin-Williams's (1998a) work on three samples of gay youths, ages fourteen to twenty-five, most of them, from an early age or from earliest childhood memories, felt that they were different from other boys their age. They experienced an overwhelming desire to be in the company of males and to touch, smell, see, and hear masculinity. These same sex-gender attractions did not seem chosen to most of these boys, but instead seemed natural or an integral part of themselves. They did not feel particularly surprised by them.

At first, the gay youths studied by Savin-Williams (1998a) could not understand why their male friends were not as preoccupied as they were with other males. However, eventually, most of them recognized that their preoccupations and feelings were not typical of other boys. And, they discovered that they should not talk openly about their attractions. They also heard from parents, friends, religious leaders, and teachers that their attractions were sick, wrong, evil, or sinful. None of these youths, however, adopted these negative views.

Many other boys studied by Savin-Williams (1998a) attributed their sense of difference to their sex-gender nonconformity or feminine appearance, behavior, and interests. Most of these boys were not interested in typical male endeavors such as competitive and aggressive sports, and they strongly disliked cultural definitions of masculinity. Perhaps because of common interests such as the arts, manners, and attraction to boys, they developed friendships with girls. They felt they were expressing their real and natural selves, but they were frequently the targets of castigation and ostracism for their nonconformity.

Others who felt different were boys who did not adopt the standard masculine characteristics, but neither did they demonstrate feminine traits. They resembled heterosexual peers who were neither particularly masculine nor feminine in behavior. During much of their childhood, these youths were loners or socialized with one or two male friends. Many felt that they faded into the background and did not stand out among their peers. Though they were not subject to the vicious, pervasive verbal abuse that their feminine counterparts received, they were the targets of ridicule because of their lack of ability in athletic pursuits or their unconventional behavior or intelligence. Another and much smaller group (about one of ten) was nearly indistinguishable from masculine heterosexual boys the same age. They participated in typical masculine pursuits, especially individual and team sports (Savin-Williams, 1998a).

Puberty

Unless their behaviors varied from expected sex-gender behavior parents allowed teens in early adolescence a detour from "normal" development. This phase was seen as temporary and attraction for persons of the same sex-gender was seen as hero-worshiping behaviors, or part of intimate friendships or adolescent crushes. Although these interpretations might soothe parents' anxieties, they created anxieties for youths who were actually developing same sex-gender or bisexual sexual identities. In their view, what they were experiencing was not temporary (Savin-Williams, 1990c), and the onset of puberty provided new meaning to their attractions to the same sex-gender (J. Hunter & Schaecher, 1987; A.D. Martin, 1982). They now interpreted these attractions as sexual (Malyon, 1981-1982).

For the gay youths studied by Savin-Williams (1998a) who connected their sexual attractions to a gay or bisexual sexual orientation, this was not always a happy occasion. Reactions to self-labeling ranged from easiness and tranquility to torture and disgust. Some felt relieved that there were no longer mysteries and that sexual and romantic feelings could now be experienced and expressed. However, clarity of sexual orientation for others frightened them immensely. A theme of fear dominated their coming out stories. For some, self-labeling could be a long, drawn-out process. It might take years or decades before they connected their sexual attractions to a nonheterosexual sexual orientation. The implications of same sex-gender attractions were particularly difficult for gay or bisexual youths with masculine characteristics. They felt considerable internal and external pressure from peers and family to conform to a heterosexual sexual orientation.

Some persons postpone dealing with what their sexual attractions might mean through denial, suppression, or repression. Others attempt to divert their attention through drugs and alcohol (Sanford, 1989) or withdrawal from social events. Others become passionately involved in academics, sports, and/or extracurricular activities (Gonsiorek, 1988). Heterosexual dating is another means for youths to blind themselves and others about their sexual orientation (Herdt, 1989; Savin-Williams, 1995b). Females may become sexually active with the other sex-gender because of greater uncertainty than males about their feelings and desires for the same sex-gender (Rosario et al., 1996). Females may also experience more pressure to participate in sexual activity with the other sex-gender (Herdt, 1989). They often report feeling pressured and coerced from peers to involve themselves in heterosexual dating (Savin-Williams, 1995b). As females are socialized to avoid interpersonal conflict, they may comply to maintain harmonious relationships with both peers and their families (Gilligan, 1982). Some youths may become sexually promiscuous with heterosexual partners, and some of the females may purposely get pregnant to cover up their sexual orientation (Sanford, 1989).

Especially if their sexual orientation is not easily identifiable by outward appearance or behavioral characteristics, LGB youths can successfully blend in with heterosexual peers and families. Even with this facade, though, sometimes peers label the attractions of these youths as not heterosexual but as lesbian, gay, or bisexual. Youths given these labels, however, are likely to repudiate them because they fear rejection and isolation (Troiden, 1988).

For those who do not directly address the implications of their same sex-gender attractions or cover them up until adulthood, the price can be high. Progression on developmental tasks in coming out is inhibited (Fontaine & Hammond, 1996). In adulthood, these persons might experience an awkward off-time social and sexual adolescence (D'Augelli, 1996b). And, they still might not be comfortable with their sexual orientation. Floyd and Stein (2002) identified five patterns of coming out in a sample of seventy-two LGB persons ages sixteen to twenty-seven. Three groups had early patterns of coming out while two had delays in either sexual activity or disclosure. Comfort with sexual orientation was highest in those with the early patterns.

Sorting Out Sexual Identity

Sometimes the delay in identifying one's sexual identity relates to the difficulties in sorting it all out. However, once early feelings of confusion and uneasiness are linked with a sexual component it is increasingly more difficult to deny what same sex-gender attractions mean. Same sex-gender sexual experiences can happen anytime after initial awareness of same sex-gender attractions, from moments to decades later. However, once sex happens with someone of the same sex-gender, this helps solidify a same sex-gender or bisexual sexual identity (Savin-Williams, 1990c). On the other hand, it is not unusual to feel uncomfortable, if not shame and guilt, about the thought of one's first sexual experiences with someone of the same sex-gender. However, at some point, the discomfort and negative internal experiences diminish and feelings about sex become positive (Savin-Williams, 1998a). Without this shift, one is unlikely to identify as lesbian, gay, or bisexual (Cass, 1979; Dank, 1971; de Monteflores & Schultz, 1978).

For even the most resistant males studied by Savin-Williams (1998a), attempts to claim either a bisexual or heterosexual sexual orientation often failed because of their experiences (including sex) with girlfriends. Some became resigned to the inevitableness of a same sex-gender sexual orientation. Many experienced an inner voice that pushed them to place honesty with one's self over and above the negative conceptions of being gay. Both self-awareness and self-identification are also aided by the development of more complex cognitive abilities (see Chapter 2) and an increasingly autonomous social life (D'Augelli, 1996b). Once at a distance from family and the hometown community, self-recognition of sexual identity among youths is often swift. Most of those who identified as gay or bisexual in college did so during their first two years (Savin-Williams, 1998a).

COMING OUT IN MIDLIFE OR LATER

Given the huge pressures in our society for persons to marry and the fact that same sex-gender sexual identity is so negatively stigmatized, it is not surprising that some lesbian and gay persons get married. This was a frequent occurrence for older lesbian and gay persons. It is also not unusual for many young persons to marry and divorce during a period of identity formation (Myers, 1989). Since lesbians usually come out several years later than gay persons, they are more likely to marry (Bell & Weinberg, 1978; Harry, 1983; Saghir & Robins, 1973; Schaefer, 1977).

Those who marry are probably "trying to do the right thing" to meet societal expectations, want a family life, or are fond of the partner (Coleman, 1981-1982b). Several older studies found that almost one-third of lesbians were married and about half of these marriages produced children (Bell & Weinberg, 1978; Saghir & Robins, 1973; Schaefer, 1977). In a review of studies on gay persons, Harry (1983) found between 14 percent and 25 percent were currently or formerly married. Approximately 10 percent were also fathers.

Men who knew they were gay while married often struggled with guilt and secrecy; some had sexual encounters with other men while married (Kimmel & Sang, 1995). Sometimes they were in a long-term liaison with another man (Bozett, 1980, 1981a,b). Others reported that they were unaware of being gay until they were divorced (Herdt, Beeler, & Rawls, 1997). A third of divorced gay men and more than three-fourths of divorced lesbians studied by Bozett (1993) were unaware of their same sex-gender attractions at the time of their marriages.

Cohler and Hostetler (2002) identified two patterns of coming out among older lesbian and gay persons. One pattern was to become aware of same sex-gender sexual wishes during childhood or adolescence. Typically those following this pattern led a quiet life in adulthood, often with partners. Their public and private lives were separated, and they did not think of their sexual orientation as relevant to their work or in the community. Older lesbian and gay persons in the second pattern had often not been aware of same sex-gender sexual desires until particular life circumstances occurred and at a time of increased visibility of LGB persons. They were mostly married and had adolescent or adult children when this awareness came about. Usually, they met another man or woman for whom they experienced same sex-gender sexual desires. The first or a subsequent same sex-gender relationship led to divorce and to establishing a long-term relationship with the newly found same sex-gender partner

(Herdt et al., 1997; Hostetler & Herdt, 1998; Ridge, Minichiello & Plummer, 1997).

In the study by Herdt et al. (1997), a mostly white, well-educated, and professional sample completed a ten-month needs assessment study for older lesbian and gay persons in Chicago in 1996. The median age when the sample members identified as lesbian or gay was twenty-two; age twenty for gay persons and age thirty for lesbians. Those who married, however, tended to come out an average of ten years later than those who did not marry, usually after the age of thirty and for a quarter of this group after the age of forty. Similar to the results of other studies reported here, some always knew they were lesbian or gay or, at least, felt captivated by same sex-gender persons. Some reported illicit encounters with same sex-gender persons while still married. Other persons reported that they were not really cognizant of being lesbian or gay until after their divorce.

Some midlife women who experienced same sex-gender desires as younger adults decided not to venture from heterosexual partnerships because of the costs of social stigma and the potential loss of motherhood (Kirkpatrick, 1989a,b). Some married women with no same sex-gender sexual experience identified as lesbian because of fantasies about other women. Yet, they also suppressed both the desires and identification (Ponse, 1980). During a reevaluation process in midlife, some woman who suppressed desires for other women chose to pursue them (Kirkpatrick, 1989a,b). For other women the pull toward same sex-gender attraction was so strong that they felt they must pursue same sex-gender relationships despite the social pressures against it (Faderman, 1991).

Several studies addressed once-married lesbians in some detail. For example, K. L. Jensen (1999) studied twenty-four women, aged twenty-nine to fifty-eight, who came out later in life. They primarily lived in the Twin Cities of Minneapolis and St. Paul, Minnesota. Most of the women had clues about their same sex-gender orientation, but they tended to stay in their marriages and tried to make them work. Six were married twenty years or longer, ten between ten and twenty years, eight between one to ten years. Nineteen of the women had children; most had two, one had three, one had four. Most enjoyed childbearing and child rearing and identified strongly with their role as mothers.

Most of the women in the K. L. Jensen (1999) sample were married for many years before they made a change in self-identification. More than half (fifteen) did not know of their same sex-gender feelings before they married. Some (nine) reported serious attractions to women after they were married. Some of these women, however, did not realize what these attractions meant. Four women consciously repressed their attractions, because they did not know how to interpret them or thought they were unacceptable. Some tried to hide their attractions, primarily because they believed that there were no other women like them. Some of the attractions were not sexual or recognized as such. Many of these women were blocked in fully knowing their attractions because of limited information and because of the pervasive heterosexist ideology. In addition, those involved with other women all experienced rejection by the other women. They did not perceive that a full relationship with a woman was available or valid for themselves. Positive same sex-gender relationship models were not available.

Even for women aware of the optional path, they did not feel free to choose it. Several reported that they were not used to making decisions based on their own needs and desires and they did not trust their judgment. Same sex-gender desires were also threatening in terms of upsetting family, other relationships, the community, and their material well-being. Consequently, they could not "let" themselves know about or act on their attractions. Eventually, however, awareness of their attractions and same sex-gender behaviors happened for these women (K.L. Jensen, 1999).

Another study focused on thirty women who identified as lesbians in midlife (Charbonneau & Lander, 1991; Lander & Charbonneau, 1990). They ranged in age from thirty-five to fifty-five and were of varied ethnic, religious, and social class backgrounds. Most were of European ancestry; 20 percent were African American or Caribbean American. Most grew up in middle- and upper-middle-class families; a third in working-class families. These women also accepted traditional definitions of the "proper" goals for women: marriage and motherhood. All but six were mothers; four of the six who had no children tried to have them but were not successful. Most of the women had two or three children; several had four to six children. The women were married for an average of 12.3 years, with a range from 1 to 32 years. One woman was never married but was engaged three times. More than half of those married remained in their marriages ten years or longer. At the time of the survey, however, none of the women were with their husbands.

This sample of midlife lesbians was unaware most of their prior adult lives of any attraction to other women and with few exceptions never considered it as a possibility. They were surprised when they fell in love with a woman or experienced sexual attraction to a woman in midlife. Even more surprising was the embracing of the label "lesbian." Some of them felt that they were always lesbians but did not know it until midlife (Charbonneau & Lander, 1991; Lander & Charbonneau, 1990).

No single event precipitated a shift in identity in midlife for these women. Instead, a combination of events evoked change or challenged them to question their heterosexuality. Many were also leaning toward nonconformity by being politically active. A majority (twenty) of them participated in political work ranging from mainstream activities such as voter registration drives to more radical activities such as antiwar demonstrations (Charbonneau & Lander, 1991). Half of the women actively participated in the women's movement. This created a climate for asking questions and looking at oneself from a different perspective. This could happen in consciousness-raising groups or from reading feminist books. For others, a particular event, such as a women's concert or an all-woman's weekend, was the catalyst for prompting the move to a lesbian identity. However, other women made no specific reference to the women's movement when discussing their move from a heterosexual to a lesbian identity, nor were they feminists (Charbonneau & Lander, 1991).

Many other turning points stood out including a parent's serious illness or death, or their own serious illness, after which they realized the transience of life and began to consider how to live the rest of their lives; divorce or the moment they first thought of leaving a marriage; time apart from men (or being celibate), which provided an opportunity to be independent and plan fulfillment of their own needs without men in their lives; changes in daily lives such as moving, entering school, leaving or entering a job, joining a consciousness-raising group, or entering therapy; discovering that a friend, work colleague, or relative was lesbian; or experiencing erotic feelings for another woman (Charbonneau & Lander, 1991).

Once these women self-identified as lesbian it was essential for them to dispel negative stereotypes about lesbians. For some, this was a slow process, but for others it happened because of a single encounter with another woman (Charbonneau & Lander, 1991).

Twenty-two women, ages forty-seven to sixty-three were interviewed by P. F. Woolf (1998). They lived in a large metropolitan city in the Pacific Northwest. Sixteen were white, the others a mixture of other racial/ethnic groups. All but one had a high school education or more; eighteen had a bachelor's degree or higher; eleven had a master's degree or higher. They had all come out between the ages of forty and fifty-five. The most common theme in these women's lives was the development of female support networks prior to their transitions. As with the women studied by Charbonneau and Lander (1991), the women also experienced at least one of a variety of transitional markers. They included female bonding, obsession with another woman, dreams/fantasy, feminist archetypes, nonconformity, a death, economic instability, negative sex with men, celibacy, promiscuity, divorce, the influence of the feminist movement, empty nest, or traumas.

Aside from changing their sexual identity, the women studied by P.F. Woolf (1998) were also described as entering another culture with a distinct set of values, codes, and norms. They also had to "normalize" their attraction to women and to shift from viewing lesbians as stigmatized to acceptable and even admirable persons to imitate. Despite some difficulties such as feeling confused and uncertain about the rules, they eventually adapted to a lesbian identity.

Sixty-two midlife and older lesbians, interviewed by T. C. Jones and Nystrom (2002), lived in Washington, Oregon, and California. Over half (59 percent) were white; ages ranged from fifty-five to ninety-five with a median age of sixty-five. Most of these women were educated beyond high school; 29 percent had some college; 21 percent a college degree, and 43 percent a graduate degree. Over half (53 percent) of the women were retired, a third (34 percent) were still employed. Household incomes ranged from under $10,000 to over $60,000, with the median income range of $30,000 to $39,000. All these women experienced a period of exploring and questioning their sexual identity, but it was common for them to repress or suppress their sexual identity. Some gave into pressures to marry. Some who married acknowledged their sexual identity only after they were divorced and their children were grown.

As many women who identified as lesbians in midlife lived a long time as self-identified heterosexuals, the change in sexual identification resulted in a radical transformation and redirection for their lives. Many results were positive such as feeling "for the first time I am me" (Charbonneau & Lander, 1991). Others described the intimacy with other women at a depth they never experienced with men, or even imagined was possible (McGrath, 1990). Along with redefinitions of sexual experiences and sexual identity, sex-gender roles were also redefined. Behaviors that before were viewed as "masculine" and unacceptable for women were now seen as acceptable.

The women studied by T.C. Jones and Nystrom (2002) grew up in the 1940s and were part of the evolution of gay pride. However, most of these women believed that while the gay rights movement had produced positive effects for younger lesbian and gay persons it had little influence on their own lives. Yet, they experienced a high level of life satisfaction.

Women and men who come out as lesbian or gay in midlife or later can also experience costs. For example, women are no longer in a primary relationship with a man, which includes privileges, fantasies of being cared for by a man, and social support. Involvement with a woman will not, in most social contexts, gain the respect and status as does a link with a man. One also has to relate to others through one's own merit (Cummerton, 1982; de Monteflores & Schultz, 1978; Groves & Ventura, 1983; Kirkpatrick, 1989a,b).

Women who identified as lesbian in midlife in the study by K.L. Jensen (1999) also felt they experienced a positive life change along with costs. However, with the exception of one woman, none of the other women mentioned the loss of entitlements via heterosexual marriage or feeling sad about the ending of a marriage, a heterosexual life, or a home. Nor did they mention the negative of having a stigmatized identity. However, they did experience fears such as not being able to take care of themselves and their children alone.

Men who had been in long-term heterosexual marriages and had little or no experience with the gay community often struggled with tasks that are associated more with adolescence rather than midlife. They were suddenly in an unfamiliar world and experienced considerable uncertainty (Herdt et al., 1997). Formerly married men also wondered whether gay persons not formerly married could understand their feelings about the importance of their children and how time-consuming children can be, the difficulties regarding divorce, the difficulties of coming out in later life, and the issues involved in making disclosures to their children (Herdt et al., 1997). The experiences of formerly married lesbians are probably similar, including lesbians who lived as single mothers or reared children from a prior marriage within a lesbian relationship (Laird, 1996).

PART II:
DISCLOSURES ACROSS
THE LIFE SPAN

Chapter 5

Disclosures: Overview

For generations, lesbian and gay culture did not exist as it does today. In the pre-Stonewall culture, one was vulnerable to the stressors of living in a highly oppressive culture. Living openly was risky and dangerous. One could lose reputation, employment, housing, friends, and family. One could even be arrested or put in a mental hospital (Fassinger, 1991; Claes & Moore, 2000). Rejection by friends and family usually meant lifelong rejection. And, most lesbian and gay persons had no backup support networks of others like them (Adelman, 1986). The isolation began to change after the Stonewall riots in June 1969. This watershed event produced a budding liberation movement and also precipitated the historical circumstances for making disclosures.

In early liberation publications, being out to oneself as lesbian or gay, but closeted, was viewed as the struggle between oppression and liberation (e.g., Jay & Young, 1972). Disclosure was seen as a political act (T.S. Stein, 1993) and a necessity to overcome oppression. Invisibility reinforces negative stereotypes and, thereby, perpetuates social oppression (D'Augelli & Garnets, 1995). Being hidden also makes it difficult to share similar concerns and to organize politically against social oppression (Dynes, 1990; Garnets, Herek, & Levy, 1990). Hidden lesbian and gay persons, not wanting to bring attention to themselves, are unlikely to push for fair and just treatment for themselves or others. Some hidden persons even support prejudice and discrimination so they will not be exposed (Shilts, 1987). Furthermore, pretenses of heterosexuality support the notion that it is bad or wrong to be lesbian or gay (Healy, 1993; Herek, 1991); secrecy

Coming Out and Disclosures
© 2007 by The Haworth Press, Inc. All rights reserved.
doi:10.1300/5423_06

implies feeling shame or guilt (Cain, 1991b; Lewis, 1979). Disclosures increased after Stonewall, but this was not the case for everyone because one still paid a heavy cost when making one's sexual orientation public. When one makes disclosures, one is socially marginalized and has a different position in society and with social institutions (Bohan, 1996; Burch, 1997; Fassinger & Miller, 1996; Gonsiorek, 1993; McCarn & Fassinger, 1996; Ponse, 1980; Rust, 2003; T.S. Stein & Cohen, 1984). And, negative responses to being lesbian, gay, or bisexual still happen. This tempers the motivation of persons in all age groups in terms of making disclosures.

DISCLOSURES AMONG YOUTHS

Adolescents who are or think they might be lesbian or gay soon recognize that they are part of a stigmatized group. They know that disclosures are not safe, and they may live in fear of exposure (J. Hunter, 1995). In a sample of 206 lesbian and bisexual youths, ages fourteen to twenty-one, some lost friends following disclosures. This could have a cascading negative effect such as increasing distress in school when rejecting friends tell others (D'Augelli, Pilkington, & Hershberger, 2002; D'Augelli, 2003).

Adolescents may wait until they are out of public school and away from home before they make disclosures. Floyd and Stein (2002) studied LGB youths, ages sixteen to twenty-seven. For some of them, sexual activity or disclosure was put off until these youths were in safer situations. This means that these events may occur during young adulthood instead of adolescence when these youths have greater independence from parental oversight and the stress from peers in high school (J. Hunter & Schaecher, 1987; Pilkington & D'Augelli, 1995). However, Chapter 6 addresses disclosures of youths to parents while still at home, albeit from different samples.

DISCLOSURES AMONG MIDLIFE PERSONS

Many midlife lesbians in the sample studied by J. Bradford and Ryan (1991) were not open about their sexual identity with many groups including family members, heterosexual friends, and work associates. Many of the midlife and older lesbians studied by T.C. Jones and Nystrom (2002) reported that they were not out or they were deliberate about whom they told about themselves. Forty self-identified lesbians, ages twenty-four to fifty-nine, were studied by S.C. Anderson and Holliday (2005). Over half (55 percent) noted that it was easier over time to be out and that they often cared less about what people think as they got older. However, a majority (72 percent) mentioned situations or locations in which passing was still necessary. This included jobs and careers; visits with family or relatives, small communities; parent-teacher meetings; visits with physicians, and confrontational interactions with authorities such as police and judges.

Some midlife women had not had the opportunity to learn about negative reactions to lesbians. So, they did not anticipate what could happen with disclosures. A large majority of the midlife women studied by Lander and Charbonneau (1990) were shocked by the verbal harassment they experienced, such as painful comments about them and being screamed at. Many experienced losses such as canceled invitations to family occasions. Since these women were unaware before of the intensity of prejudice toward same sex-gender sexual orientation, the negative reactions were sobering for them. J. Bradford and Ryan (1991) reported that midlife lesbians who experienced negative reactions were not willing to make further disclosures.

DISCLOSURES AMONG OLDER PERSONS

In the 1950s and 1960s a "homosexual" world or "secret society" existed in some locations (Gagnon & Simon, 1967b). Many older and lesbian and gay persons studied by D. Rosenfeld (2003) felt pride in having passed as heterosexual. Although most of the older gay persons studied by Hostetler (2000) did not join in the gay liberation movement, they were not hostile toward it. However, the older gay persons studied by Lee (1987) were hostile toward the liberation movement because they lost the status they had in the pre-Stonewall days. They resented the loss of their adventuresome world and subculture, and the secret signs and rituals that they controlled. They did not like pressures by gay liberationists to force openness.

Some older gay persons were largely unaware of, or indifferent to, the events surrounding gay liberation. Yet, they acknowledged that social and political changes had made life easier for gay persons (Hostetler, cited in Cohler & Galatzer, 2000). Still, many of these persons do not live much differently from how lesbian and gay persons lived in the 1940s and 1950s. Schope (2002) found in a sample from the midwest that two-thirds of the older generation raised before Stonewall (age fifty and over) had been completely closeted in school and 40 percent were currently closeted in their neighborhoods. They developed strategies of secrecy over the years to protect themselves from discrimination, and they were most likely still in place. Remaining closeted particularly includes those who live in rural and conservative communities (Rothblum, Mintz, Cowan, & Haller, 1995).

In a study of older LGB persons (average age about seventy), the ages at which disclosures were first made ranged from age ten to sixty-eight. More than half of the sample had not told both of their parents. Only 38 percent reported being known as LGB by more than three-quarters of their acquaintances. One-quarter was not known as LGB by co-workers and about half had not disclosed to employers (D'Augelli & Grossman, 2001; D'Augelli, Grossman, Hershberger, & O'Connell, 2001).

SAGE, an organization for older LGBT persons in New York City, has members who are not out to many persons in their lives. They do not open up to health care and social work providers because they fear they will not get services. In coming-out groups at SAGE, with members ranging in age from forty to eighty, many gay persons had loving marriages with women. They did not disclose their sexual identity because of the potential for major losses including their wives and children, and their jobs. Some are still struggling to be who they are while living at home with a parent for whom they are caretakers. Some, however, made disclosures soon after a divorce or the death of a spouse. Others did this after retirement when the fear of losing their livelihood no longer existed (Altman, 1999).

DISCLOSURES AMONG ETHNIC OR RACIAL PERSONS

Ethnic or racial minority lesbian and gay persons who disclose their sexual orientation are vulnerable to rejection and loneliness in their own communities (Espin, 1987; Loiacano, 1993; Tremble,

Schneider, & Apparthurai, 1989). Strong commitment to one's extended family and ethnic community as one's primary reference groups is highly valued. Ethnic and racial lesbian and gay persons, then, may be seen as violating family and community expectations because of their sexual orientation and for placing personal desires over the family and community (Kanuha, 1990). So these persons tend not to make disclosures in their families or communities, as they do not want to feel like outcasts (Espin, 1987; Loiacano, 1989; Tremble et al., 1989).

Nearly all the twenty African American gay persons age thirty-nine to seventy-three (average age of fifty-six) interviewed by Adams and Kimmel (1997) maintained ties with their biological families. However, many had never discussed their sexual identification with their families. Many reported that when they first started experimenting sexually with other men, they limited themselves to white partners so that no one in the African American community would detect their sexual identity. Six had been married; four had children.

Thirty-seven African American gay and bisexual men, ages eighteen to thirty-six, were studied by Wilson and Miller (2002). Most (twenty-six) identified as gay; others (eleven) identified as bisexual. Most were natives of Chicago and living in the south side of the city with or near their families. They used various strategies to manage their sexual minority status in both nonfriendly settings and friendly settings. One strategy was used across settings. Four types of *role-flexing strategies* were used in nonfriendly settings.

1. Altering actions, dress, and mannerisms: "butching it up"; acting in an extreme macho way, taunting and possibly acting violently toward gays, avoiding public intimacy with men; acting like a thug or hard criminal
2. Being sanctimonious or following the norms established by church teachings
3. Using deceit to conceal one's sexual identity such as lying about spending time in gay clubs, being discrete about sex with men, avoiding discussions about sexual orientation, identifying as heterosexual around heterosexuals, and maintaining sexual relations with women

4. Passivity or maintaining a quiet and reserved demeanor in the presence of heterosexuals and not saying anything when co-workers made degrading antigay comments

Other strategies used by these men included the following:

1. *Keeping the faith:* Remaining close to God, seeking advice of ministers at gay Christian organizations, attending church, and participating in worship practices/services.
2. *Changing sexual behavior:* Abstaining from same sex-gender sexual behavior to avoid the negative consequences of hetero-sexism.
3. *Standing one's ground:* Openly confronting those who speak negatively about gay persons, refusing to remain silent, or refusing to accept heterosexism by being open about one's sexual identity.

The main strategy in gay friendly contexts was to *develop a gay space or alternate family.* In these contexts, the men could be affectionate with other men and show their sexual interest in them. To cope with racism some created separate spaces for black gay men.

The strategy used in all contexts was *accepting oneself.* The men replaced negative attitudes about themselves with positive attitudes.

The strategies identified by Wilson and Miller (2002) had three functions: to avoid stigma (role flexing, changing sexual behavior), to buffer experiences of oppression (keeping the faith, creating gay-only spaces), and to attempt social change (standing one's ground and accepting self). However, as the men grew older they were more unwilling to change or use role-flexing strategies to fit in.

DILEMMAS OF DISCLOSURE

As noted, a range of stances exists on disclosure ranging from telling no one to being open at least in some arenas. As discussed, there are incentives not to disclose. Mostly, they have to do with protecting oneself. One believes one will be harmed if disclosures are made. Due to the stigma, the decision to not disclose one's sexual orientation is valid in many situations (Harry, 1993). Lesbian and gay persons are likely to encounter differential treatment by others, including ostracism, discrimination, and violence.

There are also psychological benefits associated with no disclosures. For example, hidden lesbian couples studied by Eldridge and Gilbert (1990) were found to experience high self-esteem and overall life satisfaction. Studies of older lesbian and gay persons found that no disclosure was associated with more favorable adjustment and life satisfaction (e.g., Adelman, 1991; Berger, 1982a; Friend, 1990; Lee, 1987, 1991; Quam, 1993). Adjustment to later life or high life satisfaction for older lesbian and gay persons was also related to low disclosure at work (Adelman, 1991).

There are also incentives to disclose, such as positives in psychological and interpersonal well-being, political contributions, and the negatives for well-being that can result from no disclosures. Lesbian and gay persons often disclose to others as a strategy for promoting their well-being. They feel authentic and experience higher levels of social and psychological functioning and, possibly, reduced stress and psychogenic symptoms (Herek, 2004), including lower social anxiety and depression (Schmitt & Kurdek, 1987). In addition, they experience positive identity formation (Bell & Weinberg, 1978; Coleman, 1981-1982b); identity integration (Cramer & Roach, 1988; Murphy, 1989; M. Pope, 1995; Wells & Kline, 1987); self-affirmation or validation as lesbian or gay (Harry, 1993; Wells & Kline, 1987); self-esteem (Hammersmith & Weinberg, 1973; Nemeyer, 1980); improved self-concept (Schmitt & Kurdek, 1987); personal integrity (M. Pope, 1995; Rand, Graham, & Rawlings, 1982; Wells & Kline, 1987); increased intimacy in relationships (Cramer & Roach, 1988; Sophie, 1987; Wells & Kline, 1987); decreased feelings of isolation (Murphy, 1989); and freedom from the burdens of concealment (Cramer & Roach, 1988; M.S. Weinberg & Williams, 1974).

Lesbian and gay youths also attain many advantages when they disclose their sexual identity: decreased feelings of loneliness and guilt, greater comfort and wholeness with personal identity, greater psychological adjustment and higher self-esteem, a sense of personal freedom, increased ability to merge one's sexual and romantic interests, greater access to supportive communities, increased feelings of authenticity, feeling loved and accepted for whom one is (not living a lie), and being truthful in relationships (Savin-Williams, 2001).

Another way to look at the incentives for making disclosures is the hoped-for outcomes identified by Cain (1991b), Herek (2004), and others. They include the following:

- *Relationship-building disclosures.* The goal is to attain same sex-gender friends and partners (Harry, 1993); increased closeness is especially sought (Cain, 1991b). Disclosure permits honesty and openness and a context for other kinds of self-disclosures. For example, two persons can have a conversation about topics commonly discussed in a close relationship such as the joys and stresses of one's romantic relationships or search for such relationships, feelings of fulfillment or loneliness, and mundane or momentous experiences with one's partner. Since sexual orientation is so central to personal identity, keeping it a secret from another person necessitates withholding considerable information about oneself as well as curbing spontaneity (Herek, 2004).
- *Problem-solving disclosures.* The goal is to end constant questioning about one's private life or why one was never married (Cain, 1991b).
- *Therapeutic disclosures.* The goal is to feel better. Disclosure appears to be related to enhanced mental and physical health (Herek, 2003).
- *Preventative disclosures.* The goal is to avoid anticipated difficulties with friends and employers by telling them before they discover the information from someone else (Cain, 1991b).
- *Political or ideological disclosures.* The goal is to promote political benefits through greater visibility of LGB persons (Cain, 1991b). Disclosure is viewed as a political strategy for changing attitudes and overcoming oppression (Byrne, 1993). Out and visible lesbian and gay persons can change how heterosexuals view lesbian and gay persons (Rothblum, 1994) Another political outcome is an increased chance for integration with the lesbian and gay community and for development of support systems (Gonsiorek, 1993).

There are also negative consequences of passing or hiding one's identity and a large literature on this (e.g., C.L. Cohen & Stein, 1986;

de Monteflores, 1986; Gartrell, 1984; Hetrick & Martin, 1987; A.D. Martin & Hetrick, 1988; Sophie, 1987; Spaulding, 1982). Those who do not know other lesbian and gay persons, due to lack of disclosures, can experience isolation and loneliness (e.g., Berger, 1982b; Cain, 1991b; Malyon, 1981-1982). They can also experience feelings of inferiority, negative concepts of one's self (M.S. Weinberg & Williams, 1974), guilt, shame, anxiety, and depression (J. Smith, 1988; M.S. Weinberg & Williams, 1974). They can feel deceitful (H.P. Martin, 1991) and inauthentic (Goffman, 1963; E.E. Jones et al., 1984), or that they have a false self (Winnecott, 1965). The discrepancy between public and private identities (L. Humphreys, 1972; Goffman, 1963) feels uncomfortable. They can also feel valued for what others want them to be rather than what they want to be (H.P. Martin, 1991).

Studies of adolescents reported similar negative outcomes associated with hiding one's sexual identity such as lowered self-esteem, isolation, and feeling misunderstood (Hetrick & Martin, 1987); depression, anxiety, alcohol and drug abuse, runaway behavior, and suicidality (Coleman, 1981-1982b; de Monteflores, 1986; Gartrell, 1984; Hetrick & Martin, 1987; A.D. Martin & Hetrick, 1988; Schmitt & Kurdek, 1987; J. Smith, 1988).

As noted before, some hidden lesbian and gay couples experience positive benefits from not being open, but other couples who hide or deny their relationship to family and friends can experience strains in their relationship. Their psychological adjustment is negatively affected, and secrecy also prevents the partners from attaining social support (Kurdek, 1988b; Murphy, 1989).

Passing requires both psychological and physical work and results in many practical problems. For example, some persons are partly in and partly out of the closet across different audiences. This results in categorizing people and contexts ("Who knows?" and "Who does not know?") or one's life is compartmentalized ("In what contexts does someone know or not know?") (Harry, 1993). The more audiences one is out to, the harder it may be to modify one's behavior where one is not out (Lee, 1977). This is usually a stressful way to live.

Passing takes considerable energy to make sure that leaks about one's sexual orientation do not occur (Cain, 1991b; Rust, 1993). The fear of discovery is relentless (Bell & Weinberg, 1978; Harry, 1982; M. Pope, 1995; Rofes, 1983). To be spared expected negative reactions one must do one or all of several things: not disclose, prevent others from finding out about one's self, or lie to or mislead others about one's self (H.P. Martin, 1991; Zerubavel, 1982). In addition, passing is not always successful. Disclosures can happen as accidents, or information about one's sexual orientation can be attained through sources other than the person in question. Disclosures can also be impulsive or ill advised (Gonsiorek, 1993).

OTHER FACTORS THAT INFLUENCE DISCLOSURES

Other factors also influence lesbian and gay persons to make or not make disclosures. These factors are sociocultural, stage in life, location, and personal.

Change in Sociocultural Factors

As indicated earlier, sociocultural factors for lesbian and gay persons are different today than they were prior to the Stonewall era. Visible lesbian and gay subcultures now exist, and lesbian and gay persons see themselves as part of an oppressed group instead of being deficient or deviant. This new status encourages them to come together and, through identification with each other, promotes self-esteem and self-affirmation (Adelman, 1991). J. Bradford and Ryan (1991) found that women who were active in lesbian and gay rights organizations were more likely to be open about their same sex-gender sexual orientation than those who were inactive. The women's movement has also prompted lesbians to make disclosures (deMonteflores & Schulz, 1978). Kahn (1991) also found that feminist ideology was associated with more open behavior among lesbians.

Stage in Life

It may be easier for adults to disclose than adolescents because they experience more leeway in their ability to change their audiences if reactions are too severe. Whereas the typical adolescent has a certain unchanging set of audiences (e.g, parents, siblings, school peers), adults may be able to change neighborhoods, memberships, jobs, and friends. Some persons may adapt their circumstances to make them fit their desires for disclosure, such as living in a gay ghetto or working for a lesbian and gay organization or agency. If, however, adults cannot leave a job or neighborhood for a better alternative, they may rethink their willingness to disclose (Harry, 1993).

College students who move out of predominantly heterosexual contexts can choose new audiences (Harry, 1993). They may disclose at college but not at home if parents still support them financially (A.S. Walters & Phillips, 1994). Harry found, however, that disclosure increased to about age thirty when it peaked and then declined. One interpretation of this finding is that those under age twenty-five are still invested in the heterosexual world. Gradually, they get more involved in the lesbian and gay world. Beginning in their thirties, however, they may acquire work positions requiring more caution about disclosures (see Chapter 7).

As discussed earlier, many older lesbian and gay persons remain closeted, but in other cases, being older seems to make disclosures easier. Most older gay persons studied by L.B. Brown, Alley, Sarosy, Quarto, and Cook (2001) seemed to feel that others should accept them for the way they are, and they did not shy away from being openly gay. Berger and Kelly (2001) found that compared to younger gay persons, older gay persons worried less about exposure or cared less about who knew they are gay. They were more widely known to others as gay and less concerned about the opinions of parents and other relatives. Now in retirement, most of the gay persons studied by Hostetler, cited in Cohler and Galatzer (2000), were indifferent regarding disclosure of their sexual orientations. They did not go out of their way to tell others about their sexual identity but neither did they hide it. Berger (1982a) also found that as gay persons grow older, and especially as they retire, they have less reason to hide. They are less concerned about job loss and discrimination and generally more secure emotionally and financially.

Location

Even with the sociocultural changes, lesbians and gay persons in small towns or rural areas are not as likely to make disclosures as those in larger cities. They may fear more negative attitudes and reprisals. The coming-out process may be prolonged or foreclosed and no disclosures are made. Many lesbian and gay persons from these areas move to urban settings in search of an accepting lesbian and gay community and more openness (Hanley-Hackenbruck, 1989).

Personal Variables

The largest influence on making disclosures or not is probably individual variables. This can include personality characteristics, overall psychological health, religious beliefs, and negative or traumatic experiences regarding one's sexual orientation (Hanley-Hackenbruck, 1989). Individual variation in willingness to risk going against conventional norms is also a factor. The more one will risk negative reactions when open with heterosexual audiences (Franke & Leary, 1991; Harry, 1993) the more willing one is to make disclosures. Another factor that can motivate being out is to obtain self-validation as lesbian or gay (Harry, 1993). This usually happens in lesbian and gay communities. Attempting to attain validation from heterosexual audiences is risky, as negative reactions are likely. Why then, do lesbian and gay persons disclose to heterosexual audiences? One reason is that some heterosexuals are often highly significant in one's life, and their positive validation is sought. There is a tendency, however, to disclose to highly selected heterosexual audiences that are thought to be at least somewhat accepting of one's sexual orientation (Savin-Williams, 1990a).

Chapter 6

Disclosures to Parents

LGB or T family members do not always disclose their identity to their parents. Some lesbian and gay persons studied by H.P. Martin (1991) did not make disclosures to either parent whereas in other studies of youths, fewer than 10 percent made the first disclosure to parents (D'Augelli & Hershberger, 1993; Savin-Williams, 1998a). In Cain's (1991a) sample of thirty-nine gay persons, half of them (50 percent) did not disclose to their parents. In a national survey of lesbians, 88 percent of the respondents were open to all lesbian and gay persons, but much smaller percentages were out to all family members (27 percent); 19 percent were out to no family members (J. Bradford & Ryan, 1988).

Disclosure to parents is not easy to consider, as it is one of the most anxiety-provoking and difficult disclosures that LGBT persons face (Cramer & Roach, 1988; D'Augelli, 1992; Lowenstein, 1980; G. Weinberg, 1972; Wells & Kline, 1987). There is no predicting how parents will react. LGBT youth may hear from lesbian and gay friends, counselors, or read in books or magazines that disclosure or openness and honesty are desirable and necessary for emotional well-being and self-acceptance. However, they also know that disclosure can cause great turmoil in the home, and they risk parental rejection (Myers, 1981-1982; Kurdek & Schmitt, 1987; Wells & Kline, 1987). According to Savin-Williams (1989-1990), expected parental reactions include: "'My parents won't understand'; 'My Dad will reject me, not speak to me, or throw me out of the house'; 'My mother will send me to a shrink'; 'I'll feel like I let them down'" (p. 41). Expecta-

Coming Out and Disclosures
© 2007 by The Haworth Press, Inc. All rights reserved.
doi:10.1300/5423_07

tions such as these can delay disclosure to parents or preclude all possibility of it. Transgender children also anticipate negative reactions from parents who assume not only that their children are heterosexual but that their sex-gender identification matches their biological sex (Gagné et al., 1997). Youths who have not disclosed to either parent expect more disapproval than those who have disclosed (Savin-Williams, 2001).

In a sample of 293 youths, aged fifteen to nineteen, D'Augelli, Grossman, and Starks (2005) found that over a third had parents who did not know they were LGB. Since these youths were less sex-gender atypical in childhood, they had been able to avoid parental discovery of their sexual orientation. Their fears about disclosing to parents include losing the closeness with parents, provoking parental guilt that would exacerbate things, or possibly hurting their parents if the parents blame themselves. The fear of hurting or disappointing parents may override that of rejection (Savin-Williams, 2001). Trepidation about these possible outcomes may be greater if the family has a peaceful coexistence. In such cases, youths do not want to jeopardize their status within the family and the positive relations they have with their parents (Savin-Williams, 2003; Waldner, Haugrud, & Magruder, 1999).

As LGB persons develop increasing independence from their parents as adults, the risks associated with disclosure to parents may diminish. When children are at midlife, for example, parents recognize that their child's sexual identity is not simply a phase, and they may be more accepting (Rothblum et al., 1995). Self-sufficiency, however, does not always result in disclosures. In a study of gay adults, Cramer and Roach (1988) found that the decision not to disclose resulted from wanting to continue to show deference to parents or respect for parents' feelings or beliefs. Many adult children feel responsible for their parents' well-being, and they worry about letting them down, hurting them, disappointing them, or threatening their identity as successful parents. Adelman (1991) found that some older lesbian and gay persons want to avoid conflict with or reprisal from their parents.

For those who wish not to make disclosures to one or both parents or make selective disclosures in the family, L.S. Brown (1989a) identified several patterns used to control information about one's sexual orientation. One pattern is to reduce contact with the parents to a minimum through emotional and geographical distance. However, this can result in feelings of estrangement from the parents. Another pattern, "I know you know," involves an unspoken agreement not to discuss a family member's sexual orientation, although everyone knows it. This conspiracy of silence (Mallon, 1994) may maintain stability of the family, but one's life remains unacknowledged. Yet a third pattern, "Don't tell your father," involves some family members such as the mother and supportive siblings knowing about a lesbian, gay, or bisexual family member, but they all agree not to tell father (L.S. Brown, 1989a). Those who know may also not want anyone outside the family to know. This fourth pattern, identified by Mallon (1999), is "let's keep it in the family."

The juggling of distance, collusion, and selectivity of who knows in one's family, can be temporary or last a lifetime (Herdt & Beeler, 1998). Many LGB persons end up having no relationship with their parents or having a controlled and distant one (L.S. Brown, 1989a). Secrecy, however, can create a situation in which one appears outwardly accepted but is inwardly isolated (Bell et al., 1981; Harry, 1982).

LGB children can become unhappy with the impersonal distance between themselves and their parents or feel uncomfortable or guilty about misleading them (L.S. Brown, 1989a; Cramer & Roach, 1988; Leaveck, 1994; Strommen, 1990). In addition, the absence of disclosure can result in wrong assumptions. For example, if neither person in a lesbian or gay couple is out to their families, each family may expect their "single" child to come home on holidays but may not invite the "only a roommate" partner (L.S. Brown, 1989a). Such uncomfortable situations may motivate some to make disclosures. The costs of the cover-up outweigh the risks of disclosure.

YOUTHS AND DISCLOSURE TO PARENTS

The most detailed studies of children's disclosure to parents involve adolescents. Much of the work in this area has been done by Savin-Williams (e.g., 2001).

Generally, today's LGB youths are more likely than those from earlier generations to disclose to parents and are more likely to do so at earlier ages (Savin-Williams, 1990a). Although the timing for this event ranges from age thirteen to never, on average youths who disclose to parents do it between ages eighteen and nineteen. This is down from an average age of the mid-twenties in earlier studies (Savin-Williams, 1998b). Often, this occurs while one is still in high school or occasionally, while in junior high or middle school (Savin-Williams, 1990a).

Although occurring earlier, disclosure is usually a late developmental event. It happens years after first awareness of same sex-gender attractions and after the realization that this has significant implications. In addition, and consistent across cohorts, disclosures to parents seldom occur before disclosures to supportive friends. Parents are rarely the first to be told by their children. Prior to this disclosure the child has usually integrated a same sex-gender sexual identity and has established a same sex-gender sexual or romantic relationship (Savin-Williams, 2001).

Gradually youths decide to give up their pretense of being heterosexual and tell their parents, or they drop hints so that parents eventually conclude that they have a lesbian daughter or gay son. Sometimes youths assume parents know or should know, so they offer no explicit acknowledgment (Savin-Williams, 2001).

More Mothers Know and More Are Told Before the Fathers Are Told

When youths disclose to parents, it is nearly always first to mothers. This is a consistent finding across all studies (Savin-Williams, 2001), although sometimes the initial disclosure can be to both parents simultaneously (D'Augelli & Hershberger, 1993). In D'Augelli and Hershberger's study of gay adolescents in a support group, over 60 percent first told mothers; another 25 percent told parents together; while another 10 percent told fathers first. Savin-Williams (2001) found similar results: 62 percent disclosed first to mothers; 26 percent told parents together; 12 percent told fathers first. Among 2,500 gay and bisexual male adult readers of the *Advocate,* 64 percent reported they had told their mothers, usually during their late teens or early twenties (Lever, 1994). Herdt and Boxer (1993) reported that nearly two-thirds (63 percent) of young lesbians had disclosed to their mothers. The same proportion of young lesbians studied by

Savin-Williams (1990a) had disclosed to their mothers. Almost two-thirds (65 percent) of lesbian and gay youths studied by Savin-Williams (2001) reported that they told their mothers, with many others believing their mothers knew or suspected their sexual orientation. For youths who lived at home, D'Augelli et al. (1998) reported that only 7 percent of mothers did not know or suspect.

Daughters and Mothers

The daughters studied by Savin-Williams (2001) either made a conscious decision to tell their mothers or their mothers had asked them first. In other cases, the daughters were "outed" (15 percent), or feared they would be, or it was the "right developmental time" to tell their mothers (10 percent). The daughters' primary motivation was to maintain or improve the emotional intimacy currently experienced with their mothers, although sometimes their goal was to repair the relationship. One-third of daughters disclosed to their mothers because their mothers posed the question—a reflection of the intimacy they shared—with daughters merely acknowledging the truth.

Mothers' initial reactions to learning of their daughters' sexual identity were generally perceived to be more positive than the reactions of fathers (D'Augelli et al., 1998; M.S. Weinberg et al., 1994). A quarter (25 percent) of the daughters reported mothers as being positive and supportive. However, the average mother did not noticeably react either positively or negatively. The reactions of smaller numbers of mothers were more extreme. Nearly 10 percent of mothers manifested emotional, volatile reactions, including screams and threats to cut off financial aid or to send their daughter to conversion therapy. A few mothers (4 percent) rejected or physically attacked their daughters. Since the disclosed information can threaten a mother's sense of integrity or self-concept as mother, it is possible that in such instances these mothers experienced a loss of control or power over their daughters or realignment of the relationship. Other mothers reacted less with overt anger than with denial. Even when mothers were supportive, this support could be conditional as with the admonition not to tell certain others. The most accepting mothers may fear that their daughters will experience a more difficult life (Savin-Williams, 2001).

Mothers with same sex-gender attractions themselves were perhaps the most supportive of lesbian daughters. Same sex-gender attractions were a good sign that the relationships would become the most positive in the shortest time. Just under 5 percent of the youths interviewed believed that they had a mother who either once had significant same sex-gender attractions or currently identified as lesbian or bisexual (Savin-Williams, 2001).

While most daughters did not expect an especially negative response from their mothers, over a third of the daughters (37 percent) did not disclose to them. Half this group reported that it was "not a good developmental time"; either they were "not ready to tell," or they felt that "mothers were not ready to hear the information." In other instances, they did not tell their mothers because they feared the information would "hurt their mothers" or for reasons of mothers' ethnic identification or fervent religious beliefs. No daughters suggested a lack of closeness with their mothers as a reason for nondisclosure (Savin-Williams, 2001).

Sons and Mothers

For sons who disclosed to their mothers it seemed most important to disclose to her first, because it was her support and acceptance that they most needed to have verified. Most sons described their relationship with their mothers as warm, caring, and intimate. No sons described their mothers as distant or noninvolved. Indeed, many mothers had long recognized their sons' sex-atypical mannerisms and interests as signs of being gay. However, some mothers did not appreciate the sex-atypical behavior, which created conflict in the relationship, even when mothers felt that the behavior could not be changed (Savin-Williams, 2001).

Although they might postpone it to a time when they feel more secure, sons rarely decide against disclosure to mothers. Nearly 60 percent state that the primary reason for telling their mothers was that "she asked" or else they volunteered the information "to share their life with her." Otherwise, external circumstances dictated the timing of disclosure. Over one-third reported that their mothers asked because she already suspected their sexuality. This happens in all racial and ethnic groups, social classes, and in all geographic localities. A mother may suspect something is amiss most likely because her son displays sex-atypical behavior such as not being athletic, does not show interest in girls, or has gay-appearing friends. She confronts her son, who usually reveals the truth (Savin-Williams, 2001).

Two in ten sons voluntarily told their mothers to put an end to the pretense. They longed for personal integration, honesty, a sense of genuineness, and sometimes, a return to a previous mother-son relationship that was more open and honest. For this to happen, they felt that their mothers must know all aspects of their lives. They may also have felt that they could not be truly out and gay until they shared this fact of their lives with their mothers. They often felt guilty about not disclosing to their mothers earlier. Another reason for disclosure was to elicit support from the mother in circumstances such falling in love (three in ten). Sons could also be outed by a boyfriend, another family member, or the press (Savin-Williams, 2001).

Although some sons were outed, most were as likely to disclose to their mothers in a direct fashion. Those who were more indirect left hints or clues around the house. Other mothers discovered the information by accident or through the assistance of a third party: a sibling, friend, or circumstance. Often, these discoveries were unpleasant occasions (Savin-Williams, 2001).

Mothers' initial reactions to a son's disclosures were slightly more negative than those of fathers, averaging 3.9 (slightly negative), on a scale from 1 (very supportive) to 7 (rejection); expected reactions averaged 5.1. The range of mothers' reactions, however, was wide, from extremely supportive to highly negative, the latter accompanied by screaming and threats to abandon their sons. Extreme hysterical and aggressive reactions occurred in 4 percent of the sample and were unexpected. These types of reactions were most likely to occur when the son was masculine and not sex atypical in behavior or mannerisms, and the disclosure surprised or shocked the mother (Savin-Williams, 2001).

Typically, most (nearly half) of mothers' reactions were slightly negative, characterized by denial, disparaging remarks, and discouragement. Neutral reactions including silence or a stance of neutrality were rare. None of the less-than-supportive reactions jeopardized the mother-son relationship (Savin-Williams, 2001).

Slightly more than one in ten gay youths reported that their mother offered unqualified support with their primary concern the well-being and safety of their sons. Although these mothers experienced mild forms of grief, most quickly moved to acknowledgment and to accept the situation. Two in ten mothers had more guarded albeit positive reactions. They loved their sons, were close to them, and wanted to maintain these good relations. Another group of mothers initially responded poorly but came to offer at least acknowledgment and sometimes acceptance. Many mothers became increasingly accepting once they realized that anything else would cost them their son and their ability to protect him. Most gay youths reported that they now have a positive relationship with their mothers, and they expect this to continue (Savin-Williams, 2001).

Some relationships (four in ten) did not improve, worsened, or remained the same. Mothers who initially acknowledged with acceptance often moved no further toward fully embracing their son. One in ten relationships worsened over time. A relatively rare pattern was the mother who was initially positive but then became increasingly negative. Usually, this came about from changes in the mother such as a shift in her religious beliefs (Savin-Williams, 2001).

Many sons who made no disclosures to their mothers felt that their mothers knew from other sources or would not be surprised to find out. Slightly over 10 percent delayed disclosure because they were not close to their mothers, and they felt no need to share this personal information. Others feared that bad things would happen: that she would be disappointed or hurt or that she would express moral disapproval of their sexuality. Some (30 percent) felt it was "not the right time" because they had not sufficiently progressed enough in their identity development or did not feel secure in their sexuality. One of four elected not to disclose because they knew their mothers did not have positive views of gay persons and hence would react negatively. No undisclosed youths expected their mothers to be supportive or even neutral. In fact, several anticipated threats to cut off emotional support and financial aid, and mandated conversion therapy. Several of these youths were sure that their mothers would respond negatively because of their religious beliefs, ethnicity, or because there was little evidence of her giving emotional support in the past (Savin-Williams, 2001).

Daughters and Fathers

Some daughter-father pairs experienced warmth and closeness beginning in childhood. Most daughters, however, reported that their paternal relationships were neither positive nor negative. In some cases, relations were nonexistent, or there was distant contact. Often, lack of mutual knowledge and emotional emptiness characterized these relationships. Less frequent were conflictual relationships, which ranged from neglect to occasional emotional and physical abuse (Savin-Williams, 2001).

Nearly three-quarters of young women studied by Savin-Williams (2001) who were out to their fathers reported they could not specify a precise reason for disclosing other than "the time was right," because "someone else had told him," or because the "father asked." Others "feared being outed," "wanted to hurt the father," or "wanted to share their lives with him." One in twenty disclosed to her father (as compared to one in three to mothers) because she wanted her father's support and approval, and usually received it. Nonetheless, daughters were less hopeful of bonding with their fathers than sons were, and were more likely than sons to disclose to fathers "to get it over with." Disclosure to their fathers for many daughters was the last step in exiting a heterosexual identity. They may have been in a romantic relationship and have a positive sense of themselves as lesbian, bisexual, unlabeled, or questioning.

Far more daughters than sons believed their father strongly suspected their sexual orientation or actually knew it. Fathers who knew discovered the information by accident or because someone told them (usually the mother). Typically, however, fathers chose to avoid the subject (Savin-Williams, 2001).

Often, because the mother does the telling, the daughter is not present for the father's first reaction. Some fathers respond positively, even with support. However, many fathers do not know how to react to the information and take their cues from their wives. They may not display their feelings at all. Father-daughter relationships seldom worsened or improved after disclosure. Although some improved, most changed little from their original negative, positive, or distant position (Savin-Williams, 2001).

Fathers having same sex-gender attractions did not guarantee solely positive reactions to daughters. The responses from these fathers ranged from slightly positive (one in three), to neutral (one in seven), to slightly negative (one in four) (Savin-Williams, 2001).

The expectation of a negative reaction was not the reason daughters chose not to tell their fathers. Rather, they did not disclose because either they were "not close to or intimate" with their father, or because he was "not a particularly important person in their lives." Some had "not gotten around to it." Others feared negative reactions such as losing financial support, "did not want to hurt or disappoint him," or felt that it was "not the right developmental time" (Savin-Williams, 2001).

Sons and Fathers

There is a growing tendency for sons to disclose to fathers during their adolescent or young adult years, often while still living at home. Most disclosed to fathers after disclosing to mothers, be it soon or years later. Sons sometimes disclose to fathers because "it was time he knew." Disclosure may be a last attempt to elicit support from a father (three of ten), or establish a connection with him. In contrast to daughters, sons who disclose to their fathers are more likely to do so to elicit his support. Savin-Williams (2001) reported that the goal of nearly 60 percent of sons' disclosures to their fathers was to receive support or establish a more intimate relationship.

Most sons initiated direct disclosures or responded to a direct question from their fathers. Sons who chose the direct route were fairly confident that the father would be supportive or that he already knew. Nearly all instances of indirect disclosures were the result of a third party—usually the mother—telling the father. The purpose of being indirect was to avoid an awkward and unpleasant situation. Sometimes disclosures were accidental, or a father overheard a conversation (Savin-Williams, 2001).

Most father-son relationships improved somewhat after disclosure, but little appeared to change for most of these relationships. Only about 10 percent of father-son relationships after disclosure were positive with father accepting his son. The most common reaction for 40 percent of fathers was one of support; two-thirds responded in the supportive to slightly negative range. Few fathers want to lose their sons, although many do not know what to say or how to offer support. Only a few father-son relationships deteriorated, and only 10 percent of father-son relationships became so severely impaired that they ceased to function. Moreover, when the initial reaction was negative it rarely included violence or abuse. However, some sons experienced daily recriminations from fathers because of their sex-atypical behavior. Fathers were disappointed if their sons did not become involved with male peers especially in athletics. Fathers were also frustrated if their sons did not follow in their footsteps. A more common paternal response was to express displeasure but to refrain from systematically harassing the son. Nevertheless, some fathers withdrew from their sons' lives because the son did not live up to masculine standards (Savin-Williams, 2001).

For those having fathers with suspected same sex-gender attractions, nothing suggested that their relations were any better or that the fathers were more accepting and understanding. Indeed, these fathers appeared put off by their gay sons (Savin-Williams, 2001).

One of the primary reasons 80 percent of sons gave for not disclosing to father was fear of negative reactions. They anticipated that their fathers would withhold their college money or there would be extreme conflict, verbal abuse, and perhaps even physical violence. Another primary reason for nondisclosure to fathers was that sons (three in ten) did not feel close to fathers; they were not important persons in their lives. They desired support from and intimacy with their fathers and feared that disclosure would destroy all chance of establishing a future relationship with them. Fundamental as well in not disclosing to father was the son's feeling that the present time was "not the right developmental time" (one in four) (Savin-Williams, 2001).

DISCLOSURES OF MIDLIFE AND OLDER LESBIAN AND GAY PERSONS TO PARENTS

Few studies have focused on midlife or older lesbian and gay persons and disclosure to their parents. L.B. Brown et al. (2001) found in a study of sixty-nine gay persons, ages thirty-six to seventy-nine (mostly ages fifty to sixty-five), that most of them were in regular contact with their families and that their families were aware of their sexual identity. However, a study of older LGB persons found that families rarely embraced a family member's nonheterosexual sexual identity (D'Augelli & Grossman, 2001). The relationships between older lesbian and gay persons and their families are often maintained at a distance (Altman, 1999).

ETHNIC AND RACIAL FAMILIES

Ethnic and racial lesbian and gay persons may experience additional pressures not to disclose to parents because of the particular needs and values of their ethnic group (Carmen, Gail, Neeva, & Tamara, 1991; B. Smith, 1983). Many of them are inextricably tied to their racial or ethnic communities—because of oppression and the consequent need for group bonds (Kanuha, 1990). Their communities and extended families, often their primary reference groups, provide their main social networks and support. In most racial and ethnic communities, the family also provides the basic means of survival for the culture, with family expectations taking precedence over personal wishes (Chan, 1992; Wooden et al., 1983). Hence, LGB family members feel that they must conform to acceptable outward roles (Chan, 1992). This includes accepting, without question, the cultural obligations of marriage and perpetuation of the family name (Savin-Williams, 1998b). With disclosure equivalent to putting oneself before allegiance to one's racial or ethnic group, it is seen as a betrayal. Disclosure by children risks disgrace not only for themselves but also for their families, including their ancestors (Garnets & Kimmel, 1993).

These themes appear in all family-centered cultures. However, unique issues also exist among different racial and ethnic groups (Rust, 2003). Although the discussion here is on families, it is assumed that parents are paramount in the ways that ethnic and racial LGB persons respond to their family situation and culture.

African American Families

African American lesbian and gay persons see their community as extremely rejecting of same sex-gender sexual orientation, so they feel pressured to conceal their sexual orientation (Clarke, 1983;

Gomez & Smith, 1990; Greene, 1994c, Icard, 1985-1986; Loiacano, 1993; Mays & Cochran, 1988; Poussaint, 1990, B. Smith, 1992). First, African American lesbian and gay persons may hide their same sex-gender attractions from their families often because of the conservative Christian religiosity that dominates African American communities (Bonilla & Porter, 1990; Greene, 1996) and the churches' claim that the Bible forbids same sex-gender sexual orientation because it is a sin (Crisp, Priest, & Torgerson, 1998; J.L. Peterson, 1992). Second, African American heterosexual women and men ardently want "normalcy" in their communities and feel embarrassed about lesbian and gay members (Poussaint, 1990). Third, there are strong pressures to enforce sex-gender role conformity (Icard, 1985-1986). Thus, young African American males call males "sissy" who do not conform to expected sex-gender role behavior, mannerisms, and gestures (B.E. Jones & Hill, 1996). Fourth, negative reactions to gay persons result from a perceived shortage of marriageable African American men and the implications of this for the continuation of the race (Dyne, 1980). Finally, African American women disapprove of lesbians because their status is lower than the status associated with heterosexual sexual orientation and privilege (Greene, 1997).

Although these situations have caused rejection in African American families, ambivalence, tolerance, and acceptance have emerged in recent years. Family norms of "Don't ask so they won't tell" or "Be silent and invisible" may also allow the family to accept a lesbian, gay, or bisexual family member without directly dealing with the reality of their sexual orientation and the conflicts associated with it (Manalansan, 1996; A. Smith, 1997). Gay African American men are also more accepted when they focus on their accomplishments within the African American community instead of on their sexual activities or sexual identity (Hawkeswood, 1990).

Overall, African American LGB persons are pushing for more openness and acceptance in their communities. The increase in HIV/ AIDS has forced communities to confront their existence more directly. Some political leaders now include open lesbian and gay persons in political coalitions. Most civil rights organizations support LGB civil rights and have clauses in their bylaws opposing discrimination directed at LGB persons. Open groups also now exist in a few African American churches. Also, a vibrant African American lesbian and gay culture includes literature, art, and filmmaking (Rowden, 2000).

Latino Families

For Latino lesbian and gay persons, rejection by their family and community carry more weight than rejection by mainstream society (Espin, 1987). *Familismo,* or sense of family, and respect of elders and authority figures is strong in Latino families (Parés-Avila & Montano-Lopez, 1994). Disclosure of a lesbian or gay identity is likely to result in intense disapproval by the family and community (Almaguer, 1991; Espin, 1984, 1987; Hidalgo, 1984; Morales, 1992). Latino families maintain strong conservative attitudes, cultivated by Catholicism (Carballo-Diéguez, 1989). Generally, parents do not discuss sexual matters with their children, and it is common for parents not to discuss sex with each other (González & Espin, 1996). Gender roles are clearly established (Espin, 1984, 1987; Hildalgo, 1984; Morales, 1992) as the Catholic Church also prescribes family and sex-gender roles. Men, for example, must provide for, protect, and defend the family. If a man is gay, he is viewed as deserting these obligations (Morales, 1992). In addition, the Latino culture rigidly adheres to the traditions and practices of machismo for men and *marianismo* for women. Males are expected to be dominant and independent whereas women are expected to perform behaviors that represent the virtues of the Virgin Mary (Reyes, 1992). Latino women must also honor *etiquela* that mandates patience, nurturance, passivity, and subservience (Ramos, 1994). Since Latino women must remain virtuous, some of them may live with their parents until marriage (Morales, 1992).

Males who do not model machismo are tagged with various negative labels such as the following: (a) "alien," "odd," "of another way," and "broken"; (b) "inferior" or *joto* (meaning of no significance or worth); and (c) "feminine," "butterflies," or "not masculine" (Morales, 1996). Some Latino families believe that gay persons are nonmen or that they are feminine-identified drag queens (Moraga & Hollibaugh, 1985). Unless openly "butch," lesbians are more invisible in Latino communities than gay persons are. Families may even encourage single women to participate in emotionally close friendships with other women with no presumption that these might be lesbian relationships

(Espin, 1984, 1987). Yet, if it becomes known that a daughter is linked with a lesbian partner, she may pay an even higher price than a gay son. Her violation of prescribed sex-gender role behaviors threatens the preservation of cultural continuity (Espin, 1997). Abandoning these sex-gender role expectations is also tantamount to trying to overthrow men or as threatening men's dominance and the masculine Latino cultural heritage. Such women are labeled macho or man haters (Ramos, 1994).

Latino lesbians also threaten the cultural norms of their community because they may encourage other Latino women to question their status in their families and to imagine possibilities for their independence (Trujillo, 1991). Moreover, they also force the culture to confront the sexuality of women (Espin, 1987; González & Espin, 1996). Good Latino women are not viewed as sexual. Single lesbians are more acceptable than those with sexual partners who are viewed as promiscuous and unchaste (Espin, 1984, 1987; Ramos, 1994). If a lesbian Latino who is closeted decides not to marry, she will not be questioned about her decision. Excuses involving career aspirations and asexuality are usually accepted, or there is silent tolerance (Espin, 1993).

Some open Latino lesbian and gay family members maintain a place in the family and experience quiet tolerance. This does not mean, however, that the family approves of their sexual orientation; they most likely deny it (Morales, 1996).

While less acculturated, more traditional Latino families are less likely to accept lesbian and gay family members (Chernin & Johnson, 2003). Other families display varying levels of acceptance because of differences in national origin, acculturation and assimilation statuses, socioeconomic status, educational level, and geographical residence. Traditional Latino conceptions of manhood and womanhood are moving to a more egalitarian model. This is attributed mostly to expanded education, exposure to American culture, and the influence of feminism (Marsiglia, 1998).

Latino lesbian and gay persons tend to develop support systems from compassionate family members or from the lesbian and gay community. As with African Americans, however, the gay community's racial, ethnic, and class bias can lead to similar barriers to developing a lesbian or gay identity. Hence, organizations and bars catering exclusively to Latino lesbian and gay persons have emerged (Rodriquez, 1996).

Asian American Families

The largest group of Asian Americans includes Americans of Japanese or Chinese ancestry. Confucianism has a strong influence in Eastern Asian countries such as Japan, China, and Korea (Hong, Yamamoto, & Chang, 1993). Upholding the family honor is primary, and family roles are clearly defined. Sons, particularly firstborn sons, are held in high esteem.

The Asian American family dictates the behavior and attitudes of the children (Savin-Williams, 1998b), with the most notable expectations being unquestioned obedience and unending demand for conformity (Chan, 1992). Obedience is to be shown through respect and loyalty to parents and other elders (Liu & Chan, 1996; R.A. Lopez & Lam, 1998) followed by loyalty to one's siblings and then to one's marital partner (Liu & Chan, 1996).

The demand for conformity in the Asian American family also entails expected sex-gender roles and continuation of the family line. East Asian marriages may be prearranged to provide good lineage for future generations (Nakajima, Chan, & Lee, 1996). Asian sons are the carriers of the family name, lineage, and heritage. They are expected, therefore, to marry and provide heirs (Chan, 1989, 1992); they are also expected to care for older parents (R.A. Lopez & Lam, 1998). Women are obligated to fulfill the roles of dutiful daughter, wife, and mother (Chan, 1992). Saving face is an act of sacrifice when one forgoes one's needs for the sake of the family. Many lesbian and gay Asian Americans marry to save face (Han, 2000). Women are expected to remain monogamous within a marriage. Men, however, may have male or female lovers, as long as they are married and produce sons (Nakajima, Chan, & Lee, 1996).

If children make disclosures, parents may regard this as an act of treason against the family and the culture (Greene, 1997). They may refuse to discuss the information and may put up a wall of silence (Liu & Chan, 1996; Savin-Williams, 1996). When a son discloses, he is usually perceived as selfish and disrespectful, partly because his disclosure indicates autonomous and independent thinking (Han,

2000). When a daughter discloses, she may be seen as shaming the family honor by not being a dutiful daughter and rejecting the role of wife and mother (Chan, 1987; Pamela, 1989; Shon & Ja, 1982).

The tight restrictions in the Asian American family can seem oppressive, but the family also bestows support, affection, and security (Chan, 1992; Wooden et al., 1983). Lesbian and gay children, therefore, may not be willing to risk losing their family bond by disclosure, especially to their parents (Chan, 1989). However, those more assimilated into Western culture may be more open about their sexual identity, albeit mostly in non-Asian contexts (Chan, 1997; Nakajima et al., 1996). Almost all were out to their friends (Chan, 1992). And, most Asian American lesbian and gay respondents also disclosed to someone in their family, usually first to a sister. Although more than three-quarters had disclosed to a family member, only about a quarter (26 percent) had disclosed to their parents after a mean number of 6.2 years (Chan, 1989).

The pressure from the Asian American culture drives many Asian American lesbian and gay persons to separate from their families and to assimilate into the mainstream lesbian and gay community (Nakajima et al., 1996). However, gay culture can be unsatisfying as it expects Asian American gay men to be passive and sexually submissive (Chernin & Johnson, 2003).

The situation is similar for the many Vietnamese families that immigrated to the United States as refugees following the Vietnam War. The children strive for perfection and want to conform to the Asian traditions maintained by their parents. However, fear of discovery becomes a source of mental pressure and anguish for lesbian and gay children because of their nonconformity. The Vietnamese culture, following Confucian values (Nguyen, 1992), morally and socially condemns "homosexuality" (R.A. Lopez & Lam, 1998). Cultural and sexual identity conflicts are especially acute for gay sons (R.A. Lopez & Lam, 1998; Timberlake & Cook, 1984). Vietnamese families often castigate and abandon gay sons (R.A. Lopez & Lam, 1998) and label them "lai cai," meaning "half man and half woman" (Dong, 1992).

Native American Families

In contrast to other ethnic groups, Native American lesbian and gay persons do not anticipate disapproval by the traditional community, as few Native American families repudiate relatives because of a disclosure of "difference" (L.B. Brown, 1997). Nor do they pressure them to be other than who they are (M.A. Jacobs & Brown, 1997). Membership of Native Americans in a clan, an extended family, a tribe, or a nation never changes (Tofoya, 1996).

The attitudes of more acculturated Native Americans (e.g., third and fourth generations), in contrast to other ethnic and racial groups, are often more negative. This is attributed in large part to their adoption of Western Christian religions (K.L. Walters, 1997). Even earlier traditions of acceptance from Native Americans on reservations are changing, influenced by Anglo culture (Blackwood, 1984; Whitehead, 1981; Williams, 1986). Lesbian and gay persons living on reservations may feel greater pressure to remain closeted (Owlfeather, 1988) or to move to urban areas (Greene, 1994a; Williams, 1986) where they can join Native American lesbian and gay communities. They can also more openly involve themselves in same sex-gender relationships, and they have better access to employment and educational opportunities (Lang, 1999). To attain these benefits, however, they lose support from their culture and family (Greene, 1997; Williams, 1986).

Greek American Families

Greek American families usually avoid discussing same sex-gender sexual orientation altogether. Whether adolescents or adults, lesbian and gay persons often collude with their families' wishes. Bonded by love and loyalty, these families maintain a link with their LGB children, albeit, at times, a superficial one depending on assimilation of the family into the dominant American culture. Still, many Greek Americans who are several generations removed from immigration continue to identify strongly with their Greek heritage (Fygetakis, 1997).

Chapter 7

Disclosures to Others Inside
and Outside the Family

DISCLOSURES TO OTHER FAMILY MEMBERS

Sometimes a relative such as a grandmother, aunt, uncle, or cousin is the first person that a lesbian or gay person tells about their sexual identity. Usually there is a close bond between them (D'Augelli & Hershberger, 1993). More often, however, the first person told is a close sibling (Devine, 1983-1984).

Siblings

Several studies reported that many lesbian (62 percent) and gay (72 percent) persons make disclosures to their siblings (R.-J. Green, Bettinger, & Zacks, 1996; Savin-Williams, 1998b). When older persons made disclosures to family members, they were most often to mothers or sisters. The strong preference of the African American lesbian (506) and gay (673) persons studied by Mays, Chatters, Cochran, and Mackness (1998) was to make disclosures to women in their families (both mothers and sisters). For Asian Americans, disclosures happen more often with sisters than with parents (Chan, 1989). Urban African American and Latino gay and bisexual youths, however, are less likely to disclose to siblings (30 percent) than to peers (90 percent) or mothers (50 percent). Yet, disclosures to siblings happen somewhat more often than to fathers (20 percent) (Murray, 1994).

Coming Out and Disclosures
© 2007 by The Haworth Press, Inc. All rights reserved.
doi:10.1300/5423_08

Rejection from siblings is less troublesome than rejection by parents but more troublesome than rejection from friends (Cain, 1991a). Siblings, however, are generally more accepting than rejecting (D'Augelli, 1991; Savin-Williams, 1995b). This is also the case when a transgender family member discloses to a younger sibling. This sibling typically does not view the transgender brother or sister as any different from before. The reaction of older siblings, however, will possibly be rejection (C. Rosenfeld & Emerson, 1998).

Siblings, even if accepting, may become uncomfortable if they are the only family member who knows the sexual identity of a brother or sister. They may feel like a coconspirator in a cover-up. Discomfort with this situation may lead them to out their sibling to parents with or without this person's knowledge or consent (Murray, 1994). Sometimes the lesbian or gay family member enlists a sibling to make the disclosure to parents (Strommen, 1990). Siblings may also play the role of mediator between the lesbian or gay family member and parents (Cain, 1991a). Sibling reactions to the lesbian or gay family member may affect overall family reactions, such as strengthening or modifying them (Strommen, 1990).

Lesbian and Gay Marriage Partners

Most heterosexual persons assume their marriage partner is heterosexual. Therefore, they are shocked when a partner discloses a same sex-gender sexual identity.

The little data available on disclosure by lesbian and gay persons to marital partners came from the partners rather than from the disclosing partners (Hanscombe & Forster, 1982; Kirkpatrick, Smith, & Roy, 1981; Saghir & Robins, 1980). Lesbian wives do not often disclose to husbands. However, when this happens husbands may react in a severe and angry manner (Coleman, 1985a), and some may physically abuse their wives (Hanscombe & Forster, 1982). If husbands feel extreme animosity and children are involved, wives may fear custody battles (e.g., Hanscombe & Forster, 1982; Whittlin, 1983).

Gay partners rarely disclose to their families, as they fear negative reactions from their wives and children. They also fear losing job security and social status (Strommen, 1989, 1990). In contrast, most men who identify as bisexual following marriage soon tell their partners (M.S. Weinberg et al., 1994).

Gay persons who make the choice to disclose to their families do this because they feel troubled about living a double life and want relief from anxiety and guilt (Bozett, 1980, 1981a,b, 1982; Strommen, 1989). Disclosure is thought to be a means to resolve a tense situation, but it usually results in family disruption. Although the data are limited, indirect, and anecdotal, wives of gay partners report reactions of shock, estrangement, confusion, guilt, stigma, and sense of loss. They may feel that they failed as wives (Gochros, 1985; Ross, 1983; Strommen, 1989). A forced or unwanted disclosure, as from a husband who discovers that he is HIV positive, can cause an explosive crisis. A wife does not just confront a partner's bisexual or gay sexual identity and marital infidelity but the possibility of being HIV positive also. This situation can lead to feelings of loss, betrayal, vulnerability, and uncertainty about the future (Paul, 1996).

Once disclosures are made in marriages of lesbian or gay persons with heterosexual partners, the most common result is divorce (Bozett, 1981a,b; Coleman, 1985a,b; L.E. Collins & Zimmerman, 1983; Gochros, 1985; Miller, 1979b). Coleman (1985a) found that the wife's disclosure of a bisexual or lesbian sexual identity almost always resulted in divorce. Most (97 percent) of the lesbian wives studied by Wyers (1987) were divorced compared to 78 percent of gay husbands. In the sample of married gay persons studied by Scott and Ortiz (1996), divorce occurred for 73 percent of the sample and usually between the self-acceptance and disclosure phases of coming out. Lesbians and bisexual women ended marriages more quickly because of no sexual desire for the heterosexual partner, the husband's intolerance of their sexual identities, and dislike of open marriages or secret extramarital relationships (Coleman, 1985a; Matteson, 1987). Separations and divorces are complicated and painful for the partners, children, extended family, and friends (Myers, 1989). Long-term hostility and bitterness, however, are uncommon (Bozett, 1981a,b; Gochros, 1985; Miller, 1979b; Ross, 1983).

Disclosure is not always the road to termination of a marriage. Sometimes same sex-gender sexual identity or bisexuality is integrated into a restructured arrangement such as an open, semiopen, or a sexual friendship (Brownfain, 1985; Coleman, 1985b; Gochros,

1989; Stokes & Damon, 1995; Whitney, 1990; Wolf, 1985). It may, however, be difficult to integrate the differences in sexual identity (Stokes & Damon, 1995). There will be many issues to be worked out such as disclosure to children, family, and friends; feelings of rejection; the use of money for outside relationships (Buxton, 1994); working out a new structure and set of rules; agreeing on standards regarding monogamy and multiple partners and protection from HIV/AIDS; blaming relationship difficulties on a partner's lesbian, gay, or bisexual identity; depression and anger over unfulfilled desires; and jealousy over outside relationships (Deacon, Reinkke, & Viers, 1998).

Transgender Marriage Partners

Some wives of transgender husbands find them appealing (Hunt & Main, 1997). Generally, however, the reaction of wives to the revelation of the partner's transgender identity is negative. They feel bewildered and betrayed, and wonder what other secrets the partner is hiding from them (B.F. Anderson, 1998; Emerson & Rosenfeld, 1996; Hunt & Main, 1997). Some wives feel used, left out, abandoned, or that they are no longer needed. They may become secondary to their partner's absorption in cross-dressing (Hunt & Main, 1997). These women may decide to leave their husbands, and they may disclose the transgender identity of their husbands to others (Cole et al., 2000).

One of the largest studies reported to date on women in relationships with transgender men was a six-year longitudinal study on 106 pairs. The women, members of informal discussion groups throughout the country, reported that issues of betrayal and lost trust were major obstacles to intimacy with the transgender partner. Yet, over two-thirds of them never seriously thought about divorce or separation (G.R. Brown, 1998).

Disclosure Issues for Lesbian and Gay Couples

Couples, who are family to each other, experience conflict about how to manage identity issues if they are at different levels of comfort with disclosures (L.S. Brown, 1996; Decker, 1984; Roth; 1989; Roth & B.C. Murphy, 1986). For example, if one partner decides to disclose to others, this may upset a partner who desires to stay in the closet. The less closeted partner may resent being called friend rather than partner or question whether the partner is committed to a lesbian or gay identity (Blumstein & Schwartz, 1974; Clunis & Green, 2000; Roth, 1985). Differences in openness may also create ideological conflict when only one partner is committed to working on behalf of lesbian and gay rights. The closeted partner could also be outed by association with the activist partner (Roth, 1985).

If the members of a couple are not open, they may report that passing does not affect them. However, they may be so adept at arranging their lives in response to the expectations of others (e.g., separate bedrooms, living apart) that they are unaware of the tensions and difficulties this may cause. The oppression of heterosexism can operate in subtle and nonconscious ways—even persons with a positive self-image are not totally shielded from this oppression (L.S. Brown, 1996). For example, some partners devalue same sex-gender intimacy. And some think they will eventually break up so why combine anything. Passing also limits support from other lesbian and gay persons that is often crucial to a couple's satisfaction levels (Healy, 1993). Social support also seems to be essential for relational adjustments and in the reduction of relational distress (Greene, 1994b; Kurdek, 1988a; Kurdek & Schmitt, 1987).

Disclosure to One's Children

Due to the fear of losing custody and other potential harms, such as harassment, lesbian and gay parents may keep their sexual identities secret (Patterson & Chan, 1996). Three-quarters of the lesbian and gay parents studied by Fredriksen (1999) reported that they had experienced harassment because of their sexual identities: verbal (88 percent), emotional (50 percent), physical (9 percent), or sexual (9 percent). Relationships between transgender parents and their children are often strained because of the distance these parents create with their children. Some of these parents struggle to hide existential issues, such as identity and body image, while others who cross-dress struggle to hide clothing and makeup (B.F. Anderson, 1998). The downside of secrecy, however, is that it limits intimacy between parents and children (Rohrbaugh, 1992), openness in addressing family issues (Patterson & Chan, 1996), and support from others (Matthews & Lease, 2000).

In terms of parents who make disclosures to their children, lesbian mothers are more open with their children than are gay fathers (Hanscombe & Forster, 1982; Hoeffer, 1981). Gay fathers fear that disclosure will damage their relationships with their children (Golombok, 2000). Bozett (1980) discovered that gay fathers may use indirect disclosures (e.g., demonstrating affection for a male in the children's presence) until forced to use more direct disclosures, such as when a divorce occurs and there is a need to explain the reasons for divorce.

The literature on children's reactions to parent's same sex-gender sexual identity, when it is disclosed, is sparse. Some data indicate that most children initially react negatively (Harris & Turner, 1985-1986). Midlife and older lesbians studied by T.C. Jones and Nystrom (2002) who disclosed to their children reported that many of their reactions were supportive although some of the children expressed confusion, resentment, and anger, and feared their friends' responses. Some questioned their own sexuality. If there were two or more children in a family, it was common for each of them to express different reactions. As noted before, age is a factor in how children will react. Younger children who are unaware of the stigma associated with being LGB seldom react in a negative way (Moses & Hawkins, 1986). Older children, especially adolescents, are aware of the stigma and some express resentment and fears of abuse by others (Bozett, 1987). Parents often advise their children to use discretion in what they tell their peers (Golombok, Spencer, & Rutter, 1983; C. Jones, 1978; Miller, 1979a,b).

Both lesbian mothers and gay fathers report that if they disclose to their children and others, they are happier than those who do not make these disclosures (Rand, Graham, & Rawlins, 1982). They report that openness with their children improves their relationships in the long term (Bozett, 1980; Hanscombe & Forster, 1982; Hoeffer, 1981; Miller, 1979a,b). In the study of bisexual women and men conducted by M.S. Weinberg et al. (1994), disclosures to their children led to the positive outcomes of better communication and greater closeness between the parents and children. Some children, however, never talked with their parents about their sexual identity after the disclosure, and some found it difficult to explain bisexuality to their friends.

DISCLOSURES OUTSIDE THE FAMILY

Friends

Friends generally do not withhold important personal information from each other (Cain, 1991a). Disclosures are most often first made to one's friends, especially same-age peers, as the safest and most supportive group (Herdt & Boxer, 1993; Savin-Williams, 1990 a,b, 2001). The initial person told may be another sexual-minority youth, perhaps because other same sex-gender attracted youths are now visible and available to become recipients of first disclosures (Dubé, 2000).

Close to three-quarters (73 percent) of lesbian and gay youths studied by D'Augelli and Hershberger (1993) first told a friend about their same sex-gender sexual attractions. In samples of gay youths studied by Savin-Williams (1995b, 1998a), the first person told was usually a best friend or the person they were dating. A recent Internet study of nearly 2,000 sexual-minority youths ages ten to twenty-one (mean = eighteen years) revealed that they were most likely to have disclosed to a best friend (76 percent), friends at school (66 percent), and friends outside school or work (61 percent). Far behind were mother (49 percent), brother or sister (38 percent), and father (36 percent) (OutProud, 1998). A large segment (83 percent) of a sample of older lesbian and gay persons studied by Beeler, Rawls, Herdt, and Cohler (1999) reported that most of their friends knew of their sexual identities. Bisexual women and men disclosed more to friends (and to partners, including their marital partners, or practitioners) than to others, including family members and work colleagues (Fox, 1995; M.S. Weinberg et al., 1994).

Most of the gay youths studied by Savin-Williams (1998a) reported that responses from friends following disclosure were variable. However, the vast majority of both female and male friends expressed support, acceptance, and encouragement. Gay and bisexual African American and Latino male youths from the Hetrick-Martin Institute in New York City were surprised when disclosure to friends turned out as a positive event (Rotheram-Borus et al., 1991). In the M.S. Weinberg et al. (1994) study of bisexual persons, responses by friends following disclosure were benign. However, in another sample of gay youths studied by Remafedi (1987), 41 percent reported negative reactions from friends. Pilkington and D'Augelli (1995) reported that 36 percent of gay youths and 27 percent of lesbian youths expressed fears of losing friends because of their disclosure. Many of them (43 percent gay youths and 54 percent lesbian youths) reported losing at least one friend because of disclosure.

Gay adults studied by Cain (1991a) found that it was difficult for them to disclose to friends, and it was avoided as long as possible. This was the case even when it resulted in a sense of betrayal in friends when they found out from another source. Some of these men did get around to disclosing to friends but had high expectations of them. They expected their friends to be supportive and accepting as an obligation of friendship. They felt that they were demonstrating their trust by their disclosure and thought that a "real" friend should show support. Friends who "don't come through" with support may be dropped.

The major objective given for disclosure by the gay adults studied by Cain (1991a) was closeness. Fortunately, this was a frequent outcome, although sometimes a strain developed between two previously close friends. Some recipients of the disclosures feared the discloser was sexually interested in them. This was the case for a few of the men who disclosed to friends. They hoped that their disclosures would lead to sexual encounters with previously platonic male friends. On the other hand, in cross sex-gender friendships, disclosures were made to "desexualize" the friendships.

Disclosure at College

Gay college students studied by D'Augelli (1991) were somewhere on a continuum from hidden to disclosed. Although most lesbian and gay young adults may acknowledge their sexual identity to themselves during adolescence some may not disclose it to others prior to entering a college or university, or later. Lesbian and gay students perceived more freedom to explore and disclose their identities when in college. They felt more constrained when in high school because of the norms there. Lesbian and gay social networks were also visible at college. However, disclosures may stall once these students find out that those who disclose are subjected to heterosexist attacks (Rhoads, 1994a,b, 1997).

Fears of verbal and physical abuse are a powerful disincentive to disclosures on campus (D'Augelli, 1992). G. Lopez and Chism (1993) found that demeaning comments from students and instructors in classrooms about lesbian and gay persons are also troublesome. So, many college students make conscious efforts to disguise their sexual identity such as changing pronouns to refer to dating partners (57 percent), pretending they have heterosexual dates (54 percent), refusing to discuss their personal lives (75 percent), or introducing a partner or lover as a "friend" (69 percent). Others, however, were at a point in their lives when disclosure of their sexual identity was a pressing issue (G. Lopez & Chism, 1993; Rhoads, 1993, 1994a,b, 1995). Seeing or interacting with open lesbian and gay persons on campus was an additional push to self-disclose (Rhoads, 1995).

Large classes were not comfortable for disclosures because of many unknowns in terms of students and the professors. Upper-level courses were seen as more receptive (G. Lopez & Chism, 1993). Still, negative attitudes toward same sex-gender sexual identity expressed in class or elsewhere on the campus presented a conflict. Some lesbian and gay students felt a strong commitment to challenge these attitudes, but others felt that the personal cost of emotional fatigue and resentment interfered too much with their academic pursuits and success. Some talked privately with those who made offensive remarks or engaged in other objectionable behavior. Others attempted to start a dialogue with the whole class, and some asked instructors to use them as a resource for issues on sexual identity. No student, however, felt comfortable if the instructor initiated a request for them to be a spokesperson representing lesbian and gay persons. They also thought that professors had the major responsibility for confronting heterosexist behaviors in their classroom and creating a nonheterosexist environment (G. Lopez & Chism, 1993).

Disclosures at Work

LGBT persons may be open about their sexual identities in every area of their lives except work. The workplace mirrors societal bigotry and discrimination against LGBT persons (Croteau & Lark, 1995; Woods & Lucas, 1993). Discrimination may come from employers, workers, customers, or clients (Button, 2004). Vargo (1998) cautioned that one must prepare for the possibility of being treated differently than other workers if one makes disclosures. If mistreatment is possible, one should ascertain in advance what protections the particular workplace provides such as a nondiscrimination policy. However, there is little legal protection in most workplaces. Hence, the results of disclosure in terms of prejudice and discrimination can be difficult and anxiety provoking (M.P. Levine & Leonard, 1984).

Disclosures at Work: Negatives

More than two-thirds of lesbian and gay persons think disclosure in a variety of work settings would create problems for them (M.P. Levine & Leonard, 1984; Winkelpleck & Westfield, 1982). One-third of a sample studied by Friskopp and Silverstein (1995) reported that disclosure of their sexual identity at work had hurt their career. Discrimination can result in not being hired, not being promoted, and not receiving the mentoring and support needed for advancement (Goldman, 1992). No matter what antidiscrimination policies are in effect in the workplace or how competent LGB employees are, they still anticipate that their employers and co-workers will devalue them if their sexual identity is revealed. They might lose credibility and influence (M.P. Levine & Leonard, 1984). LGB persons can also be threatened with or actually lose jobs if their sexual identity is known (Lee & Brown, 1993; Landau, 1994; Kaupman, 1991).

Transgender persons also experience negative reactions at work—harassment from other workers along with demotion, pressures to resign, or termination (Gagné et al., 1997). They may particularly have a hard time holding on to jobs following disclosure (B.F. Anderson, 1998). However, disclosures at work are usually a last step after they have taken hormones for a long time, lived some time outside the workplace in the sex-gender they are adopting, and are pursuing a legal name change. It is best to deal with these and other issues before considering disclosures at work. However, hormonal therapy can have rapid effects in some persons. A beard or breasts may develop so quickly that a fast outing at work may happen. It may help to get a lower dosage of hormones to try to slow down these physical developments (Cole et al., 2000).

LGB persons may also experience harassment in the workplace (Goldman, 1992; Woods & Lucas, 1993). Men often harass lesbians and other women in blue-collar and professional jobs traditionally held only by men (Cruikshank, 1992). B. Schneider (1984) found that 82 percent of lesbians were sexually propositioned, grabbed, pinched, or in other ways experienced unwanted sexual approaches. Kitzinger (1991) reported that gay persons also experienced harassment and physical abuse in the workplace. Heterosexual workers might not think of these behaviors as harassment but instead "just fun" (Gonsiorek, 1993).

Heterosexism encountered in the workplace was found by Waldo (1999) to be associated with decreased job satisfaction, work withdrawal, absenteeism, and intentions to quit the job. It was also positively related to psychological symptoms and to physical health problems. In another study of ninety-seven LGB persons, their experiences of heterosexism at work were associated with depression and psychological distress but not with physical symptoms (N.G. Smith & Ingram, 2004).

Responses to Heterosexism at Work

LGB persons respond to heterosexism in the workplace in different ways. Some refuse to work in heterosexist workplaces or where they have to be hidden. Some may abandon educational or career plans (Gonsiorek, 1993; Shallenberger, 1994). Five of the twelve gay persons studied by Shallenberger changed early career plans because they would not work where they could not be open about their sexual identity. Certain work settings strongly reflect a pattern of being closeted with teachers being the most closeted. Other highly closeted work settings include traditional professions such as law, medicine, dentistry, ministry, science, and technology. Settings where the closet is less closed include art, acting, and service positions such as cook, waiter, and hairdresser. Another work category that is also fairly open includes clerical and lower-level white-collar occupations (Harry, 1993). Those who are self-employed may also not be as closeted (McKirnan & Peterson, 1986).

Some lesbian and gay workers gravitate to certain jobs that are known as "safe." Some gay men quit jobs to work in lesbian and gay affirmative organizations even if it means cuts in income. Lesbians seek alternatives to discriminatory workplaces such as self-employment, fields that tolerate lesbians or employ large numbers of lesbian and gay persons, and firms owned by lesbians, women, or gay persons (M.P. Levine & Leonard, 1984). Some of these businesses serve the lesbian and gay community such as bookstores, publishing houses, and record companies (B. Schneider, 1984). Another alternative for some lesbian and gay workers is to retire early (Moses & Hawkins, 1986).

Other lesbian and gay persons enter and stay in unaccepting workplaces and never reveal their sexual identity or are selective about who they tell (Orzek, 1992). However, just the thought of disclosure at work typically creates considerable anxiety for lesbian and gay workers (Jordan & Deluty, 1998). The Teichner national telephone survey results showed that the 113 lesbian and 287 gay respondents waited an average of 4.6 years from the time they knew they were lesbian or gay until they made disclosures to co-workers. M.P. Levine and Leonard (1984) found only 23 percent of lesbians in their study informed most or all their work associates. From interviews with 13 lesbians employed in large corporations, Hall (1986) reported that about half of the sample indicated that they did not disclose their sexual identity to any co-workers.

Whether one discloses at work largely depends on an assessment of the organizational context and consequences for disclosures in that context (Day & Schoenrade, 1997). Often, one decides that secrecy is best (D'Emilio, 1983; Hetherington & Orzek, 1989). Many studies found that about three-quarters of their samples of lesbian and gay persons created various forms of subterfuge to manage information about themselves and to conceal their sexual identity at work (e.g., Hall, 1989; Kitzinger, 1991; Kronenberger, 1991; Stewart, 1991).

Lesbian and gay persons (423), studied by Button (2004), worked in 37 states, Canada, Puerto Rico, and the District of Columbia. The respondents who were in different types and sizes of organizations had been on the job for 5.9 (mean) years. This study confirmed findings from a study by Woods and Lucas (1993) on gay workers and extended the findings to lesbians. The results showed that both lesbian and gay workers manage their sexual identities in work settings through three strategies.

One strategy was *counterfeiting,* which is an active strategy of constructing a false identity (Button, 2004). This can include altering sex-gender–specific pronouns when describing a same sex-gender relationship and dropping clues about a made-up date, fiancée, or marital partner. Sometimes at social functions, gay persons were "dates" for lesbian workers and the reverse if gay workers (Byrne, 1993; Peters & Cantrell, 1993). Other means to portray a false identity include participating in activities that are sex-gender appropriate and avoiding activities and mannerisms that are stereotypically associated with being lesbian or gay (Button, 2004).

Byrne (1993) reported that leading this double life was the most common strategy used by lesbian and gay persons to hide in the workplace. A significant amount of energy was put into managing and monitoring a heterosexual act (Hall, 1989; Kitzinger, 1991; B. Schneider, 1984; Shachar & Gilbert, 1983). For example, these workers monitored their reactions to heterosexist comments and jokes (Byrne, 1993), eluded personal questions, and provided only general information about their personal lives (Button, 2004). Associations with co-workers (sometimes including known lesbian and gay persons) were superficial and restricted to work; leisure time with them was avoided (B. Schneider, 1984). Stringent boundaries were maintained between personal and work lives (Hall, 1986, 1989; Kitzinger, 1991; M.P. Levine & Leonard, 1984; Shachar & Gilbert, 1983). These workers do not place pictures of partners on office desks and rarely take partners to office functions (Byrne, 1993). They do not discuss their home life or what they do on weekends. Positive events such as engagements or anniversaries are not celebrated at work. Even painful breakups are not shared (Kitzinger, 1991).

The second strategy was *avoidance.* This strategy does not attempt to fabricate a heterosexual identity. Instead, one appears asexual (Button, 2004). Conformity to an "appropriate" sex-gender role was displayed through dresses, makeup, and long hair for women and a masculine appearance for men. The purpose was to be sure to appear like everyone else (Kitzinger, 1991). Persons who used this strategy also portrayed a strictly business image. They stayed away from situations where hints of their sexual identity might occur. Personal situations were particularly avoided because intrusive questions might be asked. This included casual lunches, cocktail parties, and other social events. They also avoided conversations about leisure time and home life (Button, 2004; M.P. Levine & Leonard, 1984; Shachar & Gilbert, 1983).

Nondisclosure at Work: Negatives

Nondisclosure at work is adaptive for lesbian and gay workers. It creates fewer problems for them as they avoid stigma, discreditability, and discrimination (D'Emilio, 1983). However, living a double life is not only tedious, as noted earlier, but living separate and private and public lives can be costly. Secrecy strategies can result in depression, hostility, anxiety, low self-esteem, ill health, and high rates of substance use (Brooks, 1991; Triandis, Kurowski, & Gelfand, 1994). Lesbian and gay graduates of the Harvard Business School were respondents in a study by Friskopp and Silverstein (1995). The researchers reported that those who remained closeted at work experienced personal and professional difficulties and losses including vulnerability to blackmail and other forms of harassment, discomfort with socializing, lack of a strong support system, inability to experience more intense and supportive relationships with heterosexuals, fewer networking opportunities with other LGB persons, more problems with personal relationships, lowered self-esteem, and diminished legal grounds in discrimination suits.

In addition, the time and attention it takes to maintain a double life may limit productivity. Problems are also created when others are avoided in a setting that focuses on team or group based efforts. Over time social isolation may create the perception that one is aloof, unfriendly, or uncommunicative. One may become alienated from others. The situation may be particularly problematic in a context in which there is no clear division between home and work. Co-workers travel to one's home or frequently contact one at home, so additional time and effort are required to maintain one's counterfeit or heterosexual image (Button, 2004).

Living a double life can also place a person in an ethical conflict (M.P. Levine & Leonard, 1984) such as when one says nothing when anti-lesbian or gay jokes are told at work (Croteau & Hedstrom, 1993). One feels dishonest (Boatwright, Gilbert, Forrest, & Ketzenberger, 1996).

Disclosures at Work: Positives

The third strategy lesbian and gay workers use and confirmed by Button (2004) is *integration*. They disclose their sexual identity and try to deal with the consequences. They communicate to others in an explicit way what their sexual identity is or in an indirect way, such as putting a picture of a same sex-gender partner on their desks. Shallenberger (1994) found that some gay persons made no effort to hide and allowed co-workers to draw their own conclusion while others sat people down and told them about themselves. Many lesbian and gay persons have reported that they felt honest, empowered, and connected after they disclosed at work. They talked freely about their personal lives and their partners (M.P. Levine & Leonard, 1984).

Friskopp and Silverstein (1995) reported that lesbians were more likely to be out in the beginning of their careers but tended to become more closeted as their careers progressed. However, gay men were more closeted in the beginning of their careers while becoming progressively more open as their careers moved along. Lesbians more easily passed as heterosexual than gay men, but they experienced more discrimination because of their sexual identity (if revealed or discovered) and being women. Yet, in this study, if a workplace was perceived as nonhostile, the results from disclosure were better than the results from no disclosures. Those who disclosed to any people at work were more comfortable with their own sexual identity, out to heterosexual friends and family, and had a partner or LGB friends who encouraged them to come out at work. Those who were most satisfied with their current out status had experienced many disclosures with heterosexual friends and relatives before revealing their sexual identity at work. Developing and using a disclosure plan was helpful, and those that did this expressed the most happiness and contentment at work.

Another positive outcome of the integration strategy is that it lays the groundwork for social changes that may reduce stigma and costs associated with disclosures of lesbian or gay identities. The continual use of counterfeiting and avoiding will limit the kinds of interpersonal encounters (e.g., educative and advocacy) that lead to social change and ultimately the creation of a more affirming climate (M. Bernstein, 1997; Creed & Scully, 2000). Still, as in other life arenas, a complex cost-benefit analysis regarding disclosure in the workplace is often necessary (Gonsiorek, 1993). One can compare the likely benefits of disclosure (e.g., honesty, support, preventing any possibility of blackmail, bringing partners to work events) to the possible costs (e.g., lost income, demotions, job loss, no promotions, deprecation, gossip, social isolation, excessive energy to monitor cues of sexual identity, harassment) (M. Pope, 1996; Vargo, 1998).

When lesbian and gay workers decide to use the integration strategy, disclosures can come through deliberation such as costs-and-benefits assessment or impulsiveness (Hall, 1989). Deevey (1993) was deliberate about making disclosures on her job as a nurse. She had a plan to help her make a thoughtful decision. She identified plus and minus factors in the hospital where she worked as a nurse. For example, she identified nurses whose support she could seek as well as potential areas of difficulty such as a lack of positive role models and potential condemnation from closeted lesbian friends. However, sometimes there is no plan and disclosures are made out of frustration in response to intolerable pressures rather than a careful decision (Kitzinger, 1991). Even when nondisclosure seems right or rational and one has well-developed skills in disclosure management, sometimes disclosure becomes more of a heart issue than a head issue. Values and meaning become more important than "objective success" (Gonsiorek, 1993). Honesty is so important for some workers that even negative reactions do not deter them from being open (Shallenberger, 1994). In her work setting, Deevey (1993) reported that at first she did not disclose because of the fear of losing her new career as a nurse. She observed, however, that lesbian and gay patients were laughed at, mistreated, or denied treatment. Anger about these and other discriminatory situations motivated her to make disclosures. In addition, she was increasingly uncomfortable with her double life at work.

PART III:
PRACTICE WITH CLIENTS
WHO ARE COMING OUT
AND MAKING DISCLOSURES

Chapter 8

Working with Clients
Who Are Coming Out

LGB clients may seek services at any stage of the coming-out process (Gonsiorek, 1982). Some desire to know whether they have a same sex-gender or bisexual sexual identity. The main task is to assist these clients in exploring and discovering whatever self-identification they feel fits them. Until and unless clients are ready to self-identify with a label other than heterosexual, it is important not to assign a label or category to them. Even if some clients claim attraction to others of the same sex-gender and have sex with them they may reject labels for these attractions and behaviors.

For those who are unclear about their sexual identity, various methods can be used to assist them. Though none of the existing scales are yet fully satisfactory, some of the multidimensional scales such as the Klein Sexual Orientation Grid (Klein et al., 1985) can be useful in assisting clients who feel confused about their sexual identity. For clients who do not like sexual identity labels, practice can focus on the various aspects in the KSOG, such as sexual behavior, fantasy, and desire for emotional or affectional intimacy related to persons of the same sex-gender. Various combinations of how lesbian, gay, bisexual persons identify themselves can also be useful for clients to review (see Chapter 1).

USE OF DEVELOPMENTAL MODELS

Coming-out models are both useful and problematic when applied to clients. They are useful because they describe the way some persons

Coming Out and Disclosures
© 2007 by The Haworth Press, Inc. All rights reserved.
doi:10.1300/5423_09

experience the coming-out process, and they pinpoint the issues that may arise at each stage and suggest ways to help. However, they make assumptions about the development of sexual identity that are not true for all persons. They also obscure or invalidate issues that arise for persons from cultural backgrounds other than Euro-American. The models are also based on a dichotomous understanding of sexuality that does not validate bisexual identity as a mature outcome (Rust, 2003). It may be best with some clients to inquire about what they have actually experienced because this may vary from the established models. A client may provide a coming-out story not addressed in the models. Clients will also vary in the timing of moving from initial discovery of same-sex sexual interests to other stages. Many variables in one's social context will affect the coming-out process and the timing of reaching the various stages or stopping and not going further.

Coming-out models also imply a stable resolution to identification when one reaches the final stages. However, some clients may not experience stability. A complication in assessment is determining what might be genuine fluidity for some clients and the need for other clients to reach a definitive and essentialist understanding of their sexual identity that matches traditional models of identity development. These dual perspectives suggest the need to adopt both constructionist and essentialist stances (Bohan, 1996). A constructionist stance suggests that identities are not universal or fixed concepts (Cass, 1996). Yet, many clients wish to hold on to their essentialist beliefs that their sexual identity was in them all along waiting to be discovered. And once discovered there will be no changes in one's identity. This stance should be respected. The practitioner's task is to support flexibility around identity questions in whatever way that is meaningful to clients.

SUGGESTED INTERVENTIONS BASED ON COMING-OUT MODELS

The following are general suggestions that Cass (1996) provided when using her coming-out model in practice (see Chapter 2):

- *Use terms that fit the client's stage of identity development.* Referring to a client as lesbian, gay, or bisexual, for example, will not likely be received well when the person is saying, "I am confused about what I'm doing" (Stage 1) or "I might be gay, lesbian, or bisexual" (beginning of Stage 2) (Cass, 1996).
- *Identify the stage where the client is.* This can facilitate a focus on the particular issues of that stage instead of on same sex-gender sexual identity generally. Talking about the ideological aspects of oppression (Stage 5), for example, will probably not be of interest when someone's main desire is to meet other lesbian and gay persons (Stage 3).
- *Accept the stage location identified by the client.* An eighteen-year-old youth who happily says, "I am a lesbian" (end of Stage 3 and onward) should not hear, "You're too young to know that." Instead, the practitioner should recognize that identity formation for this person is already in progress.
- *Avoid judging one stage as better than another stage.* Judgment should be withheld regarding clients being advanced or not in coming out because their feelings and behaviors correspond or do not correspond with any particular stage. Care should be taken to not impose clinical judgments on clients in any of the stages.

Ideas were identified by Rust (1996) and others that may also be useful for practitioners with clients at the different stages in Cass's model of identity development.

1. *Identity Confusion.* This is probably the most difficult stage for many clients as they begin to think they might be lesbian, gay, or bisexual but still present a heterosexual identity. The practitioner can encourage clients who feel confused about their sexual identity or are just beginning to explore it to discover their own needs and desires without pressure or censorship (Matteson, 1996a). One can express to confused clients that it is all right to declare a nonheterosexual identity or not; to feel confused; to go back and forth; and to change their minds. The practitioner accepts clients as they are, no matter where this process takes them (Drescher, 1998; Mallon, 1998a).

Several other issues that may arise for clients at this early stage include the effects of a change in one identity (sexual) affecting all of one's other identities. In addition, changes in self-concept often happen. Clients often have negative thoughts about themselves, or they have internalized heterosexism. The negativity needs to be challenged (Levy, 1995). Positive LGB images can help and can be attained from TV programs, libraries, bookstores, and, sometimes, in classrooms. Clients can also imagine the social implications of a lesbian, gay, or bisexual identity. Although social relationships have not yet been lost at this point, one may also have to prepare to rebuild social relationships and establish new relationships that are consistent with one's developing new identity (Rust, 2003).

Some clients will experience conflict between thinking they might be lesbian, gay, or bisexual and their religion, and they experience guilt, shame, and depression as a result. Practitioners can help these clients talk their conflicts through as well as refer them to affirmative ministers and congregations. Supportive LGB religious groups and organizations can also help such as Dignity (for Catholics), Integrity (for Episcopalians), and lesbian and gay churches such as the Metropolitan Community Churches (MCC). Bibliotherapy is also useful, including books such as the one by Helminiak (1995), *What the Bible Really Says About Homosexuality.*

2. *Identity Comparison.* At this stage, clients begin to think they might be lesbian or gay but continue to present a heterosexual identity to others. They might confide in trusted friends or counselors who might provide them with one-on-one support. Clients can consider the implications of identifying as lesbian or gay, but they have to transform the categories of lesbian or gay or dispel negative attributions to these categories before they can place themselves in one of them (de Monteflores & Schultz, 1978). While they may not be ready to seek out lesbian and gay social scenes, they might appreciate knowing that lesbian and gay communities exist and that in these communities being LGB is normal (Rust, 2003).

Other issues at this stage include the difference between how one views oneself and how others view one, and feeling that one is different from others. One also realizes that norms, ideals, and expectations based on the presumption of heterosexuality are no longer applicable to one's self. Clients should be encouraged to grieve the loss of a heterosexual identity, social relationships, and the previously taken-for-granted sense of belonging to mainstream society and culture (Rust, 2003). These persons also lose a sense of continuity or experience a psychological break between their past, present, and future. They are no longer the persons they thought they were (Cass, 1996; Rust, 2003). Since the sense of continuity in their lives is disrupted, they often look back at their pasts to find early signs of their sexual identity. The purpose of this is to find a sense of continuity. Or they might think that they cannot be anything but heterosexual, because they remember pleasurable heterosexual experiences in the past. However, this is typical in the histories of lesbian and gay persons. Not only do they have past heterosexual experiences, but many still have attractions to the other gender even after coming out as lesbian or gay (Rust, 2003). In a sample of women who identified as lesbians, Rust (2002) found that 91 percent had heterosexual relationships at some point in their lives and 43 percent of them had a heterosexual romantic or sexual relationship since coming out. Only one-third reported that they were 100 percent attracted to women. Two-thirds reported that 5 percent of their feelings of sexual attractions were associated with men.

3. *Identity Tolerance.* At this stage clients have greater commitment to a lesbian or gay identity so they are likely to want seek out LGB communities. In these communities, they will begin to see that their identities are ones they should have pride in. If they do not know locations, practitioners should be able to direct them to places such as community centers, bookstores, and special-interest groups where LGB persons congregate to meet other LGB persons. This should include specialty groups such as those for bisexual persons or ethnic, racial, or Jewish LGB persons (B. Green, 1994; Icard, 1986; Rust, 2003). Also, there are LGB newspapers and phone books that list LGB organizations. In Dallas, for example, there are the *Lambda Pages: Your Guide to Pride, Gay and Lesbian Rainbow Pages,* and *Dallas/Ft. Worth Gay Yellow Pages.* Affirmative books and articles can be helpful if local groups do not exist (Rust, 2003).

4. *Identity Acceptance.* At this stage, clients begin to make disclosures of their sexual identity to others in various arenas. Interventions related to preparing for disclosures can be used, as discussed in the Chapter 9.

5. *Identity Pride.* A client may experience conflict at this stage with a desire to be completely out but anticipates that this will create difficulties in some situation (Rust, 2003). They have to learn to manage their identities.

6. *Identity Synthesis.* Clients have worked through much of the coming-out process by this stage. They are often preparing to terminate services, as they may no longer feel a need for a practitioner.

Another way to look at the stages in the Cass model is what clients who go through these stages experience psychologically. At the first two stages, clients have not experienced the stigma and social judgments associated with gay and lesbian identities. Given this, it is usual for some clients to feel excitement about their emerging identities. And distress, although not absent (see Chapter 2 and the view of Rust [1996] earlier about the difficulty of Stage 1), tends to be lower than what may be experienced at the two middle stages where they are tested with the outcomes of disclosures, including hostility, rejection, and perhaps isolation. They also accept that they are lesbian or gay and that this is permanent (Beals & Peplau, 2005). Halpin and Allen (2004) recommended that support and resources be targeted primarily at those at the middle stages. Negotiating these stages may be associated with increased rates of depression, suicidal ideation, and suicidal attempts. However, they found that improvements came about at the two later stages (Stages 5 and 6). At these stages, lesbian and gay persons are happier and more satisfied with life, less lonely, and have a strong sense of self-esteem. Luhtanen (2003) and R.-J. Green (2002) found that certain factors are significantly associated with higher self-esteem and lower depression scores. These factors include visibility, rejection of negative stereotypes, acceptance from family, alternate sources of support and resources, involvement with other LGB persons, and feeling positive about one's sexual identity. Luhtanen noted that having a positive sexual identity was the most robust predictor of psychological well-being. Rejecting negative stereotypes was also important in the development of a positive sexual identity and in fostering psychological well-being. Beals and Peplau (2005) also found that lesbians who experienced higher levels of identity support from significant others reported higher levels of self-esteem, satisfaction with life, and overall well-being, and lower levels of depression.

SPECIAL ISSUES WITH YOUTH
WHO MAY BE COMING OUT

Adolescents and their parents may want to know how to predict LGB sexual identities. Few reliable indictors predict which youth will take this road. Yet, one's identity may shift from mere consideration of a nonheterosexual identity to certainty when (1) sexual activity happens with a same-sex partner, (2) thoughts happen that one might be lesbian, gay, or bisexual, and (3) one's attractions and fantasies about the same sex-gender persist and intensify (Rosario et al., 1996). Youths who might later define themselves as gay are more likely than others to engage in same-sex sexual behavior as teens and tend to do so for a longer time (Savin-Williams, 1990). However, many youths who identify, or eventually identify, as gay, lesbian, or bisexual also engage in heterosexual sex during their childhood and adolescence (Diamond, 1998; Rotheram-Borus, Hunter, & Rosario, 1994). With age, however, the meaning of sexual attractions, fantasies, and behaviors becomes clearer to them (Remafedi, Farrow, & Deisher, 1991). A high correspondence also increasingly emerges among desires, sexual behavior, and identity (Savin-Williams, 1995b). The data of Rosario and colleagues and Savin-Williams (1995a) indicate that once sexual identity becomes certain to a lesbian or gay youth, one's sexual activity is primarily with same-sex gender partners, with corresponding decreases of sexual activity with other-sex gender partners.

LGB youths negotiate developmental transitions when their adaptive skills can meet the demands of the transition (Herdt, 1989). If, during a sexual identity transition, confusion continues regarding same sex-gender sexual fantasies, attractions, or incidents of same sex-gender sexual contact, young persons can explore the meanings of their attractions and fantasies with a practitioner. Practitioners can provide information to help these youths clarify their sexual identities using scales such as the Klein Sexual Orientation Grid (Klein et al., 1985).

COMING-OUT ISSUES FOR BISEXUAL PERSONS

Bisexual clients may seek assistance for and express both identity concerns and system concerns. This involves how to handle the difficulties and complications of adopting a bisexual identity, how to handle multiple relationships if desired, and how to find supports for bisexual relationships. More specific potential issues identified by Matteson (1996b) and others include the following:

Exploration of bisexuality and coming out to self. Due to the prevalent dichotomized conceptions of sexual identity, those who experience sexual attractions to both sex-genders may self-identify as lesbian or gay or as heterosexual. Confusion about sexual identity is especially intense during the early stages of bisexual identity development. Practitioners can help these clients reframe their confusion as a response to society's heterosexism and to simplistic dichotomous views of sexuality (Stokes & Damon, 1995). The practitioner can also communicate that sexual identity is not dichotomous and that persons who identify as heterosexual may experience same-sex gender fantasies and same-sex gender experiences at times, and that these experiences are not evidence of being lesbian, gay, or bisexual. This removes the pressure for clients to think they are one sexual identity or another and allows them to decide for themselves what they want to identify as (M.S. Schneider, Brown, & Glassgold, 2002). Clients can also read autobiographical accounts of how other bisexual women and men successfully moved through the coming-out process (e.g., Off Pink Collective, 1988). Practitioners can provide locations of organizations for bisexual persons and additional ways for them to meet other bisexual persons. This helps clients, who are still working out their identities, to sort out the direction of their sexual feelings and behaviors (Matteson, 1996b).

Life decisions. Practitioners can assist clients to make realistic assessments of the life decisions they are contemplating. Assessment areas identified by Matteson (1996b) include the following:

- *Personal and social risk taking.* Is the client willing to take personal risks such as internalized oppression, HIV/AIDS, and harassment or bashing? Is the client willing to take social risks such as being fired from a job?
- *Sex and intimacy.* Are sex and intimacy viewed as occurring together or as separate processes? Are they associated with one or

both sex-genders? How important is each of these factors to clients? Are clients open to recreational sex?

- *Importance of the sex-gender of a partner.* Are one's attractions more for women or men? Or is the sex-gender of a partner not a significant determinant of partner choice?
- *How many partners?* Is monogamy preferred or does the client seek more than one partner?
- *Client's tolerance levels for ambiguity, confusion, and complexity.* Can clients tolerate these experiences that accompany concurrent, multiple relationships with both sex-genders? Conclusions about this can be sorted out by fantasy alone by some clients whereas for others real-life experience is necessary.

Fluidity. Is fluidity acceptable, especially in the case of a woman? Even when they acknowledge attractions to both sex-genders, women's sexual identity may remain fluid and more defined by particular relationships or social settings (Rust, 1993; Savin-Williams & Diamond, 1999).

Lack of social confirmation for bisexual attractions. Bisexual persons may have trouble attaining social validation from both heterosexual and gay and lesbian persons. In addition, because of the myths about bisexuality, such as it does not exist, they may have difficulty developing and sustaining a bisexual identity (Rust, 2003). Practitioners can affirm that attraction to persons of both sex-genders is legitimate and acceptable. This may be the only "therapy" many clients need (Fox, 1991; Stokes & Damon, 1995).

Overcoming self-oppression. Bisexual persons struggle with heterosexism because of their attractions to persons of their own sex-gender. They are also at odds with taboos about extramarital sex or multiple relationships (Matteson, 1996b). It is important for them to become acquainted with persons who are comfortable with their bisexual sexual identity. Experiences in bisexual coming-out groups and affirmative readings are helpful (Lourea, 1985; Paul, 1988).

Guilt. If clients who are exploring coming out as bisexual are presently in a committed heterosexual link, they may feel guilty if they break the expectation of sexual exclusivity. Support networks can help both the persons coming out as bisexual and their partners, who are coping with this news (Matteson, 1995).

Grief. Coming out often involves grief (Barron, 1996; Thompson, 1992) as persons recognize that earlier dreams and desires no longer work for them. Bisexual persons might have wanted monogamy and a traditional life of heterosexual marriage with children. These persons may also grieve the loss of support from some heterosexual friends and relatives.

Finding support networks. It is essential for bisexual clients to interact with positive models of bisexual identity. If clients are unaware of resources, practitioners can help them identify places where they can meet others with the same sexual identity and common interests.

Issues for previously gay or lesbian identified persons. Lesbian and gay persons are often surprised when they become captivated with someone of the other sex-gender. They may also be surprised that reentry into the world of heterosexual relations can create social difficulties for them (Matteson, 1995). Women who identified as lesbian before realizing that they were bisexual may particularly experience little support in the lesbian community (Nichols, 1988). They need support groups specifically for women like them who have been exclusively lesbian for an extended period and are now aware of heterosexual attractions—as do gay persons in the same situations (Lourea, 1985).

COMING-OUT ISSUES
FOR TRANSGENDER PERSONS

Transgender persons may seek a practitioner because of a need to understand a compulsive desire to cross-dress; the belief that they are different from others or perverted, mentally ill, or sinful; the belief that they are in the wrong body; and the strong dislike of their genitals. Common issues in the transgender client population also include shame, depression, guilt, low self-esteem, low sense of competence, social isolation, substance misuse, and suicidal behaviors. They are also dealing with secretiveness about their feelings about being in the wrong body (B.F. Anderson, 1998). An extensive list of assessment factors for use with transgender persons—including those related to health history, mental health history, legal history, sexual history, and sex-gender continuum placement is provided in the work of Cole et al. (2000) and Lev (2005).

Most transgender persons studied by Gagné et al. (1997) were in counseling. Practitioners must communicate to these clients that whatever they present about themselves is totally acceptable, and that they value and appreciate diversity (Gagné et al., 1997). Another major task for practitioners is to provide accurate and meaningful information for these clients (B.F. Anderson, 1998).

Support groups are of particular help for transgender persons to test out their identities. In these groups, they feel acceptance and may experience the freedom to be themselves for the first time. If others in these groups accept them, they often feel that they are truly transgender. Organizations, publications, and online services that focus on transgender persons are also helpful (Gagné et al., 1997).

Another concern for transgender clients is sexual reassignment surgery if they decide to pursue this course. They will likely need support before and after surgery. If persons are thinking about SRS but do not know much about it, they need concrete information about requirements of candidacy for the surgery. They also may need information about electrolysis, hormonal intervention, cosmetic surgery, and other desired resources. Reality testing and examination of future expectations are also important. Work with these clients usually takes a minimum of six months before surgery and for a continued time following surgery (B.F. Anderson, 1998).

Centers that do SRS should be recommended but only ones that do not coerce clients into specific outcomes or exclude persons deemed too young, too old, or who will not "pass" well in the new sex-gender. These centers also should not require clients to cross live full-time as a condition for initiating hormone therapy. This requirement creates a dangerous situation for hate crimes because prior to hormone treatment, these persons can be easily noticed. Only a few such centers exist in the United States, including the University of Michigan Comprehensive Gender Services Program and the University of Minnesota Program in Human Sexuality (Cole et al., 2000).

Some transgender persons have no preparation for the period following SRS. Others who relocate to "start a new life" may feel isolated and lonely. The practitioner can perform a supportive role, helping to bolster coping skills and furnishing information about community services. These clients also need assistance in coping with discrimination and victimization in society at large. For example, they need an accurate assessment of how well they pass as the new sex-gender and must prepare to cope if identified by others as transgender, if this matters to them. Practitioners can address modifications in appearance and behavior. They may also need to address relationship stressors or specific transition periods, such as when partners enter or leave their lives or when children mature (B.F. Anderson, 1998).

Persons who want SRS but cannot attain it because of health or financial reasons may require considerable support. They have to come to terms with the lack of fulfillment of their dreams of matching their bodies with their sex-gender. Practitioners can help them to cross live successfully without surgical modification of their bodies. The primary goals with all transgender clients are to experience the relief of painful feelings and self-assessments, make informed decisions, and live productive and fulfilling lives (B.F. Anderson, 1998).

Chapter 9

Working with Clients
Who Want to Make Disclosures

Some lesbians are outside the closet in everything they do and with whomever they are interacting with (Whitman et al., 2000). In an ideal world, this would be the case for all LGB persons. Same sex-gender and bisexual sexual orientations, attractions, and relationships would garner respect and positive support across all arenas (Grace, 1992). Since this is not the case, disclosure for most LGB persons is a complex, grueling, and never-finished endeavor (Gonsiorek, 1993; Kitzinger, 1991). With every new person, decisions are made whether to disclose or not (Garnets et al., 1990).

All LGB persons must decide how to manage their identities (Healy, 1993). Goffman (1963) identified two possible scenarios for persons with stigmatizing identities. One can be discredited because the stigma is immediately apparent or known beforehand. The discredited person's main task is to manage the tension in social interactions. This first scenario fits situations in which disclosures have been made so one's sexual identity is known. Passing as heterosexual fits Goffman's second scenario. The stigma of the discredited person is not immediately apparent so the management of personal information is the essential task.

If clients are debating about whether to make disclosures, they must decide what to do about them and if they are willing to cope with tensions resulting from being open. Practitioners' views about making disclosures are inappropriate to discuss with clients. Clients have the right to make their own choices about disclosures and deter-

Coming Out and Disclosures
© 2007 by The Haworth Press, Inc. All rights reserved.
doi:10.1300/5423_10

mine the direction of their lives. It is important, however, to focus on the potential dangers for clients and to be sure that they weigh them when deciding to disclose or not. Not making disclosures may be the best decision when one concludes that negative consequences will occur or that few, if any, positive consequences will result. Also, because lesbian and gay persons can be the victims of violence, maintaining safety is crucial (R.-J. Green, 2000).

PREPARING FOR DISCLOSURES

If clients want to make disclosures, practitioners can help them assess persons and situations for costs and benefits (Browning, Reynolds, & Dworkin, 1991). Barbone and Rice (1994) suggested applying the question "What's in it for me?" Disclosures should be self-serving and promote one's best interests. In a study of gay persons, Cain (1991a) found that a cost-benefit analysis was used to determine whether to make a disclosure. Without a beneficial return, such as more honesty and self-respect, or a closer relationship, disclosure may not seem worth the risks. Projecting the possible negative consequences is central in this analysis (A.S. Walters & Phillips, 1994). Clients can be asked to envision the reactions of others in their interpersonal lives through questions such as the following: "If you make disclosures, how would your mother/father, best friend/girl- or boyfriend/wife or husband/children/religious leader/employer react?" "How would you respond?" "Which friends would be supportive?" "If married, what would be the implications for your marriage and how would you feel about that?" (Rust, 2003).

If clients feel they can handle the repercussions of disclosures, they can be helped to make thoughtful choices about the issues of whom, when, where, and how (Williamson, 1998). These assessments and the other preparations discussed here are part of the pragmatic skills one needs when considering disclosures (Gonsiorek, 1993).

Whom involves which persons to tell. Clients have an uncanny ability to predict responses to startling information and can often anticipate the best and worst situations with those they might tell (Kuehlwein, 1992; Williamson, 1998). It is useful for clients to develop a list of persons they want to tell. They can also decide whom they might want to leave out of the list. Since it often takes weeks or months to work through feelings about a particular disclosure, it is best not to disclose to everyone on one's list simultaneously. Rank ordering those on the list is useful as well as taking breaks between each disclosure (Gartrell, 1984).

When involves timing and the issue of when one should or should not disclose (Williamson, 1998). In her job as a nurse, Deevey (1993) reported what she did about the timing of her disclosures to other nurses: "I chose the timing carefully, when privacy was available. I determined that extreme loneliness or anger in response to . . . [heterosexist] remarks could trigger my self-disclosure. Because both these feelings expanded my vulnerability, I tried to postpone self-disclosure until I felt reasonably secure" (p. 22). Clients should make disclosures when they are feeling positive about themselves rather than when they are feeling vulnerable. They should also feel prepared instead of making impulsive or reactive disclosures (Gartrell, 1984).

Where involves variations such as making disclosures in private or public settings, such as at home versus at a restaurant (Williamson, 1998). One should determine where one would feel most comfortable making a disclosure.

How involves the style of disclosure such as a subtle statement, a strong statement, or a matter-of-fact statement (Williamson, 1998). The strongest or the most forward type of disclosure is the Queer Nation approach. Here, lesbian and gay persons announce their sexual identity publicly by every act they do, with the accompanying attitude that it is unimportant whether other persons like them or not (Esterberg, 1996). Most persons use a more subtle approach such as when a lesbian, in response to being asked about her weekend, says "I had a date with a woman" (M. Pope, 1995).

Some clients may need coaching on various ways to make disclosures as well as time to prepare (Williamson, 1998). Role-play is useful for rehearsing various approaches to telling others and practicing projected disclosure conversations (Gartrell, 1984; Mallon, 1998b). The practitioner and client can play both sides of an interchange, and the role-play can be audio- or videotaped and played back for critique and revision. Clients can practice styles of delivery and word choices. They can practice making disclosures in a proud, affirmative, and direct manner. This communicates that they feel good about themselves and their lives. Rehearsals and practice can improve confidence and skill at handling a difficult disclosure such as disclosure to parents. Repeated practice, using standard communication and assertion techniques, is also helpful (Kuehlwein, 1992).

Scenarios for practice and role-plays, presented by Deevey (1993), are useful examples of how to word disclosures that match a particular purpose:

- "I know you know . . . , but I wanted to bring it out in the open. I am a lesbian" (p. 22). With this approach sensitivity from the listener is anticipated.
- "You are an open-minded person. . . . I've decided to be more open about my lesbian relationship with Lana" (p. 22). This is an approach to use with persons one wants to keep as friends and colleagues. So one appeals to strengths in the recipients such as maturity.
- "I need your support for a risk I want to take. I'm starting to tell people about the lesbian community that I am part of " (p. 22). This approach enlists assistance from the listener.
- "I want to share something with you, since you have talked so openly with me. . . ." (p. 22). This approach can be used when the goal is to build friendships based on honesty and equality in self-disclosures. It is most effective with peers.

GETTING READY TO TELL ONE'S PARENTS

Since disclosures to parents are usually the most difficult to make, the rest of this chapter focuses on LGBT children and their parents. Some useful considerations in deciding whether to make disclosures to one's parents were provided by R.-J. Green (2000, 2002):

1. preexisting levels of closeness, openness, and conflict;
2. time shared together;
3. importance of the family for sex-gender identity and economic support;
4. availability of other forms of support; and
5. cost/benefit appraisal of the anticipated responses of family members.

Many LGBT persons finally decide to disclose their sexual identity or sex-gender expression to their parents mainly because of the internal costs from not doing this. For example, they may feel guilty about misleading their parents (Leaveck, 1994; Strommen, 1990) or feel uncomfortable with the wall between themselves and their parents (L.S. Brown, 1989a; Cramer & Roach, 1988). Yet, they may still fear the outcomes of disclosing to their parents.

It is helpful for clients who have decided to disclose to parents to make their strongest fears explicit in words. They may be able to desensitize their worst fears or feel that they can live through them if they happen (Kuehlwein, 1992). Also, they need to practice making the first disclosure to parents a positive one. When children use positive words in their initial disclosure to parents (e.g., "I am lesbian and happy"), both they and their parents adjust more easily. An adjustment is more difficult when the first disclosure contains negative information (e.g., "I have a problem because I am gay") or even neutral information (e.g., "I am gay"). Disclosures should also not be equivocal, such as "I think I am gay" (Ben-Ari, 1995). Equivocation fosters denial in parents, or they might think that their children can change their minds or get "fixed" through "therapy" (Scasta, 1998).

Parents typically have internalized a negative view of LGB or T identities and apply it to their child (Mallon, 1999). This view is filtered through the coping mechanisms typically used by parents (R.-J. Green, 2002; R.-J. Green & Mitchell, 2002). Clients need to avoid defending their sexual identity or sex-gender expression with parents who have rigid moral beliefs. Nor should they defer to heterosexist remarks or prejudicial statements about transgender persons (Gartrell, 1984). The practitioner can model a steady and resilient response to intense parental reactions (Williamson, 1998). If clients anticipate outright rejection, they need sufficient resources such as support systems to help them deal with the situation (Scasta, 1998). Adolescents especially need resources because they are usually emotionally or financially dependent on parents. If they contemplate negative reactions, such as verbal and physical harm or eviction from the home, they may want to hold off disclosures until they are in a more favorable emotional and financial position (D'Augelli, Hershberger, & Pilkington, 1998; Vargo, 1998). However, if they insist on making disclosures, they should develop a safety plan. For example, if parents throw them out of the house whom can they contact for emotional and financial support? Where can they live? They need a list of contact persons, their locations and phone numbers, and local services, including emergency assistance (Vargo, 1998).

WORKING WITH PARENTS AFTER THE DISCLOSURE

Parents are rarely unaffected upon first learning of their child's LGBT identity, but there is no uniform way they respond (Greene, 1994b; Robinson, Walters, & Skeen, 1989). Neither are they likely to progress in an orderly way as stage theories suggest (Savin-Williams, 2001).

Parents' Reactions

Rarely does the initial response by parents represent full support and understanding, but this is a response that is unlikely to continue (Savin-Williams, 2001). Theorists have categorized various reactions that white parents may experience into stages (e.g., McCubbin & Patterson, 1983; Neisen, 1987; Robinson et al., 1989). The stage approaches of Savin-Williams and Dubé (1998), Savin-Williams (2001), and others are summarized here, although the extent of parents who experience the various reactions in these stages is not known.

First, parents may experience an initial reaction of *shock.* They usually move on to other emotions, but shock can intrude into the daily life of some parents for a long time (Savin-Williams, 2001). Besides shock, parents may feel estranged from their child; this person suddenly is a stranger or someone they no longer know. They may not know how to act with this person (B.E. Bernstein, 1990).

Second, parents experience *denial and isolation.* They may pretend the disclosure did not happen or refuse to believe it and not acknowledge it. They may dismiss it as experimentation, rebellion, or a passing phase. Or, if they acknowledge the information in the disclosure, they may feel isolated if they think they are in a unique situation (Savin-Williams, 2001).

Third, parents experience *anger, agitation, or even rage.* They can feel anger toward what they think are external causes of their child's same sex-gender desires (such as thinking their child was seduced by another person). Or, they can feel guilty if they think that bad parenting might have caused this to happen and fear they will be judged as doing something wrong as parents. They sometimes try to recall past situations, even during the prenatal period that perhaps "caused" their child's "problem" (B.E. Bernstein, 1990). Some parents feel that they destroyed their children's lives (Fairchild & Hayward, 1979). Parents are influenced by numerous sources including psychoanalytic and psychological theories, religious exhortations, and public opinion (B.E. Bernstein, 1990). They may believe older theories that blamed the mother primarily and the father secondarily for same-sex attractions in children (Scasta, 1998). If parents do not feel responsible for their child's sexual orientation they may angrily ask their children why they did this to them (C. Griffin, Wirth, & Wirth, 1986; Robinson et al., 1989).

Fourth, parents may *bargain* or try to make various exchanges with their child. For example, they might agree to not throw a child out of the house or not end an allowance if, for example, the child agrees to "convert" back to being heterosexual. Or they may bargain for the child to tell no one else. Some parents, who feel guilty that they have a LGB child or think this came about because of poor parenting skills, may make pacts to be good so that this situation will change (Savin-Williams, 2001).

Fifth, parents may experience *emotions* such as *depression, grief, and shame*. One-quarter to one-half of parents studied by Ben-Ari (1995) experienced these emotional states. If others discover the facts about their child, parents may feel even greater humiliation and shame. Some parents experience profound grief, as if their child were dead (Robinson et al., 1989), while other parents declare that their child no longer has a role or identity as a family member (L.E. Collins & Zimmerman, 1983; DeVine, 1983-1984). Some parents are disappointed and sad because they now have no hopes of grandchildren and continuation of family lines (B.E. Bernstein, 1990; Scasta, 1998). Parents who feel ashamed of their child's sexual orientation will not want to expose themselves to possible rejection from others who may disapprove. So they will not turn to family, physicians or mental health professionals, or the church. Parents sometimes distance themselves even from close friends if they think they will be rejecting (B.E. Bernstein, 1990; C. Rosenfeld & Emerson, 1998).

Sixth, parents reach the final stage of *acceptance.* Most studies report acceptance levels to be just under 50 percent for both parents (D'Augelli et al., 1998; Remafedi, 1987). Acceptance may come with the passage of time when parents realize that all efforts to change the situation have not done so. They no longer see their child's sexual orientation as temporary—nor is it kept a secret (Savin-Williams, 2001). They revise their dreams for their child and come to accept the new identity of their child (L.S. Brown, 1989a; Strommen, 1989, 1990). Accepting parents also gain the perspective that a lesbian or gay identity is only one part of the total child they love (Strommen, 1990). Eventually, the child's sexual identity is not a focus (Savin-Williams, 2001).

The ideal goal is for parents to convey love for their children (Vargo, 1998) and help them create a positive identity (Hammersmith, 1987). Only a few parents, however, become proud parents of an LGB child. Indeed, most parents remain somewhat ambivalent (Savin-Williams, 2001). Some may not accept that their child's condition is moral or normal. Even if parents think same sex-gender sexual orientation is a natural variation of sexuality, many still feel embarrassed by one of their children being lesbian, gay, or bisexual (B.E. Bernstein, 1990). On the other hand, disclosures can create an opportunity for transformation for parents (Mallon, 1999). Savin-Williams (1996) suggested that once parents become comfortable with same sex-gender or bisexual sexual orientations they may invest in social change as a way to help improve the lives of LGB persons. Youths feel affirmed when parents join with actions to counter heterosexism and become social activists in schools and communities. However, most families go no further than accommodating and adapting to their child's disclosure.

The reactions of parents with a transgender child are similar to those in families with a lesbian, gay, or bisexual member (K. Ellis & Eriksen, 2002; Emerson & Rosenfeld, 1996). Parents (as well as other family members) who discover a member's cross sex-gender behavior often experience *shock and denial.* They may be able to keep up the denial if the person does not assume a full-time cross sex-gender role or lives away from home. The predominant feeling following shock and denial is *anger.* Often, the parents direct frustration and scapegoating at the transgender child for upsetting the family with "crazy" ideas or behaviors. They blame this child for any family difficulties.

Parents also *bargain* with their transgender children. They may threaten them with disinheritance if they will not behave "normally" or at least keep cross-dressing or sexual reassignment surgery secret. Parents may offer money for their children to go to college or begin a business (Emerson & Rosenfeld, 1996; C. Rosenfeld & Emerson, 1998).

As the reality of a transgender child sets in further, parents and other family members may experience *depression, weeping, physical illness, or suicide.* The transgender child may also experience these reactions. Sometimes family members withdraw or start using drugs. If discord in the family escalates, the parents may pursue divorce (Emerson & Rosenfeld, 1996; C. Rosenfeld & Emerson, 1998).

For parents with more moderate emotions, a family ceremony can help the family accept the "rebirth" of the transgender member and start a new beginning. The goal is to accept "what is." This can assist the adjustment to change, reestablish communication among family members, and normalize what is at first incomprehensible behavior (C. Rosenfeld & Emerson, 1998). Parents reach *acceptance* when they confront the loss of the child they once knew and no longer try to force their child to change. They shift their focus to concerns about the welfare of their transgender child (Emerson & Rosenfeld, 1996; C. Rosenfeld & Emerson, 1998).

Accepting versus Nonaccepting Parents

Parents may or may not come to terms with a LGBT child. A positive relationship between parents and children before the disclosure may be a good omen for a positive resolution following disclosure (Savin-Williams & Dubé, 1998). Some families move toward more closeness following a child's disclosure. The information can open up communication and intimacy within the family. Hence, families can become stronger, closer, and more honest (Mallon, 1999). Even conservative religious parents who love their child unconditionally can respond in an accepting, loving manner (Savin-Williams, 2001). Transgender children who make disclosures to parents often believe that the relationship bond will weather the strain. Given time and space to adjust to the information, responses from their parents mostly become accepting, tolerant, and supportive (Gagné et al., 1997).

Other parents, including liberal parents, who have a poor relationship with their lesbian, gay, or bisexual child, can initially react negatively and with rage. Progressing from an initially positive base also does not predict that the relations will remain positive or improve; some deteriorate. Progressing from an initially negative reaction, relations can stay bad, deteriorate, or improve, if only slightly (Savin-Williams, 2001). Parents cannot be moved further than they are ready to move and while some parents may reach intellectual acceptance, it may take much longer for them to achieve emotional acceptance (Wren, 2002).

Rejecting parents of LGBT children accept the negative stereotypes about them and do not stop applying these negative views to their child. They blame this person for causing disruption in the family and negating their role in the family. They idealize and long for their child's old family role. Feeling estranged, they are unable to identity with their child's feelings (Strommen, 1990). Rejecting parents also cannot allow their children to develop in their own way. They show no support for their children's personal development that includes an exploration of alternative sexual identities and sex-gender expressions (Laird, 1996). They do not realize that part of what is going on with their children is what happens in any family as the children begin to show value differences, develop autonomy, and put more emphasis on relationships and interests outside the family (L.S. Brown, 1989a).

Since some parents remain rejecting and never reach acceptance, their children may regret ever having disclosed to them, because relations with them and the whole family are now strained and damaged (L.S. Brown, 1989a; DeVine, 1983-1984; McDonald, 1983-1984; Strommen, 1989). Parents who are rejecting and offending may later blame themselves for family rifts. The rifts, however, may take years to repair, if a repair is even possible (Mattison & McWhirter, 1995). If parents trivialized what their children told them, they may hear nothing more from them (L.S. Brown, 1989a; Strommen, 1989, 1990).

Practitioners can help clients to understand that future relationships with rejecting parents are largely dependent on the parents' willingness to expunge themselves of heterosexism and prejudicial attitudes toward transgender persons through self-examination and education (Gartrell, 1984). Sanders and Kroll (2000) recommended that the processes that are restraining and demeaning be named, such as *heterosexism*. For the children, empathy and patience may diffuse angry responses to parents who are rejecting by placing their negative reactions into context. For example, they can be encouraged to recall how long it took them to accept their sexual orientation (Kuehlwein, 1992). Still, rejecting parents are difficult to contend with and being in this situation can affect one's mental health (D'Augelli, 2003).

Sometimes parents who cannot move beyond intense emotions require intervention. For example, if their grief is severe, the practitioner can encourage them to go through "regrieving." They discuss the disclosure event in more detail so that they can fully experience their grief. If anger is severe, anger control sessions may be necessary (Coenen, 1998). If religion is a barrier to moving beyond grief and anger, the practitioner should refer the parents to affirmative clergy. Also, affirmative material from some mainline denominations is available on same sex-gender sexual orientation and religion (Hammersmith, 1987).

If motivated, parents can also learn skill-building techniques for resolving disputes and communication impasses. For example, they can be instructed in how to replace inappropriate communications, such as accusatory statements or lecturing, with positive communications, such as active listening, with accompanying positive nonverbal behaviors. Cognitive restructuring is useful for identifying and challenging unrealistic beliefs and faulty cognitions. More appropriate cognitions can be modeled and the parents can rehearse them (Coenen, 1998).

ANSWERING PARENTS' QUESTIONS

Aside from the reactions parents may experience when LGBT children make disclosures to them, they will also probably ask many questions about same sex-gender sexual orientation or sex-gender expression. Typical questions and some ways to address them follow:

How did this happen? Most parents want to know how or why their child is lesbian, gay, bisexual, or transgender. They want to know the cause to help them make sense of what happened with their child. However, they should be informed that the cause of nonheterosexual sexual orientations or sex-gender expression is not known (B.E. Bernstein, 1990).

Is it permanent? Most parents want to know whether the expressed sexual orientation or sex-gender expression of their child is permanent. Or can their child change? Is this just a passing phase? (B.E. Bernstein, 1990; Emerson & Rosenfeld, 1996). Parents need to be helped to conquer false hopes for change, although some will not surrender these hopes easily (Mallon, 1998b). Sexual identity can be fluid, and persons can modify their same sex-gender sexual behavior but not their attractions. If the child is transgender, the practitioner must help parents to realize that this child is not going through a phase either and is unlikely to quit pursuing strong desires for changes in sex-gender expression (C. Rosenfeld & Emerson, 1998).

What kind of future is there for my child? Parents envision their child living a lonely life and never having children or stable relationships. Parents also worry about prejudice and violence against their child (B.E. Bernstein, 1990; Robinson et al., 1989). If the child is male, the greatest concern is HIV/AIDS (Robinson et al., 1989). Parents need accurate, unbiased information about same sex-gender sexual orientation, sex-gender expression, and HIV/AIDS (Williamson, 1998). It can be useful to use bibliotherapy or assigned readings on these and other pertinent topics (Neisen, 1987). Meeting other LGB persons who live happy lives can also be constructive for these parents. Most will have close friends and a partner.

What about disclosures outside the family? If parents decide that others should know about their child, the issue arises of who should make the disclosure. The practitioner should discuss the issue of "outing" or when someone else announces a person's sexual orientation or sex-gender expression without that person's permission. When this happens, the person may not be able to handle the public disclosure. It should always be the person's choice to make these disclosures, and parents should honor this (Cabaj, 1996).

A POSITIVE VISION FOR PARENTS

Parents need a vision of a positive outcome and the knowledge that other families have successfully met the same challenges they are experiencing. Parents also need to know that they will require time as well as stamina for their adjustment to the new realities they face (Hammersmith, 1987). Many affirmative books now exist, some written by parents (e.g., C. Griffin et al. 1986; Muller, 1987; Rafkin, 1987). Books by parents provide views on developing an accepting and affirmative family environment for LGBT members (L.S. Brown, 1989a). Reading about the progress of other parents can provide parents hope that they can also reach acceptance. It can help to know that other parents also struggled to reach this goal.

There are also helpful Web sites, such as My Child Is Gay! Now What Do I Do? (available at www.pe.net/~bidstrup/parents.htm). Parents can be assigned readings from the professional literature, such as the findings of Beeler and DiProva (1999) that identified twelve themes in family stories on having a lesbian or gay child. These themes reflect how families responded to disclosures over time and how they integrated a lesbian or gay child into the family.

SUPPORT GROUPS FOR PARENTS AND CHILDREN

Parents with LGBT children need love and support (Cole et al., 2000). Those who can develop sources of social support are better able to recover and regain stability (McCubbin & Patterson, 1983). It is important, therefore, for practitioners to help parents with LGBT children expand their sources of support. Extended family members and friends can help parents adapt to their new status, especially if they can offer a different and affirmative perspective (Savin-Williams, 1996). Extended family members may also be able to assist parents to adapt if, for example, they have lesbian or gay children or have had same sex-gender attractions themselves (Savin-Williams, 2001). Support groups can provide opportunities to share information about parents' progression and where to get assistance and additional support (McCubbin & Patterson, 1983; Williamson, 1998). Meeting other parents of lesbian, gay, or transgender children also helps these parents know that they do not need things all worked out yet.

Practitioners should have available local support resources such as Parents, Families, and Friends of Lesbians and Gays (PFLAG; available at www.pflag.org). What is best about support groups such as PFLAG is that they help parents overcome the barriers preventing them from loving their child unconditionally (Savin-Williams, 1998a; Savin-Williams & Dubé, 1998).

PFLAG subscribes to the view that same sex-gender sexual orientation and sex-gender expression are not choices or sins. It challenges parents to examine their values and to empathize with their child's stigmatized situation (Strommen, 1990). Becoming acquainted with lesbian, gay, bisexual, or transgender adults can also happen via PFLAG and can cause a dramatic shift in adjustment. These adults become mentors who help the parents deconstruct their negative images about lesbian, gay, and transgender persons and reconstruct new meanings about them. Parents see firsthand how these persons turned out. They realize that being lesbian, gay, or transgender is not synonymous with deviance and immorality. They will also see what might lie ahead for their child and discover ways to participate in their child's life as they reconstruct their parenting roles. Fears of the unknown diminish and their connection to their children is revitalized (Saltzburg, 2004).

PFLAG is not just for parents. LGBT children also join to find support in their struggles with their parents. Meeting accepting parents of other LGBT persons can often give them hope for their own parents. They learn strategies for dealing with their parents, and even can find parental substitutes who will listen to them when their own parents will not (Rust, 2003).

Chapter 10

Working in Larger Arenas
to Facilitate Disclosures

When key places where LGB persons get educated and work become affirmative, more of these persons will make disclosures. However, the most important changes must be directed at heterosexism at
the societal level because this affects these and all other arenas that
LGB persons may be part of. However, this task is the most difficult
to make headway on.

PUBLIC SCHOOLS

Many public school personnel tolerate prejudice, discrimination,
and violence perpetrated on LGBT youths (Herdt & Boxer, 1993)
and are often the perpetrators (Sanford, 1989). LGBT students hear
heterosexist and prejudicial statements from principals, teachers,
counselors, and coaches (Uribe & Harbeck, 1991). In addition, these
school officials often fail to take a stance against physical and emotional abuse perpetrated by other youths or intervene on behalf of the
abused. Teachers and other school personnel may act as if the abuse
does not exist (Sanford, 1989). Or, if they notice it, they often "blame
the victim" for harassment and assaults (McManus, 1991). In effect,
this sanctions continued victimization of these students (Rofes,
1993-1994). However, schools are now being pressured in courts to
provide a safe environment for all students including those who are
LGB or T.

Coming Out and Disclosures
© 2007 by The Haworth Press, Inc. All rights reserved.
doi:10.1300/5423_11

Students are suing school systems for failing to protect them. For example, in 1996, the U.S. Court of Appeals for the Seventh Circuit ruled in favor of Jamie Nabozny, a high school student who claimed that his school violated his guarantee of equal protection (*Nabozny v. Podlesny,* 1996). He was not protected even after persistent complaints to school personnel about antigay harassment and violence. Although the school provided other students protection from other forms of harassment and abuse, Nabozny's complaints were repeatedly ignored or dismissed by school personnel. The defendants (the school district, the district administrator, two principals, and one assistant principal) were ordered to pay one million dollars for Nabozny's medical expenses and damages (Logue, 1997). Defendants in another case (*Iversen v. Kent School,* 1998), involving similar issues, settled out of court for $40,000 in Ohio. The case focused on a student who alleged that during his years in middle and high school that school personnel refused to protect him from verbal and physical harassment because he was gay.

Schools may not be able to promise full safety but can do more to protect LGBT youths (D'Augelli, 1996a). First, the school culture must change. The leadership must inspire a shared vision of a hostile-free or safe school. The leadership must also firmly insist that violence, harassment, hate, and ignorance are unacceptable because these behaviors are morally wrong. Schools should be inclusive, meaning that they provide information about our diverse world and teach skills to manage differences. Inclusive schools are places of growth and possibilities for all students. These goals call for multiple levels of participation and support from the top leadership down (Camille, 2002; Chen-Hayes, 2001; Cook & Pawlowski, 1991; D'Augelli, 1996a; Friend, 1998; Giorgis, Higgins, & McNab, 2000; P. Griffin, Lee, Waugh, & Beyer, 2004; G. Hollander, 2000; S.T. Russell, 2005; Safe Schools Coalition of Washington State, 1996; Taylor, 2000; Uribe, 1994). More specific affirmative and inclusive actions include the following:

- Establish policies that protect LGBT students from harassment, discrimination, or violence such as having zero tolerance for harassment, thoroughly investigating incidents of harassment, educating perpetrators, educating the parents of those involved, supporting and protecting those who are harassed, educating staff to prevent future incidents, and educating the student body.

- Model affirmation of diversity, dignity, and respect for all persons.
- Educate adults working in schools about diverse sexual orientations and sex-gender expression.
- Provide parents opportunities to learn about sexual orientations and sex-gender expression.
- Provide support groups for parents of LGBT students.
- Increase knowledge about LGBT youths through film series, lectures, and LGBT organizations.
- Provide peer support groups for any students who want to learn more about heterosexism, sexual identity, and sex-gender expression.
- Require stigma-free language, forbidding the use of terms such as "fag" or "dyke."
- Forbid jokes about LGBT persons.
- Avoid judgments of "normal/abnormal" or "good/bad."
- Use inclusive language such as "Who are you dating?" instead of "Who is your boyfriend or girlfriend?"
- Provide strictest confidence for students who disclose a non-heterosexual sexual orientation or sex-gender expression, if this is requested.
- Create safe, harassment-free zones such as a classroom or counseling room; LGBT students can go to these zones if they are feeling unsafe; the eventual goal is for all school zones to be safe for these students.
- Designate certain staff to be available to share the concerns of LGBT students. Faculty and staff can serve as role models, but will need protection by the school from harassment or from losing their jobs.
- Establish affirmative peer support groups and counseling services, including semester-long coming-out groups.
- Establish an alliance group (e.g., Gay-Straight Alliance) as an opportunity for all students to work on common projects.
- Incorporate LGBT issues throughout the curriculum and in school-sponsored organizations.

- Include in the curriculum accurate information about LGBT persons who contributed to the scientific, social, economic, political, and cultural richness of current and prior generations.
- Place LGBT educational materials, pamphlets, and posters in visible locations.
- Include LGBT-affirming books in the school library and a list of supportive local resources such as churches, mental health clinics, and LGBT community organizations.
- Make school-sponsored social functions such as proms and dances inclusive with invitations that make it clear that all individuals and couples are welcome.
- Provide activities for LGBT youths only, such as dances and movies.

In 1985, a Los Angeles high school had the first specialized school-based program for lesbian and gay students—Project 10. It provided discussion, support, and advocacy for them, as well as training and education for school personnel and administrators (Uribe, 1994). It also promoted a code of conduct for students and faculty to ensure safety for lesbian and gay students. Project 10 is now in use throughout the Los Angeles Unified School District. The district has formed a Gay and Lesbian Education Commission empowered to make recommendations to the Board of Education regarding lesbian and gay youths (Greeley, 1994). The Project 10 model is also in use in the San Francisco Unified School District, as well as in several other schools in California and in other states (Rofes, 1989).

Fourteen model programs focusing on preventing harassment of LGBT youths in schools were identified by Henning-Stout, James, and Macintosh (2000). All the programs have common elements that contribute to their success:

Guiding Ideas

- Respond directly to harassment issues.
- Take a preventive approach for students at risk.

Goals

- Increase safety for all children and youths.
- Counter heterosexism in the school and community cultures.

Objectives

- Listen to everyone involved, including perpetrators and harassed students.
- Engage personnel who have legitimate power, are trusted, and are likely to be followed in program development, implementation, and maintenance.
- Provide support and resources for those involved in the program development, implementation, and maintenance.
- Support dialogues on issues of difference, beliefs, and understandings and model affirmative stances.
- Provide training on conflict resolution and mediation, and the structure and space for practicing the training.
- Recognize the many paths to attain the goals.
- Evaluate systematically the effects of the program on creating a safe environment and countering heterosexist bias.

Processes

- Identify issues in the local community, such as assaults on LGBT persons.
- Develop coalitions with allies.
- Gather information such as the history of harassment in the school and community, the political climate, pertinent laws, and potentials for backlash.
- Plan actions and present information and programs with confidence.
- Implement actions such as policy changes, nondiscrimination clauses, staff development programs, community education programs, curriculum supplements, and support groups.

Additional information on how to foster an understanding of heterosexism in schools, and interventions to curb it, is available from the Gay, Lesbian, and Straight Teachers Network. This is the largest national organization that addresses heterosexism in public schools. The Network is located at 122 W. 26th Street, Suite 1100, New York, NY 10001 (available at www.glstn.org/respect). It publishes updated material on books and videos as well as a module for staff development in schools. Another resource is "Anti-Homophobia Training for

School Staff and Students," available at www.glstn.org/pages/sections/ library/schooltools/031.artie.

More programs are needed in community settings. For some students, community programs such as support groups may be more comfortable than school programs (Gerstel, Feraios, & Herdt, 1989; Greeley, 1994; Singerline, 1994). Several alternative schools are also now available such as the Harvey Milk School, an alternative high school for LGBT youths. The Hetrick-Martin Institute, a private agency in New York for LGBT youths, runs the school.

Unfortunately, the affirmative initiatives discussed here are rare. Most schools deny the presence of LGBT students or ignore their needs. Those seeking to meet the needs of LGBT youths in mainstream schools often face the opposition of heterosexist parents, school boards, and others in the community (Fontaine & Hammond, 1996; Rofes, 1989). An example of this opposition occurred in a school district in a suburb of Dallas. A workshop to train middle school counselors in how to help lesbian and gay youths was canceled because of protests from local ministers and other Christian conservatives. A local resident who was also a state executive member of the Republican Party did not want the counselors trained by persons from a local lesbian and gay counseling center because these persons would not present a balanced view that "homosexuality" is sinful. Nor would they present information on religious-based counseling to change same sex-gender sexual orientation (McCoy, 1999).

COLLEGE CAMPUSES

Colleges and universities should act to ensure that LGBT students accomplish their educational goals without fear, harassment, discrimination, or violence by taking affirmative action (D'Augelli, 1989a; D'Emilio, 1990; Herek, 1994; Obear, 1991; Schoenberg, 1989; Slater, 1993; Tierney, 1992a,b; Waldo, 1998). Examples of affirmative actions that can be taken are as follows:

- Include sexual orientation in the mission and nondiscrimination policy statements of the college or university; verify that the whole campus is aware of such policies and that students understand intolerable behaviors.

- Refuse to tolerate hate-motivated attacks on LGBT students; the highest officers of the institution should correct underlying difficulties associated with such attacks.
- Do not allow organizations that discriminate against LGBT students to operate on campus.
- Require the campus counseling center and health center to have counselors and health workers who specialize in the concerns of LGBT students.
- Urge the president, other administrators, and faculties to show in behaviors their desire to learn more about the diversity of their students, including those who are LGBT.
- Encourage faculty and staff networks of "allies" to demonstrate their support and respect for LGBT students by wearing buttons and hanging posters in their offices to reflect affirmative views.
- Challenge students to develop the building blocks for valuing diversity, such as relativistic thinking, openness to new ideas, and a belief in civil rights for all persons.
- Sponsor educational panels of LGBT students in residence halls, classrooms, fraternities, and sororities.
- Promote interactions between heterosexual and LGBT students.
- Include materials on LGBT persons in campus libraries.
- Provide LGBT courses and scholarships.
- Support LGBT student organizations in the college or university; provide resources to procure speakers and to sponsor dances and other social events.

Programs such as Safe Zone and similar initiatives are now available on many college campuses to provide a more positive campus climate for LGBT students and employees. For instance, as part of the Safe Zone program at the University of Wyoming, students, staff, and faculty volunteers provide two-hour training sessions on LGBT topics, including myths and stereotypes; definitions and terminology; resources to help participants better understand sexual orientation; and ways to support LGBT students and promote a positive campus environment for everyone. Aside from educating the program participants, other goals include modeling nonheterosexist behaviors and attitudes; confronting overt heterosexist incidents; and advocating for social change (Conklin, 1999).

WORKPLACE

Protective legislation at the national level is critical to reducing discrimination in workplaces, but even more important is a supportive or LGBT-friendly workplace. Ragins and Cornwell (2001) reported from a national sample of 534 lesbian and gay employees that this factor was the key to whether discrimination was perceived as operating in their workplaces. And, the workplace must show movement beyond slogans or just talking about nondiscrimination if it wants to be affirmative.

Actions can be taken to contribute to a supportive or affirmative workplace where LGBT persons can be open with no fear of discrimination, harassment, or violence. Top management must be committed to affirmative actions and supervisors, managers, and co-workers must have positive attitudes toward these actions (Ankeny, 1991; Lee & Brown, 1993). Various scholars provided examples of affirmative actions in the workplace (Brooks, 1991; Byrne, 1993; H. Jacobs, 1994; Kitzinger, 1991; Kronenberger, 1991; Lee & Brown, 1993; M.P. Levine & Leonard, 1984; Mickens, 1994; Ragins & Cornwell, 2001; Woolsey, 1991). Recommended actions include the following:

- Follow a goals and timetables model—goals are numerical targets for hiring or promoting qualified LGBT workers; timetables set the deadlines for achieving the goals.
- Include lesbian and gay domestic partnerships and nonbiological children in employee benefit packages and family leave policies.
- Develop an explicit policy prohibiting discrimination based on sexual orientation or sex-gender expression.
- Establish zero tolerance for heterosexist behaviors in the workplace, including antilesbian and antigay jokes and derogatory comments.
- Intervene when difficulties arise, such as verbal harassment from heterosexual workers.
- Conduct and require participation in diversity training programs and workshops to change attitudes and sensitize employees to the perspectives and concerns of LGBT employees.
- Talk with open LGBT workers to identify their concerns.
- Facilitate support groups for LGBT workers.

- Foster contact between LGBT and heterosexual co-workers, as this is one of the most powerful means of reducing heterosexism.
- Provide LGBT affirmative contacts within the organization.
- Include same sex-gender partners in company social events.
- Provide information on organizations helpful to LGBT workers (e.g., Gay Teachers Association, Lesbian and Gay People in Medicine, High Tech Gays).

Companies have been rated on their nondiscrimination policies. For example, Mickens (1994) identified the 100 best companies for lesbian and gay persons. *The Advocate* (2005) produces a yearly list of shining Fortune 10 companies offering protections to lesbian and gay workers. The Human Rights Campaign's 2005 Corporate Equality Index assesses many items listed earlier in various corporations; available at www.hrc.org/Template.cfm?Section=About_HRC_Work Net.

If management has yet to propose affirmative changes, individuals or small groups within an organization can start an employee resource group. These groups can provide some or all the following functions:

1. support for isolated LGBT employees;
2. safety in a group for taking actions such as pointing out biased behaviors in the organization, when it may be ineffective to do this alone;
3. legitimacy of being an organizational group;
4. diverse talents for the many group responsibilities;
5. expansion of potential solutions through the diverse perspectives of a group;
6. financial assistance through dues for group events, conferences, or producing written materials;
7. alliances with other groups with "diversity" goals such as those representing women or racial and ethnic persons; and
8. developing a large enough group to influence the organizational culture (Gore, 2000).

The downside of making workplaces affirmative is that they become targets of bigoted groups. These groups spend enormous energy and resources on countering affirmative actions. For example, a coalition of conservative religious groups may regularly protest against diversity training and partner benefits and call for boycotts of companies that they believe promote "homosexuality." Religious and social conservatives branded American Airlines as among the "worst offenders" in the late 1990s, and persons were asked to not fly on this airline. Due to the "immoral ideologies" of Disney, by offering medical benefits to partners of lesbian and gay employees, the Southern Baptist Convention passed a resolution calling on its membership to stop patronizing the Walt Disney Company and its subsidiaries, including Disney World and Disneyland (Caldwell, 1997).

CHANGE AT THE SOCIETAL LEVEL

Heterosexism is probably the most relevant environmental or structural issue affecting the openness of LGB persons or affecting whether they will even admit to themselves that they are LGB. These persons will not be liberated from heterosexism until mainstream society views them as full and equal citizens. This goal, however, seems remote, if not unreachable, because curtailing heterosexism is no easy task (Herek, 1995).

Negative stereotypes and attitudes about LGBT persons are difficult to change. Once integrated into one's belief system, stereotypes are highly resistant to modification even if one wishes to not engage in stereotypical thinking (Herek, 2004). One can experience guilt, discomfort, or other negative feelings about one's stereotyped thinking, but it is unlikely to be undone (Deine & Monteith, 1993). This is because an automatic mental process controls one's thinking and one tends to use the most readily available information about a target group to apply to the group (Tvesky & Kahneman, 1973).

Negative stereotypes also fulfill certain psychological functions, identified by Herek (1995) as experiential, social identity, and ego defensive. The *experiential function* helps persons to decide to accept LGB persons or not, based on their interactions with them. If the interactions are amiable, they generally accept LGB persons but if unpleasant this may lead to negative attitudes that are generalized to all LGB persons.

The *social identity function* increases one's self-esteem through the following two interrelated components: *value expressive* and *so-*

cial expressive. First, significant values are usually tied to and affirm one's self-concept. For example, a fundamentalist Christian may express hostile attitudes about lesbian and gay persons to affirm a self-concept as a good Christian. The second component involves a person's sense of belonging to a significant reference group that can strengthen certain social values. When one expresses values of the reference group, one gains acceptance, approval, and love from the group. Approval comes by regarding LGB persons either favorably or unfavorably, depending on the particular slant of the reference group.

The *ego-defensive function* occurs when hostility about lesbian and gay persons represents an unconscious defensive strategy. This allows some persons to avoid internal conflict about unacceptable parts of themselves, such as attraction to persons of the same sex-gender.

Perpetrators of violence against LGBT persons may play out several or all the functions, or act from multiple motives. An example is acting out violence to boost the cohesiveness among group members, show antagonism toward the sexual and sex-gender role violations of gay persons (the most common victims), and affirm for the attackers their own heterosexual orientation and masculine sex-gender role identity (Herek, 1992b). Violence in the first instance is social expressive because affiliation with one's peer group is maintained. In the second instance the violence is value expressive because certain values such as upholding moral authority reinforce the self-concepts of the perpetrators. Franklin (2000) referred to persons in this group as *"antigay ideology"* perpetrators who think of themselves as social norms enforcers; they are punishing gay persons for moral transgressions. Violence in the third instance is ego defensive because of the emphasis on one's heterosexuality and masculinity (Herek, 1995). Franklin called perpetrators who are trying to prove their "masculine" identity to their peers: *"peer dynamics"* perpetrators. If the attackers subordinate older, white men (assumed to be members of the dominant elite), they experience an enhancement of their own masculinity and status (Connell, 1995). Violence is also ego defensive when perpetrators attack or castigate someone because that person symbolizes the unacceptable parts of themselves. They are probably unaware, however, of the motivations that underlie their hostile and violent behaviors (Herek, 1995).

Franklin (2000) identified several other groups who are violent toward LGBT persons: *"self-defense"* perpetrators who attack someone whom they interpret as flirting with them or propositioning them, suggesting that they think they have cultural permission for violence based on *"homosexual innuendo"* and *"thrill-seeker"* perpetrators who feel socially alienated and powerless.

Stopping violence and other manifestations of heterosexism requires changes at both the institutional and individual levels. Change at the institutional level is difficult to achieve except through legal means (Rubenstein, 1996). Change at the individual level is also difficult to attain because it necessitates a transformation in the consciousness of heterosexual persons.

CHANGE AT THE INDIVIDUAL LEVEL

Personal contact is the most consistently influential factor in reducing prejudice (Herek & Glunt, 1993), because it challenges misconceptions that, in turn, can change cognitions. So, disclosure of one's identity to family members, friends, and co-workers is an important way to challenge psychological heterosexism at the individual level (Herek, 1992a). This is most likely to happen in the context of a close relationship. The lesbian or gay person manages the disclosure process so that the heterosexual person can learn what it means to be lesbian or gay and that this person is like other lesbian or gay persons. It helps if there is a juxtaposition or inconsistency between one's stereotypes and one's experiences with a lesbian or gay person. This can facilitate rejection of stereotypes while fostering attitude change. The heterosexual person is likely to experience cognitive dissonance. If the dissonance is resolved in favor of a friend or relative, the outcome may be more favorable. And it also helps if one has contact with more than one lesbian or gay person. Then the friend or relative will not be seen as atypical (Roothbart & John, 1985).

Herek (1995) also pointed out that it is necessary to use strategies that match the functions served by holding prejudicial attitudes. The contact strategy, for example, may work best with persons who hold heterosexist attitudes because they serve an experiential function. Their attitudes are shaped by experience. Attitudes may not change through personal contact if they serve a value-expressive function. A strategy of creating dissonance between the person's prejudices and another significant value, such as personal freedom, may have a stronger influence in these situations. Attitudes supporting the value-expressive function may also change if a respected authority, such as a minister, presents a more positive view of same sex-gender or bisexual sexual orientation, grounded in religious teachings. Close contact is also unlikely to have any positive influence on attitudes that serve an ego-defensive function because it may arouse anxiety and heighten defensiveness. If one has fears about one's own sexual orientation, close contact is unlikely to be beneficial. Attitudes that express a social-expressive function may change if one's reference groups change (e.g., from conservative to more liberal). If cultural norms about heterosexism change, the attitudes of reference groups and individuals are likely to shift accordingly. Yet, there is no evidence of any significant shift in norms, as heterosexism remains strongly entrenched in our culture. Sears and Williams (1997) presented an array of other methods for attempting to change heterosexist attitudes including those suitable for changing racism. Not only should heterosexism be eradicated but also all forms of social bigotry (Bohan & Russell, 1999).

References

Adam, B.D. (1987). *The rise of the lesbian and gay movement.* Boston: Twayne.

Adams, C.L., & Kimmel, D.C. (1997). Exploring the lives of older African American gay men. In B. Greene (Ed.), *Ethnic and cultural diversity among lesbians and gay men* (pp. 132-151). Thousand Oaks, CA: Sage Publications.

Adelman, M. (1986). *Long time passing.* Boston: Alyn.

Adelman, M. (1991). Stigma, gay lifestyles, and adjustment to aging: A study of later-life gay men and lesbians. In J.A. Lee (Ed.), *Gay midlife and maturity* (pp. 1-32). Binghamton, NY: The Haworth Press.

Adelman, M. (2000). *Midlife lesbian relationships: Friends, lovers, children, and parents.* Binghamton, New York: The Haworth Press.

Advocate (2005, September). *Best companies: Welcoming workplaces,* pp. 55-60.

Alexander, C.J. (1998). Treatment planning for gay and lesbian clients. *Journal of Gay & Lesbian Social Services, 8,* 95-106.

Allen, P.G. (1984). Beloved women: The lesbian in American Indian culture. In T. Darty & S. Potter (Eds.), *Women-identified women* (pp. 83-96). Palo Alto, CA: Mayfield.

Almaguer, T. (1991). Chicano men: A cartography of homosexual behavior. *A Journal of Feminist Culturalist Studies, 3,* 75-100.

Altman, C. (1999). Gay and lesbian seniors: Unique challenges of coming out in later life. *Siecus Report, 27,* 14-17.

American Psychological Association, Committee on Lesbian and Gay Concerns (1991). Avoiding heterosexist language. *American Psychologist, 46,* 937-974.

Anderson, B.F. (1998). Therapeutic issues in working with transgendered clients. In D. Denny (Ed.), *Current concepts of transgendered identity* (pp. 215-226). New York: Garland.

Anderson, S.C., & Holliday, M. (2005). Normative passing in the lesbian community: An exploratory study. *Journal of Gay & Lesbian Social Services, 17,* 25-38.

Anhalt, K., & T.L. Morris (2003). Developmental and adjustment issues of gay, lesbian, and bisexual adolescents: A review of the empirical literature. In L.D. Garnets & D.C. Kimmel (Eds.). *Psychological perspectives on lesbian, gay, and bisexual experiences* (pp. 571-601). New York: Columbia University Press.

Ankeny, D.C. (1991). Creating the statistical portion of an affirmative action plan. *Tulane Law Review, 65,* 1183, 1205.

Armour, S. (2005). When an employee switches gender, what's a company to do? *USA Today.* 1, 2 B, (June 10).

Coming Out and Disclosures
© 2007 by The Haworth Press, Inc. All rights reserved.
doi:10.1300/5423_12

Badgett, M.V.L. (1996). Employment and sexual orientation: Disclosure and discrimination in the workplace. *Journal of Gay & Lesbian Social Services, 4*, 29-52.

Bailey, J.M. (1996). Gender identity. In R.C. Savin-Williams & K.M. Cohen (Eds.), *The lives of lesbians, gays, and bisexuals: Children to adults* (pp. 71-93). Ft. Worth, TX: Harcourt Brace.

Ball, S. (1994). A group model for gay and lesbian clients with chronic mental illness. *Social Work, 39*, 109-115.

Balsam, K.F., Rothblum, E.D., & Beauchaine, T.P. (2005). Victimization over the life span: A comparison of lesbian, gay, bisexual, and heterosexual siblings. *Journal of Counseling and Clinical Psychology, 73*, 477-487.

Barbone, S., & Rice, L. (1994). Coming out, being out, and acts of virtue. *Journal of Homosexuality, 27*, 91-110.

Barr, R.F., & Catts, S.V. (1974). Psychiatry opinion and homosexuality: A short report. *Journal of Homosexuality, 1*, 213-215.

Barron, J. (1996). Some issues in psychotherapy with gay and lesbian clients. *Psychotherapy, 33*, 611-616.

Beals, K.P., & Peplau, L.A. (2005). Identity support, identity devaluation, and well-being among lesbians. *Psychology of Women Quarterly, 29*, 140-148.

Beeler, J., & DiProva, V. (1999). Family adjustment following disclosure of homosexuality by a member: Themes discerned in narrative accounts. *Journal of Marital and Family Therapy, 25*, 443-459.

Beeler, J.A., Rawls, T.W., Herdt, G.H., & Cohler, B.J. (1999). Needs of older lesbians and gay men in Chicago. *Journal of Gay and Lesbian Social Services, 9*, 31.

Bell, A.P., & Weinberg, M.S. (1978). *Homosexualities: A study of diversity among men and women.* New York: Simon & Schuster.

Bell, A.P., Weinberg, M.S., & Hammersmith, S.K. (1981). *Sexual preference: Its development in men and women.* Bloomington, IN: Indiana University.

Ben-Ari, A. (1995). The discovery that an offspring is gay: Parents', gay men's, and lesbians' perspectives. *Journal of Homosexuality, 30*, 89-112.

Berger, R.M. (1982a). *Gay and gray: The older homosexual man.* Binghamton, NY: The Haworth Press.

Berger, R.M. (1982b). The unseen minority: Older gays and lesbians. *Social Work, 27*, 236-242.

Berger, R.M., & Kelly, J.J. (2001). What are older gay men like? An impossible question? *Journal of Gay & Lesbian Social Services, 13*, 55-64.

Berkey, B.R., Perelman-Hall, T., & Kurdek, L.A. (1990). The multidimensional scale of sexuality. *Journal of Homosexuality, 19*, 67-87.

Bernstein, B.E. (1990). Attitudes and issues of parents of gay men and lesbians and implications for therapy. *Journal of Gay & Lesbian Psychotherapy, 1*, 37-53.

Bernstein, G.S. (1992). How to avoid heterosexual bias in language. *Behavior Therapist, 15*, 161.

Bernstein, M. (1997). Celebration and suppression: The strategic use of identity by the lesbian and gay movement. *American Journal of Sociology, 103*, 531-565.

Berrill, K.T. (1990). Anti-gay violence and victimization in the United States. *Journal of Interpersonal Violence, 5*, 274-294.

Berrill, K.T. (1992). Organizing against hate on campus: Strategies for activists. In G.M. Herek & K.T. Berrill (Eds.), *Hate crimes: Confronting violence against lesbians and gay men* (pp. 259-269). Newbury Park, CA: Sage Publications.

Bérubé, A. (1990). *Coming out under fire: The history of gay men and women in World War Two.* New York: Free Press.

Bieber, I., Dain, H.J., Dince, P.R., Drellich, M.G., Grand, H.G., Gundlach, R.H., Kremer, M.W., Rifkin, A.H., Wilbur, C.B., & Bieber, T.B. (1962). *Homosexuality: A psychoanalytic study.* New York: Basic.

Birch, E. (2002, June 10). Priest abuse problem isn't a gay issue. *Dallas Morning News,* p. 17A.

Blackwood. E. (1984). Sexuality and gender in certain Native American tribes: The case of the cross-gender females. *Signs,* 10, 27-42.

Blumstein, P., & Schwartz, P. (1974). Lesbianism and bisexuality. In E. Goode and R.R. Troiden (Eds.), *Sexual deviance and sexual deviants* (pp. 278-295). New York: Morrow.

Blumstein, P., & Schwartz, P. (1977). Bisexuality: Some social psychological issues. *Journal of Social Issues,* 33, 30-45.

Blumstein, P., & Schwarz, P. (1990). Intimate relationships and the creation of sexuality. In D.P. McWhirter, S.A. Sanders, & J.M. Reinisch (Eds.), *Homosexuality/heterosexuality: Concepts of sexual orientation* (pp. 307-320). New York: Oxford University Press.

Boatwright, K.J., Gilbert, M.S., Forrest, L., & Ketzenberger, K. (1996). Impact of identity development upon career trajectory: Listening to the voices of lesbian women. *Journal of Vocational Behavior,* 48, 210-228.

Bockting, W.O. (1999). From construction to context: Gender through the eyes of the transgendered. *Siecus Report,* 28, 3-7.

Bodlund, O., & Kullgren, G. (1996). Transsexualism—General outcome and prognostic factors: A five-year follow-up study of nineteen transsexuals in the process of changing sex. *Archives of Sexual Behavior,* 25, 303-316.

Bohan, J.S. (1996). *Psychology and sexual orientation: Coming to terms.* New York: Routledge.

Bohan, J.S., & Russell, G.M. (1999). Conceptual frameworks. In J.S. Bohan & G.M. Russell (Eds.), *Conversations about psychology and sexual orientation* (pp. 11-30). New York: New: York University Press.

Bonilla, J., & Porter, J. (1990). A comparison of Latino, black, and non-Hispanic white attitudes toward homosexuality. *Hispanic Journal of Behavioral Sciences,* 12, 437-452.

Boxer, A.M., Cook, J.A., & Herdt, G. (1991). Double jeopardy: Identity transitions and parent-child relationships among gay and lesbian youth. In K. Pillemer & K. McCartney (Eds.), *Parent-child relations throughout life* (pp. 59-92). Hillsdale, NJ: Lawrence Erlbaum.

Bozett, F.W. (1980). Gay fathers: How and why they disclose their homosexuality to their children. *Family Relations,* 29, 173-179.

Bozett, F.W. (1981a). Gay fathers: Evolution of the gay-father identity. *American Journal of Orthopsychiatry,* 51, 552-559.

Bozett, F.W. (1981b). Gay fathers: Identity conflict resolution through integrative sanctioning. *Alternative Lifestyles,* 4, 90-107.

Bozett, F.W. (1982). Heterogeneous couples in heterosexual marriages: Gay men and straight women. *Journal of Marital and Sexual Therapy,* 8, 81-89.

Bozett, F.W. (1987). Children of gay fathers. In F.W. Bozett (Ed.), *Gay and lesbian parents* (pp. 39-57). New York: Praeger.

Bozett, F.W. (1993). Gay fathers: A review of the literature. In L.D. Garnets & D.C. Kimmel (Eds.), *Psychological perspectives on lesbian and gay male experiences* (pp. 437-457). New York: Columbia University Press.

Bradford, J., & Ryan, C. (1988). *National lesbian health care survey: Final report.* Washington, DC: National Lesbian and Gay Health Foundation.

Bradford, J., & Ryan, C. (1991). Who we are: Health concerns of middle-aged lesbians. In B.J. Warshow, & A.J. Smith (Eds.), *Lesbians at midlife: The creative transition* (pp. 147-163). San Francisco: Spinsters Book Company.

Bradford, M. (2004). The bisexual experience: Living in a dichotomous culture. *Journal of Bisexuality,* 4, 7-23.

Brady, S., & Busse, W.J. (1994). The gay identity questionnaire: A brief measure of homosexual identity formation. *Journal of Homosexuality,* 26, 1-22.

Broad, K.L. (2002). GLBT? Gender/sexuality movement and transgender collective identity (de)constructions. *International Journal of Sexuality and Gender studies,* 7, 241-264.

Brooks, S.E. (1991). Resources. In N.J. Evans & V.A. Walls (Eds.). *Beyond tolerance: Gays, lesbians, and bisexuals on campus* (pp. 213-232). Alexandria, VA: American College Personnel Association.

Brown, G.R. (1998). Women in the closet: Relationships with transgendered men. In D. Denny (Ed.), *Current concepts of transgendered identity* (pp. 353-371). New York: Garland.

Brown, L.B. (1997). Women and men, not-men and not-women, lesbians and gays: American Indian gender-style alternatives. *Journal of Gay & Lesbian Social Services,* 6, 5-20.

Brown, L.B., Alley, G.R., Sarosy, S., Quarto, G., & Cook, T. (2001). Gay men: Aging well! *Journal of Gay & Lesbian Social Services,* 13, 41-54.

Brown, L.S. (1989a). Lesbians, gay men and their families: Common clinical issues. *Journal of Gay & Lesbian Psychotherapy,* 1, 65-77.

Brown, L.S. (1989b). New voices, new visions: Toward a lesbian/gay paradigm for psychology. *Psychology of Women Quarterly,* 13, 445-458.

Brown, L.S. (1995). Therapy with same-sex couples: An introduction. In N.S. Jacobson & S. Guttman (Eds.), *Clinical handbook of couple therapy* (pp. 274-291). New York: Guilford Press.

Brown, L.S. (1996). Ethical concerns with sexual minority patients. In R.P. Cabaj & T.S. Stein (Eds.), *Textbook of homosexuality and mental health* (pp. 897-916). Washington, DC: American Psychiatric Press.

Brownfain, J.J. (1985). A study of the married bisexual male: Paradox and resolution. *Journal of Homosexuality,* 11, 173-188.

Browning, C., Reynolds, A.L., & Dworkin, S.H. (1991). Affirmative psychotherapy for lesbian women. *Counseling Psychologist,* 19, 177-196.

Bryant, S., & Demian (1998). Terms of same-sex endearment. *Siecus Report, 26,* 10-13.

Buhrke, R. (1989). Female student perspectives on training in lesbian and gay issues. *Counseling Psychologist,* 17, 629-636.

Buhrke, R., & Douce, L. (1991). Training for counseling psychologists in working with lesbian women and gay men. *Counseling Psychologist, 19,* 216-234.

Bullough, B., & Bullough, V. (1997). Are transvestites necessarily heterosexual? *Archives of Sexual Behavior,* 26, 1-12.

Bullough, V.L. (1994). *Science in the bedroom: A history of sex research.* New York: Basic Books.

Bullough, V.L. (1998). Alfred Kinsey and the Kinsey report: Historical overview and lasting contributions. *Journal of Sex Research,* 35, 127-131.

Burch, B. (1997). *Other women: Lesbian/bisexual experience and psychoanalytic views of women.* New York: Columbia University Press.

Burke, P. (1993). *Family values: Two moms and their son.* New York: Random House.

Burn, S.M. (2000). Heterosexuals' use of "fag" and "queer" to deride one another: A contributor to heterosexism and stigma. *Journal of Homosexuality,* 40, 1-11.

Button, S.B. (2004). Identity management strategies utilized by lesbian and gay employees. *Group & Organization Management,* 29, 470-494.

Buxton, A.P. (1994). *The other side of the closet: The coming-out crisis for straight spouses and families.* New York: John Wiley & Sons.

Byrne, J.S. (1993). Affirmative action for lesbians and gay men: A proposal for true equality of opportunity and work force diversity. *Yale Law & Policy Review,* 11, 47-108.

Cabaj, R.P. (1996). Gay, lesbian, and bisexual mental health professionals and their colleagues. In R.R. Cabaj & T.S. Stein (Eds.), *Textbook of homosexuality and mental health* (pp. 33-39). Washington, DC: American Psychiatric Association.

Cain, R. (1991a). Relational contexts and information management among gay men. *Families in Society,* 72, 344-352.

Cain, R. (1991b). Stigma management and gay identity development. *Social Work,* 36, 67-73.

Caldwell, D.K. (1997, March). "Pro-gay" companies targeted: Conservatives say values compromised. *The Dallas Morning News,* G1, 4.

Camille, L. (2002). The impact of belonging to a high school gay/straight alliance. *High School Journal,* 85, 13-26.

Carballo-Diéguez, A. (1989). Hispanic culture, gay male culture, and AIDS: Counseling implications. *Journal of Counseling and Development,* 68, 26-30.

Carmen, Gail, Neena, & Tamara (1991). Becoming visible: Black lesbian discussions. In Feminist Review (Eds.), *Sexuality: A reader* (pp. 216-244). London: Virago.

Carroll, L., Gilroy, P.J., & Ryan, J. (2002). Counseling transgendered, transsexual, and gender-variant clients. *Journal of Counseling & Development,* 80, 131-139.

Cass, V.C. (1979). Homosexual identity formation: A theoretical model. *Journal of Homosexuality,* 4, 219-235.

Cass, V.C. (1984). Homosexual identity formation: Testing a theoretical model. *Journal of Sex Research,* 20, 143-167.

Cass, V.C. (1990). The implications of homosexual identity formation for the Kinsey model and scale of sexual preference. In D.P. McWhirter, S.A. Sanders, & J.M Reinisch (Eds.), *Homosexuality/heterosexuality: Concepts of sexual orientation* (pp. 239-266). New York: Oxford University.

Cass, V.C. (1996). Sexual orientation identity formation: A western phenomenon. In R.P. Cabaj & T. S. Stein (Eds.), *Textbook of homosexuality and mental health* (pp. 227-251). Washington, DC: American Psychiatric Press.

Castells, M. (1983). *The city and the grassroots: A cross cultural theory of urban social improvements.* Berkeley, CA: University of California Press.

Cazenave, N.A. (1984). Race, socioeconomic status, and age: The social context of American masculinity. *Sex Roles,* 11, 639-656.

Chan, C.S. (1987). Asian lesbians: Psychological issues in the "coming out" process. *Asian American Psychological Association Journal,* 12, 16-18.

Chan, C.S. (1989). Issues of identity development among Asian-American lesbians and gay men. *Journal of Counseling and Development,* 68, 16-20.

Chan, C.S. (1992). Cultural considerations in counseling Asian American lesbians and gay men. In S. Dworkin & F. Gutiérrez (Eds.), *Counseling gay men and lesbians* (pp. 115-124). Alexandria, VA: American Association for Counseling and Development.

Chan, C.S. (1995). Issues of sexual identity in an ethnic minority: The case of Chinese American lesbians, gay men, and bisexual people. In A.R. D'Augelli & C.J. Patterson (Eds.), *Lesbians, gay, and bisexual identities over the lifespan* (pp. 87-101). New York: Oxford.

Chan, C.S. (1997). Don't ask, don" tell, don't know: The formation of a homosexual identity and sexual expression among Asian American lesbians. In B. Greene (Ed.), *Ethnic and cultural diversity among lesbians and gay men* (pp. 240-248). Thousand Oaks, CA: Sage Publications.

Chapman, B.E., & Brannock, J.C. (1987). Proposed model of lesbian identity development: An empirical examination. *Journal of Homosexuality,* 14, 69-80.

Charbonneau, D., & Lander, P. (1991). Redefining sexuality: Women becoming lesbian in midlife. In B. Sang, J. Warshow, & A. Smith (Eds.), *Lesbians at midlife: The creative transition* (pp. 35-43). San Francisco: Spinsters.

Chen-Hayes, S.F. (2001). Counseling and advocacy with transgendered and gender-variant persons in schools and families. *Journal of Humanistic Counseling, Education, and Development,* 40, 34-48.

Chernin, J.N., & Johnson, M.R. (2003). *Affirmative psychotherapy and counseling for lesbians and gay men.* Thousand Oaks, CA: Sage.

Ciro, D., Surko, M., Bhandarkar, K. Helfgott, Penke, K, & Epstein, I. (2005). Lesbian, gay, bisexual, sexual orientation questioning adolescents seeking mental health services: Risk factors, worries, and desire to talk about them. *Social Work in Mental Health,* 3, 213-234.

Claes, J.A., & Moore, W.R. (2000). Issues confronting lesbian and gay elderly: The challenge for health and human services providers. *Journal of Health and Human Services Administration,* 23, 181-202.

Clarke, C. (1983). The failure to transform: Homophobia in the black community. In B. Smith (Ed.), *Home girls: A black feminist anthology* (pp. 197-2708). New York: Kitchen Table—Women of Color.

Clunis, D.M., & Green, G.D. (2000). *Lesbian couples: A guide to creating healthy relationships.* Seattle, WA: Seal Press.

Coenen, M.E. (1998). Helping families with homosexual children: A model for counseling. *Journal of Homosexuality,* 36, 73-85.

Cohen, C.J., & & Stein, T.S. (1986). Reconceptualizing individual psychotherapy with gay men and lesbians. In T.S. Stein & C.J. Cohen (Eds.). *Contemporary perspective on psychotherapy with lesbians and gay men* (pp. 27-54). New York: Plenum.

Cohen, K.M., & Savin-Williams, R.C. (1996). Developmental perspectives on coming out to self and others. In R.C. Savin-Williams & K.M. Cohen (Eds.), *The lives of lesbians, gays, and bisexuals children to adults* (pp. 113-151). Ft. Worth, TX: Harcourt Brace.

Cohen-Kettenis, P.T., & Van Goozen, S.H.M. (1997). Sex reassignment of adolescent transsexuals: A follow up study. *Journal of the American Academy of Adolescent Psychiatry,* 36, 263-271.

Cohler, B. J., & Boxer, A. (1984). Middle adulthood: Settling into the world-persons, time, and context. In D. Offer & M. Sabshin (Eds.), *Normality and the life-course* (pp. 145-203). New York: Basic.

Cohler, B.J., & Galatzer, A. (2000). *The course of gay and lesbian lives: Social and psychoanalytic perspectives.* Chicago: University of Chicago Press.

Cohler, B.J., Galatzer-Levy, R.M., Boxer, A., & Irvin, F. (2000). Adolescence and youth: Realizing gay and lesbian sexual identity. In B.J. Cohler & R.M. Galatzer-Levy (Eds.), *The course of gay and lesbian lives: Social and psychoanalytic perspectives* (pp. 144-192). Chicago: University of Chicago Press.

Cohler, B.J., & Hostetler, A.J. (2002). Aging, intimate relationships, and life story among gay men. In R.S. Weiss & S.A. Bass (Eds.), *Challenges of the third age: Meaning and purpose in later life* (pp. 137-160). Oxford, England: Oxford University Press.

Cole, S.S., Denny, D., Eyler, A.E., & Samons, S.L. (2000). Issues of transgender. In L.T. Szuchman & F. Muscarella (Eds.), *Psychological perspectives on human sexuality* (pp. 149-195). New York: John Wiley & Sons.

Coleman, E. (1978). Toward a new model of treatment of homosexuality: A review. *Journal of Homosexuality,* 3, 345-359.

Coleman, E. (1981-1982a). Bisexual and gay men in heterosexual marriage: Conflicts and resolutions in therapy. *Journal of Homosexuality,* 7, 93-101.

Coleman, E. (1981-1982b). Developmental stages of the coming-out process. *Journal of Homosexuality,* 7, 31-43.

Coleman, E. (1985a). Bisexual women in marriages: Conflicts and resolutions in therapy. *Journal of Homosexuality,* 11, 87-99.

Coleman, E. (1985b). Integration of male bisexuality and marriage. *Journal of - Homosexuality,* 11, 189-207.

Collins, J.F. (2000). Biracial-Bisexual individuals: Identity coming of age. *International Journal of Sexuality and Gender Studies,* 5, 221-253.

Collins, L.E., & Zimmerman, N. (1983). Homosexual and bisexual issues. In J.C. Hansen, J.D. Woody, & R.H. Woody (Eds.), *Sexual issues in family therapy* (pp. 82-100). Rockville: Aspen.

Conklin, S.C. (1999). Wyoming horror breaks dam of silence on violence based on sexual orientation. *Siecus Report,* 27, 8-11.

Connell, R.W. (1995). *Masculinities.* Berkeley: University of California Press.

Cook, A.T., & Pawlowski, W. (1991). *Youth and homosexuality.* Issue Paper 3. Washington, DC: Parents and Friends of Lesbians and Gays.

Coombs, M. (1998). Sexual disorientation: Transgendered people and same-sex marriage. *UCLA Women's Law Journal,* 8, 217-266.

Cotten-Huston, A.L., & Waite, B.M. (2000). Anti-homosexual attitudes in college students: Predictors and classroom interventions. *Journal of Homosexuality,* 38, 117-133.

Cramer, D.W., & Roach, A.J. (1988). Coming out to mom and dad: A study of gay males and their relationships with their parents. *Journal of Homosexuality,* 15, 79-91.

Creed, W.E., & Scully, M.A. (2000). Songs of ourselves: Employees' deployment of social identity in workplace encounters. *Journal of Management Inquiry,* 9, 391-412.

Crisp, D., Priest, B., & Torgerson, A. (1998). African American gay men: Developmental issues, choices, and self-concept. *Family Therapy,* 25, 161-168.

Crocker. J., & Major, B. (1989). Social stigma and self-esteem: The self-protective properties of stigma. *Psychological Review,* 96, 608-630.

Cronin, D.M. (1974). Coming out among lesbians. In E. Goode & R.R. Troiden (Eds.), *Sexual deviance and sexual deviants* (pp. 268-277). New York: Morrow.

Croteau, J.M., & Hedstrom, S.M. (1993). Integrating commonality and difference: The key to career counseling with lesbian women and gay men. *The Career Development Quarterly,* 41, 201-209.

Croteau, J.M., & Lark, J.S. (1995). A qualitative investigation of biased and exemplary student affairs practice concerning lesbian, gay, and bisexual issues. *Journal of College Student Development,* 36, 472-482.

Cruikshank, M. (1992). *The gay and lesbian liberation movement.* New York: Routledge.

Cummerton, J. (1982). Homophobia and social work practice with lesbians. In A. Weick & S.T. Vandiver (Eds.), *Women, power and change* (pp. 104-113). Washington, DC: National Association of Social Workers.

Dank, B. (1971). Coming out in the gay world. *Psychiatry,* 34, 180-197.

D'Augelli, A.R. (1989a). Gay men's and lesbians' experiences of discrimination, harassment, and indifference in a university community. *American Journal of Community Psychology,*17, 317-321.

D'Augelli, A.R. (1989b). Homophobia in a university community: Views of prospective resident assistants. *Journal of College Student Development,* 30, 546-552.

D'Augelli, A.R. (1991). Gay men in college: Identity processes and adaptations. *Journal of College Student Development,* 32, 140-146.

D'Augelli, A.R. (1992). Lesbian and gay male undergraduates' experiences of harassment and fear on campus. *Journal of Interpersonal Violence,* 7, 18-29.

D'Augelli, A.R. (1994). Identity development and sexual orientation: Toward a model of lesbian, gay, and bisexual development. In E.J. Trickett, R.J., Watts, & D. Birman, D. (Eds.), *Human diversity* (pp. 312-333). San Francisco, CA.

D'Augelli, A.R. (1996a). Enhancing the development of lesbian, gay, and bisexual youths. In E.D. Rothblum & L.A. Bond (Eds.), *Preventing heterosexism and homophobia* (pp. 124-150). Thousand Oaks, CA: Sage.

D'Augelli, A.R. (1996b). Lesbian, gay, and bisexual development during adolescence and young adulthood. In R.P. Cabaj & T.S. Stein (Eds.). *Textbook of homosexuality and mental health* (pp. 267-287).Washington, DC: American Psychiatric.

D'Augelli, A.R. (1998, February). *Victimization history and mental health among lesbian, gay, and bisexual youths.* Paper presented at the biennial meetings of the Society for Research on Adolescence, San Diego, CA.

D'Augelli, A.R. (2002). Mental health problems among lesbian, gay, and bisexual youths ages 14-21. *Clinical Child Psychology,* 7, 433-456.

D'Augelli, A.R. (2003). Lesbian and bisexual female youths aged 14-21: Developmental challenges and victimization experiences. *Journal of Lesbian Studies,* 7, 9-29.

D'Augelli, A.R., & Garnets, L.D. (1995). Lesbian, gay, and bisexual communities. In A.R. D'Augelli & C.J. Patterson (Eds.), *Lesbians, gay, and bisexual identities over the lifespan* (pp. 293-320). New York: Oxford University Press.

D'Augelli, A.R., & Grossman, A.H. (2001). Disclosure of sexual orientation, victimization, and mental health among lesbian, gay, and bisexual older adults. *Journal of Interpersonal Violence,* 16, 1008-1027.

D'Augelli, A.R., Grossman, A.H., Hershberger, S.L., & O'Connell, T.S. (2001). Aspects of mental health among older lesbian, gay, and bisexual adults. *Aging & Mental Health,* 5, 149-158.

D'Augelli, A.R., Grossman, A.H., & Starks, M.T. (2005). Parents' awareness of lesbian, gay, and bisexual youths' sexual orientation. *Journal of Marriage and Family,* 67, 474-482.

D'Augelli, A.R., & Hershberger, S.L. (1993). Lesbian, gay, and bisexual youth in community settings: Personal challenges and mental health problems. *American Journal of Community Psychology,* 21, 421-448.

D'Augelli, A.R., Hershberger, S.L., & Pilkington, N.W. (1998). Lesbian, gay, and bisexual youth and their families: Disclosure of sexual orientation and its consequences. *American Journal of Orthopsychiatry,* 68, 361-371.

D'Augelli, A.R., Pilkington, N.W., & Hershberger, S.L. (2002). Incidence and mental health impact of sexual orientation victimization of lesbian, gay, and bisexual, youths in high school. *School Psychology Quarterly,* 17, 148-167.

D'Augelli, A.R., & Rose, M.L. (1990). Homophobia in a university community: Attitudes and experiences of heterosexual freshmen. *Journal of College Student Development,* 31, 484-491.

Davis, J.A., & Smith, T.W. (1993). *General social surveys, 1972-1993: Cumulative codebook.* Chicago: National Opinion Research Center.

Day, N.E., & Schoenrade, P. (1997). Staying in the closet versus coming out: Relationships between communication about sexual orientation and work attitudes. *Personnel Psychology,* 50, 147-163.

Deacon, S.A., Reinke, L., & Viers, D. (1998). Cognitive-behavioral therapy for bisexual couples: Expanding the realms of therapy. *The American Journal of Family Therapy,* 24,242-258.

Dean, L., Wu, S., & Martin, J.L. (1992). Trends in violence and discrimination against gay men in New York City: 1984-1990. In G.M. Herek, & K.T. Berrill (Eds.), *Hate crimes: Confronting violence against lesbians and gay men* (pp. 46-64). Newbury Park, CA: Sage Publications.

Decker, B. (1984). Counseling gay and lesbian couples. *Journal of Social Work and Human Sexuality,* 2, 39-52.

Deevey, S. (1993). Lesbian self-disclosure: Strategies for success. *Journal of Psychosocial Nursing,* 16, 35-37, 39.

Degges-White, S., Rice, B., & Myers, J.E. (2000). Revisiting Cass' theory of sexual identity formation: A study of lesbian development. *Journal of Mental Health Counseling,* 22, 318-333.

Deine, P.G., & Monteith, M.J. (1993). The role of discrepancy associated affect in prejudice reduction. In D.M. Mackie & D.L. Hamilton (Eds.). *Affect, cognition, and stereotyping: Interactive processes in group perception* (pp. 31-44). San Diego: Academic Press.

D'Emilio, J. (1983). *Sexual politics, sexual communities: The making of a homosexual minority in the United States, 1940-1970.* Chicago: University of Chicago.

D'Emilio, J. (1990). The campus environment for gay and lesbian life. *Academe,* 76, 16-19.

de Monteflores, C. (1986). Notes on the management of difference. In T. Stein & C. Cohen (Eds.), *Contemporary perspectives in psychotherapy with lesbians and gay men* (pp. 73-101). New York: Plenum.

de Monteflores, C., & Schultz. S. (1978). Coming out: Similarities and differences for lesbians and gay men. *Journal of Social Issues,* 34, 59-72.

Dempsey, C. (1994). Health and social issues of gay, lesbian, and bisexual adolescents. *Families in Society: The Journal of Contemporary Human Services,* 75, 160-167.

Denny, D. (1997). Transgender: Some historical, cross-cultural, and contemporary models and methods of coping and treatment. In B. Bullough, V. L. Bullough, & J. Elias (Eds.), *Gender blending* (pp. 33-47). Amherst, NY: Prometheus Books.

Denny, D. (1999). Transgender in the United States: A brief discussion. *Siecus Report,* 28, 8-13.

DeVine, J.L. (1983-1984). A systematic inspection of affectional preference orientation and the family of origin. *Journal of Social Work and Human Sexuality,* 2, 9-17.

Devor, H. (1997). *Female-to-male transsexuals in society.* Bloomington, IL: Indiana University Press.

Diamond, L.M. (1996). *Attraction and identity: Evidence for sexual fluidity among young lesbian, bisexual, and heterosexual women.* Unpublished master's thesis, Cornell University, Ithaca, New York.

Diamond, L.M. (1998). Development of sexual orientation among adolescent and young adult women. *Developmental Psychology,* 34, 1085-1095.

Diamond, L.M. (2003). Was it a phase? Young women's relinquishment of lesbian/bisexual identities over a 5-year period. *Journal of Personality and Social Psychology,* 84, 352-364.

Diamond, L.M. (2005). A new view of lesbian subtypes: Stable versus fluid identity trajectories over an 8-year period. *Psychology of Women Quarterly,* 29, 119-128.

DiAngelo, R. (1997). Heterosexism: Addressing internalized dominance. *Journal of Progressive Human Services,* 8, 5-21.

Dong tinh luyen ai co phai la can benh hay khong [Is homosexuality a disease?] (1992, January 31). *The [Orange County] Vietnamese Weekly Newspaper,* 4-5.

Donovan, J.M. (1992). Homosexual, gay, and lesbian: Defining words and sampling populations. In H.L. Minton (Ed.), *Gay and lesbian studies* (pp. 27-47). Binghamton, NY: The Haworth Press.

Drescher, J. (1998). Contemporary psychoanalytic psychotherapy with gay men: With a commentary on reparative therapy of homosexuality. *Journal of Gay & Lesbian Psychotherapy,* 2, 51-74.

DuBay, W.H. (1987). *Gay identity: The self under ban.* Jefferson, NC: McFarland.

Dubé, E.M. (1997). *Sexual identity and intimacy development among two cohorts of sexual minority men.* Unpublished master's thesis, Cornell University, Ithaca, New York.

Dubé, E.M. (2000). The role of sexual behavior in the identification process of gay and bisexual males. *Journal of Sex Research,* 37, 123-132.

Dyne, L. (1980, September). Is DC becoming the gay capitol of America? *Washingtonian,* pp. 96-101, 133-141.

Dynes, W.R. (1990). Heterosexuality. In W.R. Dynes (Ed.), *Encyclopedia of homosexuality* (pp.532-535). New York: Garland.

Dynes, W.R., & Donaldson, S. (1992). General introduction. In W.R. Dynes & S. Donaldson (Eds.), *Homosexuality and psychology, psychiatry, and counseling* (pp. v-xx). New York: Garland.

Eldridge, N.S., & Gilbert, L.A. (1990). Correlates of relationship satisfaction in lesbian couples. *Psychology of Women Quarterly,* 14, 43-62.

Elias, M. (2002, July 16). Is homosexuality to blame for the child sexual abuse crisis now plaguing the Catholic church? *USA Today,* p. 6D.

Eliason, M.J. (1995). Attitudes about lesbian and gay men: A review and implications for social service training. *Journal of Gay & Lesbian Social Services,* 2, 73-90.

Eliason, M.J. (1997). The prevalence and nature of biphobia in heterosexual undergraduate students. *Archives of Sexual Behavior,* 26, 317-326.

Ellis, A.L., & Mitchell, R.W. (2000). Sexual orientation. In L.T. Szuchman & F. Muscarella (Eds.), *Psychological perspectives on human sexuality* (pp. 196-231). New York: Wiley.

Ellis, K., & Eriksen, M.K. (2002). Transsexual and transgenderist experiences and treatment options. *Family Journal: Counseling and Therapy for Couples and Families,* 10, 289-299.

Emerson, S., & Rosenfeld, C. (1996). Stages of adjustment in family members of transgender individuals. *Journal of Family Psychotherapy,* 7, 1-12.

Espin, O.M. (1984). Cultural and historical influences on sexuality in Hispanic/Latin women: Implications for psychotherapy. In C. Vance (Ed.), *Pleasure and danger: Exploring female sexuality* (pp. 149-163). London: Routledge & Kegan Paul.

Espin, O.M. (1993). Issues of identity in the psychology of Latina lesbians. In L.D. Garnets & D.C. Kimmel (Eds.), *Psychological perspective on lesbian and gay male experiences* (pp. 349-363). New York: Columbia University Press.

Espin, O.M. (1997). Crossing borders and boundaries: The life narratives of immigrant lesbians. In B. Greene (Ed.), *Ethnic and cultural diversity among lesbians and gay men* (pp. 191-215). Thousand Oaks, CA: Sage Publications.

Esterberg, K.G. (1994). Being a lesbian and being in love: Constructing identity through relationships. *Journal of Gay & Lesbian Social Services,* 1, 57-82.

Esterberg, K.G. (1996). Gay cultures, gay communities: The social organization of lesbians, gay men, and bisexuals. In R.C. Savin-Williams & K.M. Cohen (Eds.), *The lives of lesbian, gay men, and bisexuals: Children to adults* (pp. 377-391). Ft. Worth, TX: Harcourt Brace.

Esterberg, K.G. (1997). *Lesbian and bisexual identities: Constructing communities, constructing selves.* Philadelphia: Temple University Press.

Evans, N., & Levine, H. (1990). Perspectives on sexual orientation. *New Directions for Student Services,* 51, 49-58.

Faderman, L. (1981). *Surpassing the love of men: Romantic friendship and love between women from the Renaissance to the present.* New York: Morrow.

Faderman, L. (1984-1985). The new "gay" lesbians. *The Journal of Homosexuality,* 10, 85-95.

Faderman, L. (1991). *Odd girls and twilight lovers: A history of lesbian life in twentieth-century America.* New York: Penguin.

Fairchild, B., & Hayward, N. (1979). *Now that you know: What every parent should know about homosexuality.* New York: Harcourt, Brace, Jovanovich.

Fassinger, R.E. (1991). The hidden minority: Issues and challenges in working with lesbians and gay men. *Counseling Psychologist,* 19, 157-176.

Fassinger, R.E. (1994, February). *Sexual orientation and identity development: Human dignity for all?* Invited address at the 20th annual Maryland Student Affairs Conference, University of Maryland, College Park, Maryland.

Fassinger, R.E. (1995). From invisibility to integration: Lesbian identity in the workplace. *The Career Development Quarterly,* 44, 148-166.

Fassinger, R.E., & Miller, B.A. (1996). Validation of an inclusive model of sexual minority identity formation on a sample of gay men. *Journal of Heterosexuality,* 32, 53-78.

Feinberg, L. (1996). *Transgender warriors: Making history from Joan of Arc to "RuPaul."* Boston: Beacon Press.

Feldman, D.A., & Johnson, T.M. (1986). *The social dimension of AIDS: Methods and theory.* New York: Praeger.

Ficarrotto, T. (1990). Racism, sexism, and erotophobia: Attitudes of heterosexuals toward homosexuals. *Journal of Homosexuality,* 19, 111-116.

Firestein, B.A. (1996). Bisexuality as paradigm shift: Transforming our disciplines. In B.A. Firestein (Ed.), *Bisexuality: The psychology and politics of an invisible minority* (pp. 263-303). Thousand Oaks, CA: Sage.

Floyd, F.J., & Stein, T.S. (2002). Sexual orientation identity formation among gay, lesbian, and bisexual youths: Multiple patterns of milestone experiences. *Journal of Research on Adolescence*, 12, 167-191.

Fontaine, J.H., & Hammond, N.L. (1996). Counseling issues with gay and lesbian adolescents. *Adolescence*, 31, 817-830.

Fox, R.C. (1991). Development of a bisexual identity: Understanding the process. In L. Hutchins & L. Káahumanu (Eds.), *Bi any other name: Bisexual people speak out* (pp. 29-36). Boston: Alyson.

Fox, R.C. (1995). Bisexual identities. In A.R. D'Augelli & C.J. Patterson (Eds.) (1995). *Lesbians, gay, and bisexual identities over the life span* (pp. 48-86). New York: Oxford.

Fox, R.C. (1996). Bisexuality in perspective: A review of theory and research. In B.A. Firestein (Ed.). *Bisexuality: The psychology and politics of an invisible minority* (pp. 3-50). Thousand Oaks, CA: Sage.

Fox, R.C. (2000). Bisexuality in perspective: A review of theory and research. In B. Greene & G.L. Croom (Eds.), *Education, research, and practice in lesbian, gay, bisexual, and transgendered psychology: A resource manual*, Vol. 5 (pp. 161-206). Thousand Oaks, CA: Sage Publications, Inc.

Franke, R., & Leary, M. (1991). Disclosure of sexual orientation by lesbians and gay men: A comparison of private and public processes. *Journal of Social and Clinical Psychology*, 10, 262-269.

Franklin, K. (2000). Antigay behaviors among young adults: Prevalence, patterns, and motivators in a noncriminal population. *Journal of Interpersonal Violence*, 15, 339-362.

Freedman, M. (1971). *Homosexuality and psychological functioning*. Belmont, CA: Brooks Cole.

Fredriksen, K.I. (1999). Family caregiving responsibilities among lesbians and gay men. *Social Work*, 44, 142-155.

Friend, R.A. (1990). Older lesbian and gay people: Responding to homophobia. *Marriage and Family Review*, 14, 241-263.

Friend, R.A. (1998). Heterosexism, homophobia, and the culture of schooling. In S. Books (Ed.), *Invisible children in the society and its schools* (pp. 137-166). Mahwah, New Jersey: Erlbaum.

Friskopp, A., & Silverstein, S. (1995). *Straight jobs, gay lives*. New York: Scribner's.

Fygetakis, L.M. (1997). Greek American lesbians: Identity odysseys of honorable good girls. In B. Greene (Ed.), *Ethnic and cultural diversity among lesbians and gay men* (pp. 152-190). Thousand Oaks, CA: Sage Publications.

Gagné, P., & Tewksbury, J.R. (1999). Knowledge and power, body and self: An analysis of knowledge systems and the transgendered self. *The Sociological Quarterly*, 40, 59-83.

Gagné, P., Tewksbury, R., & McGaughey, D. (1997). Coming out and crossing over: Identity formation and proclamation in a Transgender community. *Gender & Society*, 11, 478-508.

Gagnon, J.H. (1989). Disease and desire. *Daedalus*, 118, 47-77

Gagnon, J.H., & Simon, W. (1967b). *Sexual deviance*. New York: Harper & Row.

Gagnon, J.H., & Simon, W. (1968). Sexual deviance in contemporary America. *Annals of the American Academy of Political and Social Science,* 376, 106-122.

Garnets, L., Herek, G.M., & Levy, B. (1990). Violence and victimization of lesbians and gay men: Mental health consequences. *Journal of Interpersonal Violence,* 5, 366-383.

Garnets, L.D., & Kimmel, D.C. (1993). Cultural diversity among lesbians and gay men. In L.D. Garnets & D.C. Kimmel (Eds.), *Psychological perspectives on lesbian and gay male experiences* (pp. 331-337). New York: Columbia University.

Garnets, L.D., & Peplau, L.A. (2001). A new paradigm for women' sexual orientation: Implications for therapy. *Women in Therapy,* 24, 111-121.

Gartrell, N. (1984). Combating homophobia in the psychotherapy of lesbians. *Women & Therapy,* 3, 13-29.

Gay victim of beating in Wyoming dies (1998, October 13). *Dallas Morning News,* A3.

GenderPAC (1998). *First national study on transviolence.* Waltham, MA: Author.

Germain, C.B. (1991). *Human behavior and the social environment.* New York: Columbia University.

Gerstel, C.J., Feraios, A.J., & Herdt, G. (1989). Widening circles: An ethnographic profile of a youth group. *Journal of Homosexuality,* 17, 75-92.

Gilligan, C. (1982). *In a different voice: Psychological therapy and women's development.* Cambridge, MA: Harvard University Press.

Giorgis, C., Higgins, K., & McNab, W.L. (2000). Continuing education health issues of gay and lesbian youth: Implications for school. *Journal of Health Education,* 31, 28-36.

Gochros, J.S. (1985). Wives' reactions to learning that their husbands are bisexual. *Journal of Homosexuality,* 11, 101-113.

Gochros, J.S. (1989). *When husbands come out of the closet.* Binghamton, NY: The Haworth Press.

Gock, T. (1985, August). *Psychotherapy with Asian/Pacific gay men: Psychological issues, treatment approach and therapeutic guidelines.* Paper presented at the meeting of the Asian-American Psychological Association, Los Angeles, CA.

Gock,T.S. (1992). Asian-Pacific islander issues: Identity integration and pride. In B. Berzon (Ed.), *Positively gay* (pp. 247-252). Berkeley, CA: Celestial Arts.

Goffman, E. (1963). *Stigma: Notes on the management of spoiled identity.* Englewood Cliffs, NJ: Prentice Hall.

Golden, C. (1987). Diversity and variability in women's sexual identities. In Boston Lesbian Psychologies Collective (Eds.), *Lesbian psychologies: Explorations and challenges* (pp. 19-34). Urbana: University of Illinois Press.

Golden, C. (1994). Our politics, our choices: The feminist movement and sexual orientation. In B. Greene & G.M. Herek (Eds.), *Lesbian and gay psychology: Theory, research, and clinical application.* Thousand Oaks, CA: Sage.

Golden, C. (1996). What's in a name? Sexual self-identification among women. In R.C. Savin-Williams & K.M. Cohen (Eds.), *The lives of lesbians, gays, and bisexuals: Children to adults* (pp. 229-249). Ft. Worth, TX: Harcourt Brace.

Golden, C. (1997, Winter). Do women choose their sexual identity? *The Harvard Gay & Lesbian Review,* pp. 18-20.

Goldman, J. (1992, September). Coming out strong. *California Lawyer,* pp. 13, 30-36, 86-67.

Golombok, S. (2000). Parents' sexual orientation: Heterosexual or homosexual? In S. Golombok (Ed.), *Parenting: What really counts?* (pp. 45-60). Philadelphia: Routledge.

Golombok, S., Spencer, A., & Rutter, M. (1983). Children in lesbian and single-parent households: Psychosexual and psychiatric appraisal. *Journal of Child Psychology,* 24, 551-572.

Gomez, J., & Smith, B. (1990, Spring). Taking the home out of homophobia. *Outlook,* 8, 32-37.

Gonsiorek, J.C. (1982). Introduction to mental health issues and homosexuality. *American Behavioral Scientist,* 25, 267-383.

Gonsiorek, J. (1988). Mental health issues of gay and lesbian adolescents. *Journal of Adolescent Health Care,* 9, 114-122.

Gonsiorek, J.C. (1993). Threat, stress, and adjustment: Mental health and the workplace for gay and lesbian individuals. In L. Diamant (Ed.), *Homosexual issues in the workplace* (pp. 242-263). Washington, DC: Taylor & Francis.

Gonsiorek, J.C. (1995). Gay male identities: Concepts and issues. In A.R. D'Augelli & C.J. Patterson (Eds.), *Lesbians, gay, and bisexual identities over the life span* (pp. 24-47). New York: Oxford University Press.

González, F.J., & Espin, O.M. (1996). Latino men, latino women, and homosexuality. In R.P. Cabaj & T.S. Stein (Eds.), *Textbook of homosexuality and mental health* (pp. 583-601). Washington, DC: American Psychiatric Press.

Gore, S. (2000). The lesbian and gay workplace: An employee's guide to advancing equity. In B. Greene & G.L. Croom (Eds.), *Psychological perspectives on lesbian and gay lives.* Vol. 5 (pp. 282-302). Thousand Oaks, CA: Sage.

Grace, J. (1992). Affirming gay and lesbian adulthood. In N.J. Woodman (Ed.), *Lesbian and gay lifestyles: A guide for counseling and education* (pp. 33-47). New York: Irvington.

Gramick J. (1984). Developing a lesbian identity. In T. Darty & S. Potter (Eds.), *Women-identified women* (pp. 31-44). Palo Alto, CA: Mayfield.

Greeley, G. (1994). Service organizations for gay and lesbian youth. *Journal of Gay and Lesbian Social Services,* 1, 111-130.

Green, B. (1994). African American lesbians and other culturally diverse people in psychodynamic psychotherapies: Useful paradigms or oxymoron? *Journal of Lesbian Studies,* 8, 57-77.

Green, J., & Brinkin, L. (1994, September). *Investigation into discrimination against transgender people.* San Francisco Human Rights Committee.

Green, R. (1972). Homosexuality as a mental illness. *International Journal of Psychiatry,* 10, 77-128.

Green, R. (1987). *"Sissy boy syndrome" and the development of homosexuality.* New Haven, CT: Yale University Press.

Green, R.-J. (2000). "Lesbians, gay men, and their parents:" A critique of LaSala and the prevailing clinical "wisdom." *Family Process,* 39, 257-266.

Green, R.-J. (2002). Coming out to family . . . in context. In E. Davis-Russell (Ed.), *California School of Professional Psychology handbook of multicultural educa-*

tion, research, intervention, and training (pp. 277-283). San Francisco, CA: Jossey-Bass.

Green, R.-J., Bettinger, M., & Zacks, E. (1996). Are lesbian couples fused and gay male couples disengaged? Questioning gender straight jackets. In J. Laird & R.-J. Green (Eds.), *Lesbians and gays in couples and families* (pp. 185-231). San Francisco: Jossey-Bass.

Green, R.-J., & Mitchell, V. (2002). Gay and lesbian couples in therapy: Homophobia, relational ambiguity, and social support. In A.S. Gurman & N.S. Jacobson (Eds.), *Clinical handbook of couple therapy* (pp. 536-568), New York: Guilford Press.

Greene, B. (1986). When the therapist is white and the patient is black: Considerations for psychotherapy in the feminist heterosexual and lesbian communities. In D. Howard (Ed.), *The dynamics of feminist therapy* (pp. 41- 65). Binghamton, NY: The Haworth Press.

Greene, B. (1994a). Ethnic minority lesbians and gay men: mental health and treatment issues. *Journal of Consulting and Clinical Psychology, 62*, 243-251.

Greene, B. (1994b). Lesbian and gay sexual orientations: Implications for clinical training, practice, and research. In B. Greene & G.M. Herek (Eds.), *Lesbian and gay psychology: Theory, research, and clinical applications* (pp. 1-24). Thousand Oaks, CA: Sage.

Greene, B. (1994c). Lesbian women of color: Triple jeopardy. In L. Comas-Diaz & B. Greene (Eds.), *Women of Color* (pp. 389-427). New York: Guilford.

Greene, B. (1996). Lesbians and gay men of color: The legacy of ethnosexual mythologies in heterosexism. In E.D. Rothblum & L.A. Bond (Eds.), *Preventing heterosexism and homophobia* (pp. 59-70). Thousand Oaks, CA: Sage Publications.

Greene, B. (1997). Ethnic minority lesbians and gay men: Mental health and treatment issues. In B. Greene (Ed.), *Ethnic and cultural diversity among lesbians and gay men* (pp. 216-239). Thousand Oaks, CA: Sage Publications.

Greene, B., & Croom, G. (2000) (Eds.). *Education, research, and practice in lesbian, gay, bisexual, and transgendered psychology: A resource manual,* Vol. 5. Thousand Oaks, CA: Sage Publications.

Griffin, C., Wirth, M., & Wirth, A. (1986). *Beyond acceptance: Parents of lesbians and gays talk about their experiences.* Englewood Cliffs, NJ: Prentice Hall.

Griffin, P., Lee, C., Waugh, J., & Beyer, C. (2004). Describing roles that gay-straight alliances play in schools: From individual support to social change. *Journal of Gay and Lesbian Issues in Education, 1*, 7-22.

Gross, A.E., Green, S.K., Storck, J.T., & Vanyur, J.M. (1980). Disclosure of sexual orientation and impressions of male and female homosexuals. *Personality and Social Psychology Bulletin, 6*, 307-314.

Grossman, A.H., D'Augelli, A.R., & O'Connell, T.S. (2001). Being lesbian, gay, bisexual, and 60 or older in North America. *Journal of Gay and Lesbian Social Services, 13*, 23-40.

Groves, P.A., & Ventura, L.A. (1983). The lesbian coming out process: Therapeutic considerations. *The Personnel and Guidance Journal, 62*, 146-149.

Gruskin, E.P. (1999). Treating lesbians and bisexual women: *Challenges and strategies for health professionals.* Thousand Oaks, CA: Sage Publications.

Guidry, L.L. (1999). Clinical intervention with bisexuals: A contextualized understanding. *Professional Psychology: Research and Practice,* 30, 22-26.

Gurwitz, S.B., & Marcus, M. (1978). Effects of anticipated interaction, sex, or homosexual stereotypes on first impression. *Journal of Applied Social Psychology,* 8, 47-56.

Haldeman, D.C. (1994). The practice and ethics of sexual orientation conversion therapy. *Journal of Counseling and Clinical Psychology,* 62, 221-227.

Hall, M. (1986). The lesbian corporate experience. *Journal of Homosexuality,* 12, 59-75.

Hall, M. (1989). Private experiences in the public domain: Lesbians in organizations. In J. Hearn, D.L. Sheppard, P. Tancred-Sheriff, & G. Burrell (Eds.), *The sexuality of organizations* (pp. 125-138). Newbury Park, CA: Sage Publications.

Halpin, S.A., & Allen, M.W. (2004). Changes in psychological well-being during stages of gay identity development. *Journal of Homosexuality,* 47, 109-126.

Hammersmith, S.K. (1987). A sociological approach to counseling homosexual clients and their families. In E. Coleman (Ed.), *Integrated identities for gay men and lesbians: Psychotherapeutic approaches for emotional well-being* (pp. 173-190). Binghamton, NY: Harrington Park Press.

Hammersmith, S.K., & Weinberg, M.S. (1973). Homosexual identity: Commitment, adjustment, and significant others. *Sociometry,* 36, 56-79.

Han, S. (2000). Asian American gay men's (dis)claiming masculinity. In P.M. Nardi (Ed.), *Gay masculinities* (pp. 206-223). Thousand Oaks, CA: Sage Press.

Hancock, K.A. (1995). Psychotherapy with lesbians and gay men. In A.R. D'Augelli & C.J. Patterson (Eds.), *Lesbian, gay, and bisexual identities over the lifespan* (pp. 398-432). New Yrok: Oxford University Press.

Hanley-Hackenbruck. P. (1989). Psychotherapy and the "coming out" process. *Journal of Gay & Lesbian Psychotherapy,* 1, 21-39.

Hanscombe, G.E., & Forster, J. (1982). *Rocking the cradle: Lesbian mothers: A challenge in family living.* Boston: Alyson.

Harris, M.B., & Turner, P.H. (1985-1986). Gay and lesbian parents. *Journal of Homosexuality,* 12, 101-113.

Harry, J. (1982). *Gay children grown up.* New York: Praeger.

Harry, J. (1983). Gay male and lesbian relationships. In E. Macklin & R. Rubin (Eds.), *Contemporary families and alternative lifestyles: Handbook on research and theory* (pp. 216-234). Beverly Hills, CA: Sage.

Harry, J. (1993). Being out: A general model. *Journal of Homosexuality,* 26, 25-39.

Hartman, A. (1996). Social policy as a context for lesbian and gay families: The political is personal. In J. Laird & R.-J. Green (Eds.), *Lesbians and gays in couples and families* (pp. 69-85). San Francisco: Jossey-Bass.

Hawkeswood, W.G. (1990). *I'm a black man who just happens to be gay. The sexuality of black gay men.* Paper presented at the American Anthropological Association Annual Meeting, New Orleans.

Healy, T. (1993). A struggle for language: Patterns of self-disclosure in lesbian couples. *Smith College Studies in Social Work,* 63, 247-263.

Helminiak, D.A. (1995). *What the Bible really says about homosexuality.* San Francisco, CA: Alamo Square Press.

Hencken, J., & O'Dowd, W. (1977). Coming out as an aspect of identity formation. *Gay Academic Union Journal,* 1, 18-26.

Henning-Stout, M., James, S., & Macintosh, S. (2000). Reducing harassment of lesbian, gay, bisexual, transgender, and questioning youth in schools. *School Psychology Review,* 29, 180-191.

Herdt, G.H. (1989). Gay and lesbian youth, emergent identities, and cultural scenes at home and abroad. *Journal of Homosexuality,* 17, 1-42.

Herdt, G.H. (1992). "Coming out" as a rite of passage: A Chicago study. In G.H. Herdt & A. Boxer (Eds.), *Gay culture in America: Essays from the field* (pp. 29-65). Boston: Beacon.

Herdt, G. (1997). *Same sex, different cultures.* Boulder, CO: Westview Press.

Herdt, G., & Beeler, J. (1998). Older gay men and lesbians in families. In C.J. Patterson & A.R. D'Augelli (Eds.), *Lesbian, gay, and bisexual identities in families: Psychological perspectives* (pp. 177-196). New York: Oxford University Press.

Herdt, G., Beeler, J., & Rawls, T.W. (1997). Life course diversity among older lesbians and gay men: A study in Chicago. *Journal of Gay, Lesbian, and Bisexual Identity,* 2, 231-246.

Herdt, G.H., & Boxer, A. (1992). Introduction: Culture, history, and life course of gay men. In G. Herdt (Ed.), *Gay culture in America: Essays from the field* (pp. 1-28). Boston: Beacon.

Herdt, G.H., & Boxer, A. (1993). *Children of the horizons: How gay and lesbian teens are leading a way out of the closet.* Boston: Beacon.

Herek, G.M. (1988). Heterosexual's attitudes toward lesbians and gay men: Correlates and gender differences. *Journal of Sex Research,* 25, 451-477.

Herek, G.M. (1989). Sexual orientation. In H. Tierney (Ed.), *Women's Studies Encyclopedia* (Vol. 1) (pp. 344-346). New York: Greenwood.

Herek, G.M. (1991). Myths about sexual orientation: A lawyer's guide to social science research. Law and Sexuality. *Review of Lesbian and Gay Legal Issues,* 1, 133-172.

Herek, G.M. (1992a). Homophobia. In W.R. Dynes (Ed.), *Encyclopedia of homosexuality* (pp. 552-555). New York: Garland Publications.

Herek, G.M. (1992b). Psychological heterosexism and anti-gay violence: The social psychology of bigotry and bashing. In G.M. Herek & T. Berrill (Eds.). *Hate crimes: Confronting violence against lesbians and gay men* (pp. 149-169). Newbury Park, CA: Sage.

Herek, G.M. (1993). Documenting prejudice against lesbians and gay men on campus: The Yale sexual orientation survey. *Journal of Homosexuality,* 25, 15-30.

Herek, G.M. (1994). Assessing heterosexuals' attitudes toward lesbian and gay men. In B. Greene & G.B. Herek (Eds.), *Lesbian and gay psychology: theory, research, and clinical applications* (pp. 206-228). Thousand Oaks, CA: Sage

Herek, G.M. (1995). Psychological heterosexism in the United States. In A.R. D'Augelli & C.J. Patterson (Eds.), *Lesbian, gay, and bisexual identities over the lifespan: Psychological perspectives* (pp. 321-346). New York: Oxford.

Herek, G.M. (2000). The psychology of sexual prejudice. *Current Direction in Psychological Science,* 9, 19-22.

Herek, G.M. (2002). Gender gaps in public opinion about lesbians and gay men. *Public Opinion Quarterly,* 66, 40-66.

Herek, G.M. (2003). Why tell if you're not asked? Self-disclosure, intergroup contact, and heterosexuals' attitudes toward lesbians and gay men. In L.D. Garnets & D.D. Kimmel (Eds.), *Psychological perspectives on lesbian, gay, and bisexual experiences* (pp. 270-298). New York: Columbia University Press.

Herek, G.M. (2004). Beyond "homophobia:" Thinking about sexual stigma and prejudice in the twenty-first century. *Sexuality Research and Social Policy,* 1, 6-24.

Herek, G.M., Cogan, J.C., & Gillis, J.R. (2002). Victim experiences in hate crimes based on sexual orientation. *Journal of Social Issues,* 58, 319-339.

Herek, G.M., Gillis, J.R., & Cogan, J.C. (1999). Psychological sequelae of hate-crime victimization among lesbians, gay, and bisexual adults. *Journal of Consulting and Clinical Psychology,* 67, 945-951.

Herek, G.M., & Glunt, E. (1993). Interpersonal contact and heterosexuals' attitudes toward gay men: Results from a national survey. *The Journal of Sex Research,* 30, 239-244.

Hershberger, S.L., & D'Augelli, A.R. (1995). The impact of victimization on the mental health suicidality of lesbian, gay, and bisexual youths. *Developmental Psychology,* 31, 65-74.

Hetherington, C. (1991). Life planning and career counseling with gay and lesbian students. In N.J. Evans & V.A. Wall (Eds.), *Beyond tolerance: Gays, lesbians, and bisexuals on campus* (pp. 131-145). Alexandria, VA: American College Personnel Association.

Hetherington, C., & Orzek, A. (1989). Career and life planning with lesbian women. *Journal of Counseling and Development,* 68, 52-57.

Hetrick, E.S., & Martin, A.D. (1987). Developmental issues and their resolution for gay and lesbian adolescents. *Journal of Homosexuality,* 14, 25-44.

Hidalgo, H.A. (1984). The Puerto Rican lesbian in the United States. In T. Darty and S. Potter (Eds.), *Women-identified women* (pp. 105-115). Palo Alto, CA: Mayfield.

Hoeffer, B. (1981). Children's acquisition of sex-role behavior in lesbian mothers' families. *American Journal of Orthopsychiatry,* 51, 536-643.

Hollander, G. (2000). Questioning youth: Challenges to working with youths forming identities. *School Psychology Review,* 29, 173-179.

Hollander, J., & Haber, L. (1992). Ecological transition: Using Bronfenbrenner's model to study sexual identity change. *Health Care for Women International,* 13, 121-129.

Homosexuals said to face unique midlife issues (1994, July). *Psychiatric News,* 29, 10.

Hong, S.M. (1984). Australian attitudes towards homosexuality: A comparison with college students. *The Journal of Psychology,* 117, 89-95.

Hong, W., Yamamoto, J., & Chang, D.S. (1993). Sex in a Confucian society. *Journal of the American Academy of Psychoanalysis & Dynamic Psychiatry,* 21, 405-419.

Hooker, E. (1967). The homosexual community. In. J.H. Gagnon & W. Simon (Eds.), *Sexual Deviance* (pp. 167-184). New York: Harper & Row.

Horowitz, J.L., & Newcomb, M.D. (2001). A multidimensional approach to homosexual identity. *Journal of Homosexuality, 42*, 1-19.

Hostetler, A.J. (2000). Lesbian and gay lives across the adult years. In B.J. Cohler & R.M. Galatzer (Eds.), *The course of gay and lesbian lives: Social and psychoanalytic perspectives* (pp. 193-251). Chicago: University of Chicago Press.

Hostetler, A., & Herdt, G. (1998). Culture, sexual lifeways and developmental subjectivities: Rethinking sexual taxonomies. *Social Research, 65*, 249-290.

Humphreys, L. (1972). *Out of the closets: The sociology of homosexual liberation.* Englewood Cliffs, NJ: Prentice Hall.

Humphreys, N.A., & Quam, J.K. (1998). Middle-aged and old gay, lesbian, and bisexual adults. In G.A. Appleby & J.W. Anastas (Eds.), *Not just a passing phase: Social work with gay, lesbian, and bisexual people* (pp. 245-267). New York: Columbia University Press.

Hunt, S., & Main, T.L. (1997). Sexual orientation confusion among spouses of transvestites and transsexuals following disclosure of spouse's gender dysphoria. *Journal of Psychology and Human Sexuality, 9*, 39-52.

Hunter, J. (1990). Violence against lesbian and gay male youth. *Journal of Interpersonal Violence, 5*, 295-300.

Hunter, J. (1995). At the crossroads: Lesbian youth. In K. Jay (Ed.) *Dyke life: A celebration of the lesbian experience* (pp. 50-60). New York: Basic Books.

Hunter, J., & Schaecher, R. (1987). Stresses on lesbian and gay adolescents in schools. *Social Work in Education, 9*, 180-189.

Hunter, J., & Schaecher, R. (1990). Lesbian and gay youth. In M.J. Rotheram-Borus, J. Bradley, & N. Obolensky (Eds.). *Planning to live: Evaluating and treating suicidal teens in community settings* (pp. 297-316). Tulsa: University of Oklahoma Press.

Hunter, S., & Hickerson, J. (2003). *Affirmative practice: Understanding and working with lesbian, gay, bisexual, and transgender persons.* Washington, DC: NASW Press.

Hunter, S., Shannon, C., Knox, J., & Martin, J.I. (1998). *Lesbian, gay, and bisexual youth and adults: Knowledge for human services practice.* Thousand Oaks, CA: Sage.

Hutchins, L., & Káahumanu, L. (1991). *Bi any other name: Bisexual people speak out.* Boston: Alyson.

Icard, L. (1985-1986). Black gay men and conflicting social identities: Sexual orientation versus racial identity. *Journal of Social Work and Human Sexuality, 4*, 83-93.

Iversen v. Kent School (1998). [Online]. Available at www.safeschools-wa.org/iversen.html.

Jackson, D., & Sullivan, R. (1994). Developmental implications of homophobia for lesbian and gay adolescents: Issues in policy and practice. *Journal of Gay & Lesbian Social Services, 1*, 93-109.

Jacobs, H. (1994). A new approach for gay and lesbian domestic partners: Legal acceptance through relational property theory. *Duke Journal of Gender Law & Policy,* 1, 159-172.

Jacobs, M.A., & Brown, L.B. (1997). American Indian lesbians and gays: An exploratory story. *Journal of Gay and Lesbian Social Services,* 6, 29-41.

Jay, K., & Young, A. (Eds.), (1972). *Out of the closets: Voices of gay liberation.* New York: Douglas/Links.

Jay, K., & Young, A. (1979). *The gay report: Lesbians and gay men speak out about sexual experiences and lifestyles.* New York: Summit.

Jeffreys, S. (1994). The queer disappearance of lesbians: Sexuality in the academy. *Women's Studies International Forum,* 17, 459-472.

Jensen, K.L. (1999). *Lesbian epiphanies: Women coming out in later life.* Binghamton, NY: Harrington Park Press.

Jensen, L., Gambles, D., & Olsen, J. (1988). Attitudes toward homosexuality: A cross-sectional analysis of predictors. *The International Journal of Social Psychiatry,* 34, 47-57.

Johansson, W. (1990). Prejudice. In W.R. Dynes (Ed.), *Encyclopedia of homosexuality* (pp. 1031-1033). New York: Garland.

Johns, D.J., & Probst, T.M. (2004). Sexual minority identity formation in an adult population. *Journal of Homosexuality,* 47, 81-90.

Johnson, M.E., Brems, C., & Alford-Keating, P. (1997). Personality correlates of homophobia. *Journal of Homosexuality,* 34, 57-69.

Jones, B.E., & Hill, M.J. (1996). African American lesbians, gay men, and bisexuals. In R.P. Cabaj & T.S. Stein (Eds.), *Textbook of homosexuality and mental health* (pp. 549-561).

Jones, C. (1978). *Understanding gay relatives and friends.* New York: Seabury.

Jones, E.E., Farina, A., Hastorf, A.H., Markus, H.J., Miller, D.T., & Scott, R.A. (1984). *Social stigma: The psychology of marked relationships.* New York: Freeman.

Jones, M.A., & Gabriel, M.A. (1999). Utilization of psychotherapy by lesbians, gay men, and bisexuals: Findings from a nationwide survey. *American Journal of Orthopsychiatry,* 69, 209-219.

Jones, T.C., & Nystrom, N.M. (2002). Looking back . . . looking forward: Addressing the lives of lesbians 55 and older. *Journal of Women & Aging,* 14, 59-76.

Jordan, K.M., & Deluty, R.H. (1998). Coming out for lesbian women: Its relation to anxiety, positive affectivity, self-esteem, and social support. *Journal of Homosexuality,* 35, 41-63.

Jost, K. (2000). Gay-rights update. *CQ Researcher,* 10-307-327.

Kahn, M.J. (1991). Factors affecting the coming out process for lesbians. *Journal of Homosexuality,* 21, 47-70.

Kanuha, V. (1990). Compounding the triple jeopardy: Battering in lesbian of color relationships. *Women and Therapy,* 9, 169-184.

Kaupman, G. (1991, February 29). Cracker Barrel waffles on anti-gay policy. *Southern Voice,* p. 1.

Kehoe, M. (1989). *Lesbians over 60 speak for themselves.* Binghamton, NY: Harrington Park Press.

Kimmel, D.C., & Sang, B.E. (1995). Lesbians and gay men in midlife. In A.R. D'Augelli & C.J. Patterson (Eds.), *Lesbian, gay, and bisexual identities over the lifespan: Psychological perspectives* (pp. 190-214). New York: Oxford.

Kinnish, K.K., Strassberg, D.S., & Turner, C.W. (2005). Sex differences in the flexibility of sexual orientation: A multidimensional retrospective assessment. *Archives of Sexual Behavior,* 34, 173-183.

Kinsey, A.C., Pomeroy, W.B., & Martin, C.E. (1948). *Sexual behavior in the human male.* Philadelphia: W.B. Saunders.

Kinsey, A.C., Pomeroy, W.B., Martin, C.E., & Gebbard, P.H. (1953). *Sexual behavior in the human female.* Philadelphia: W.B. Saunders.

Kirkpatrick, M. (1989a). Lesbians: A different middle-age? In J. Oldham & R. Liebert (Eds.), *New psychoanalytic perspectives: The middle years* (pp. 35-148). New Haven, CT: Yale University.

Kirkpatrick, M. (1989b). Middle age and the lesbian experience. *Women's Studies Quarterly,* 1-2, 87-86.

Kirkpatrick, M., Smith, C., & Roy, R. (1981). Lesbian mothers and their children: A comparative survey. *American Journal of Orthopsychiatry,* 51, 545-551.

Kirp, D.L. (1999). Martyrs and movies. *American Prospect,* 11, 52-53.

Kite, M.E. (1984). Sex differences in attitudes towards homosexuals: A meta-analytic review. *Journal of Homosexuality,* 10, 69-89.

Kitzinger, C. (1991). Lesbian and gay men in the workplace: Psychosocial issues. In M. J. Davidson & J. Earnshaw (Eds.), *Vulnerable workers: Psychosocial and legal issues* (pp. 223-257). New York: John Wiley & Sons.

Kitzinger, C., & Wilkinson, S. (1995). Transitions from heterosexuality to lesbianism: The discursive production of lesbian identities. *Developmental Psychology,* 31, 95-104.

Klein, F. (1990). The need to view sexual orientation as a multivariate dynamic process: A theoretical perspective. In D.P. McWhirter, S.A. Sanders, & J.M. Reinisch (Eds.), *Homosexuality/heterosexuality: Concepts of sexual orientation* (pp. 277-282). New York: Oxford University.

Klein, F. (1993). *The bisexual option* (2nd ed.). Binghamton, NY: Harrington Park Press.

Klein, F., Sepekoff, B., & Wolf, T.J. (1985). Sexual orientation: A multi-variable dynamic process. *Journal of Homosexuality,* 11, 35-49.

Kourany, R.F.C. (1987). *Suicide among homosexual adolescents,* 13, 111-117.

Kronenberger, G.K. (1991). Out of the closet. *Personnel Journal,* 70, 40-44.

Kuehlwein, K.T. (1992). Working with gay men. In A. Freeman & F.M. Dattilio (Eds.), *Comprehensive casebook of cognitive therapy* (pp. 249-255). New York: Plenum Press.

Kuiper, A.J. (1991). *Transsexualiteit; evaluatie van de ge slachtsaanpassende behandeling.* Amsterdam: Free University Press.

Kuiper, A.J., & Cohen-Kettenis, P.T. (1988). Sex reassignment surgery: A study of 141 Dutch transsexuals. *Archives of Sexual Behavior,* 17, 439-457.

Kurdek, L.A. (1988a). Relationship quality of gay and lesbian cohabiting couples. *Journal of Homosexuality,* 15, 93-118.

Kurdek, L.A. (1988b). Perceived social support in gays and lesbians in cohabiting relationships. *Journal of Personality and Social Psychology,* 54, 504-509.

Kurdek, L.A., & Schmitt, J.P. (1987). Perceived emotional support from family and friends in members of homosexual, married, and heterosexual cohabiting couples. *Journal of Homosexuality,* 14, 57-68.

Laird, J. (1996). Family-centered practice with lesbian and gay families. Families in society: *Journal of Contemporary Human Services,* 77, 559-572.

LaMar, L., & Kite, M. (1998). Sex differences in attitudes towards homosexuals: A meta-analytic review. *Journal of Homosexuality,* 10, 69-89.

Landau, D.A. (1994). Employment discrimination against lesbians and gays: The incomplete legal response of the United States and the European Union. *Duke Journal of Comparative and International Law,* 4, 335-361.

Lander, P.S., & Charbonneau, C. (1990). The new lesbian in midlife: Reconstructing sexual identity. In J. Hurtig, K. Gillogly, & T. Gulevich (Eds.), *Michigan Discussions in Anthropology,* 9, 1-14.

Lang, S. (1999). Lesbians, men-women and two-spirits: Homosexuality and gender in Native American cultures. In E. Blackwood & S. Wieringa (Eds.), *Female desires: Same-sex relations and transgender practices across cultures* (pp. 91-116). New York: Columbia University Press.

Laris, M. (2000, October 1). City examines its attitudes after shooting at gay bar. *Dallas Morning News,* A4.

Laumann, E.D., Gagnon, J.H., Michael, R.T., & Michaels, S. (1994). *The social organization of sexuality: Sexual practices in the United States.* Chicago: University of Chicago Press.

Leaveck, A. (1994). *Perceived parental reactions to same-sex sexual orientation disclosure: A search for predictors.* Unpublished doctoral dissertation, Central Michigan University, Mount Pleasant.

Lee, J.A. (1977). Going public: A study in the sociology of homosexual liberation. *Journal of Homosexuality,* 3, 49-78.

Lee, J.A. (1987). What can homosexual aging studies contribute to theories of aging? *Journal of Homosexuality,* 13, 43-71.

Lee, J.A. (1991). Can we talk? Can we really talk? Communication as a key factor in the maturing homosexual couple. In J.A. Lee (Ed.), *Gay midlife and maturity* (pp. 143-168). Binghamton, NY: The Haworth Press.

Lee, J.A., & Brown, R.G. (1993). Hiring, firing, and promoting. In L. Diamant (Ed.), *Homosexual issues in the workplace* (pp. 45-62). Washington, DC: Taylor & Francis.

Lev, A. I. (2005). *Transgender emergence: Therapeutic guidelines for working with gender-variant people and their families.* Binghamton, NY: The Haworth Press.

Lever, J. (1994, August 23). Sexual revelations. *The Advocate,* pp. 17-24.

Levine, H. (1997). A further exploration of the lesbian identity development process and its measurement. *Journal of Homosexuality,* 34, 67-78.

Levine, M.P. (1979). Employment discrimination against gay men. *International Review of Modern Sociology,* 9, 151-163.

Levine, M.P., & Leonard, R. (1984). Discrimination against lesbians in the work force. *Signs,* 9, 700-710.

Levy, E.F. (1995). Feminist social work practice with lesbian and gay clients. In N. Van Den Bergh (Ed.), *Feminist practice in the 21st century* (pp. 278-294). Washington, DC: NASW Press.

Lewis, S. (1979). *Sunday's women: Lesbian life today.* Boston: Beacon.

Liang, C.T.H., & Alimo, C. (2005). The impact of white heterosexual students' interactions on attitudes toward lesbian, gay, and bisexual people: A longitudinal study. *Journal of College Student Development, 46,* 237-250.

Linton, S. (1998). *Claiming disability: Knowledge and identity.* New York: New York University Press.

Little, B.J. (1996). Therapist sexual orientation, gender, and counseling practices as they relate to ratings of helpfulness by gay and lesbian clients. *Journal of Counseling Psychology, 41,* 394-401.

Little, B.J. (1997). Gay and lesbian clients' selection of therapists and utilization of therapy. *Psychotherapy, 34,* 11-18.

Little, B.J. (1999). Recent improvement in mental health services to lesbian and gay clients. *Journal of Homosexuality, 37,* 127-137.

Liu, P., & Chan, C.C. (1996). Lesbian, gay, and bisexual Asian Americans and their families. In J. Laird & R-J. Green (Eds.), *Lesbians and gays in couples and families: A handbook for therapists* (pp. 137-152). San Francisco: Jossey-Bass.

Logue, P.M. (1997). Near $1 million settlement raises standard for protections of gay youth. [Online]. Available at www.lambdalegal.org/cgi-bin/pages/documents.

Loiacano, D.K. (1989). Gay identity issues among black Americans: Racism, homophobia, and the need for validation. *Journal of Counseling & Development, 68,* 21-25.

Loiacano, D.K. (1993). Gay identity issues among black Americans: Racism, homophobia, and the need for validation. In L. Garnets & D. Kimmel (Eds.), *Psychological perspectives on lesbian and gay male experiences* (pp. 364-375). New York: Columbia University Press.

Lopez, G., & Chism, N. (1993). Classroom concerns of gay and lesbian students. *College Teaching, 41,* 97-103.

Lopez, R.A., & Lam, B.T. (1998). Social supports among Vietnamese American gay men. *Journal of Gay & Lesbian Social Services, 8,* 29-50.

Lowenstein, S.F. (1980). Understanding lesbian women. *Social Casework, 61,* 29-38.

Lourea, D.N. (1985). Psycho-social issues related to counseling bisexuals. *Journal of Homosexuality, 11,* 51-62.

Luhtanen, R.K. (2003). Identity, stigma management, and well-being: A comparison of lesbian/bisexual women and gay/bisexual men. *Journal of Lesbian Studies, 7,* 85-100.

Mackelprang, R.W., Ray, J., & Hernandez-Peck, M. (1996). Social work education and sexual orientation: Faculty, student, and curriculum issues. *Journal of Gay & Lesbian Social Services, 5,* 17-31.

Mallon, G.P. (1994). Counseling strategies with gay and lesbian youth. *Journal of Gay & Lesbian Social Services, 1,* 75-91.

Mallon, G. (1997). When schools are not safe places; Gay, lesbian, bisexual, and transgender young people in educational settings. *Reaching Today's Youth, 2,* 41-45.

Mallon, G. (1998a). Knowledge for practice with gay and lesbian persons. In G.P. Mallon (Ed.), *Foundations of social work practice with lesbian and gay persons* (pp. 1-30). Binghamton, NY: The Haworth Press.

Mallon, G.P. (1998b). Social work practice with gay men and lesbians within families. In G.P. Mallon (Ed.), *Foundations of social work practice with lesbian and gay persons* (pp. 145-180). Binghamton, NY: The Haworth Press.

Mallon, G.P. (1999). Gay and lesbian adolescents and their families. *Journal of Gay & Lesbian Social Services,* 10, 69-88.

Malyon, A.K. (1981-1982). Psychotherapeutic implications of internalized homophobia in gay men. *Journal of Homosexuality,* 7, 56-59.

Manalansan, M.F., IV. (1996). Double minorities: Latino, black, and Asian men who have sex with men. In R.C. Savin-Williams & K.M. Cohen (Eds.), *The lives of lesbian, gay men, and bisexuals: Children to adults* (pp. 393-425). Ft. Worth, TX: Harcourt Brace.

Marmor, J. (1972). Homosexuality: Mental illness or moral dilemma? *International Journal of Psychiatry,* 10, 114-117.

Marmor, J. (1980). Overview: The multiple roots of homosexual behavior. In J. Marmor (Ed.), *Homosexual behavior: A modern reappraisal* (pp. 3-22). New York: Basic.

Marsiglia, F.F. (1998). Homosexuality and Latinos/as: Towards an integration of identities. *Journal of Gay & Lesbian Social Services,* 8, 113-125.

Marszalek, J.F., III, & Cashwell, C.S. (1998). The gay affirmative development (GLAD) model: Applying Ivey's developmental counseling therapy model to Cass's gay identity development model. *Adultspan Journal,* 1, 13-31.

Marszalek, J.F., Cashwell, C.S., Dunn, M.S., & Jones, K.H. (2004). Comparing gay identity development theory to cognitive development: An empirical study. *Journal of Homosexuality,* 48, 103-123.

Martin, A.D. (1982). Learning to hide: Socialization of the gay adolescent. *Adolescent Psychiatry,* 10, 52-64.

Martin, A.D., & Hetrick, E.S. (1988). The stigmatization of the gay and lesbian adolescent. *Journal of Homosexuality,* 15, 163-183.

Martin, H.P. (1991). The coming-out process for homosexuals. *Hospital and Community Psychiatry,* 42,150-162.

Martinez, D.G. (1998). Mujer, Latina, lesbian—Notes on the multidemsionality of economic and sociopolitical injustice. *Journal of Gay & Lesbian Social Services,* 8, 99-112.

Mason-John, V., & Khambatta, A. (1993). *Making black waves: Lesbians talk.* London: Scarlett Press.

Massey, S.G., & Ouellette, S.C. (1996). Homosexual bias in the identity self-portraits of gay men, lesbians, and bisexuals. *Journal of Homosexuality,* 32, 57-76.

Matteson, D.R. (1987). The heterosexually married gay and lesbian parent. In F.W. Bozett (Ed.), *Gay and lesbian parents* (pp. 138-161). New York: Praeger.

Matteson, D.R. (1995). Counseling with bisexuals. *Individual Psychology,* 51, 144-159.

Matteson, D.R. (1996a). Counseling and psychotherapy with bisexual and exploring clients. In B.A. Firestein (Ed.), *Bisexuality: The psychology and politics of an invisible minority* (pp. 185-213). Thousand Oaks, CA: Sage Publications.

Matteson, D.R. (1996b). Psychotherapy with bisexual individuals. In R.P. Cabaj & T.S. Stein (Eds.), *Textbook of homosexuality and mental health* (pp. 433-449). Washington, DC: American Psychiatric Press.

Matthews, C.R., & Lease, S.H. (2000). Focus on lesbian, gay, and bisexual families. In R.M. Perez, K.A. DeBord, & K.J. Bieschke (Eds.), *Handbook of counseling and psychotherapy with lesbian, gay, and bisexual clients* (pp. 249-273). Washington, DC: American Psychological Association.

Mattison, A.M., & McWhirter, D.P. (1995). Lesbians, gay men, and their families: Some therapeutic issues. *The Psychiatric Clinics of North America, 18,* 123-137.

Maurer, L. (1999). Transgressing sex and gender: Deconstruction zone ahead? *Siecus Report, 28,* 14-21.

Mays, V.M. (1985). Black women working together: Diversity in same sex relationships. *Women's Studies International Forum, 8,* 67-71.

Mays, V.M., Chatters, L.M., Cochran, S.D., & Mackness, J. (1998). African American families in diversity: Gay men and lesbians as participants in family networks. *Journal of Comparative Family Studies, 29,* 73-87.

Mays, V.M., & S.D. Cochran. (1988). The black women's relationship project: A national survey of black lesbians. In M. Shernoff & W. Scott (Eds.), *The sourcebook on lesbian/gay health care* (2nd. ed.) (pp. 54-62). Washington, DC: National Lesbian and Gay Health Foundation.

McCarn, S.R., & Fassinger, R.E. (1996). Revisioning sexual minority identity formation: A new model of lesbian identity and its implications for counseling and research. *Counseling Psychologists, 24,* 508-534.

McCoy, J. (1999, February). Workshop cancelled on gay, lesbian youths. *The Dallas Morning News,* A35.

McCubbin, H., & Patterson, J. (1983). The family stress process: The double ABCX model of adjustment and adaptation. *Marriage and Family Review, 6,* 7-37.

McDonald, G.J. (1982). Individual differences in the coming out process for gay men: Implications for theoretical models. *Journal of Homosexuality, 8,* 47-60.

McDonald, G.J. (1983-1984). A little bit of lavender goes a long way: A critique of research on sexual orientation. *Journal of Sex Research, 19,* 94-100.

McDougall, G.J. (1993). Therapeutic issues with gay and lesbian elders. *Clinical Gerontologist, 14,* 45-57.

McGrath, E. (1990, August). *New treatment strategies for women in the middle.* Paper presented at the annual convention of the American Psychological Association, Boston.

McKenna, W., & Kessler, S.J. (2000). Retrospective response. *Feminism & Psychology, 10,* 66-72.

McKirnan, D., & Peterson, P. (1986, October 2). Preliminary social issues survey results available. *Windy City Times,* pp. 2, 8.

McManus, M. (1991). Serving lesbian and gay youth. *Focal Point, 5,* 1-4.

Messing, A.E., Schoenberg, R., & Stephens, R.K. (1983-1984). Confronting homophobia in health care settings: Guidelines for social work practice. *Journal of Social Work & Human Sexuality,* 2, 65-74.

Mickens, E. (1994). *The 100 best companies for gay men and lesbians.* New York: Pocket.

Miller, B. (1979a). Gay fathers and their children. *Family Coordinator,* 28: 544-552.

Miller, B. (1979b). Unpromised paternity: Life-styles of gay fathers. In M.P. Levine (Ed.), *Gay men: The sociology of male homosexuality* (pp. 239-252). New York: Harper and Row.

Minton, H.L., & McDonald, G.J. (1983-1984). Homosexual identity formation as a developmental process. *Journal of Homosexuality,* 9, 91-104.

Moore, D.L., & Norris, F.H. (2005). Empirical investigation of the conflict and flexibility models of bisexuality. *Journal of Bisexuality,* 5, 5-25.

Moraga, C., & Hollibaugh, A. (1985). What we're rolling around in bed with. In A. Snitow, C. Stansell, & S. Thompson (Eds.). *Powers of desire: The politics of Sexuality* (pp. 394-405). New York: Monthly Review.

Morales, E. (1983, August). *Third world gays and lesbians: A process of multiple identities.* Paper presented at the American Psychological Association, Anaheim, CA.

Morales, E.S. (1990). Ethnic minority families and minority gays and lesbians. *Marriage and Family Review,* 14, 217-239.

Morales, E.S. (1992). Counseling Latino gays and Latina lesbians. In S. Dworkin & F. Gutiérrez (Eds.), *Counseling gay men and lesbians: Journey to the end of the rainbow* (pp. 125-139). Alexandria, VA: American Association for Counseling and Development.

Morales, E.S. (1996). Gender roles among Latino gay and bisexual men: Implications for family and couple therapy. In J. Laird & R.-J. Green (Eds.). *Lesbians and gays in couples and families: A handbook for therapists* (pp. 272-297). San Francisco: Jossey-Bass.

Morin, S.F., & Rothblum, E.D. (1991). Removing the stigma: Fifteen years of progress. *American Psychologist,* 32, 629-637.

Moses, A.E., & Hawkins, R.O., Jr. (1986). *Counseling lesbian women and gay men: A life issues approach.* Columbus, OH: Merrill.

Muller, A. (1987). *Parents Matter.* New York: Naiad.

Murphy, B.C. (1989). Lesbian couples and their parents: The effects of perceived parental attitudes on the couple. *Journal of Counseling and Development,* 68, 46-51.

Murphy, B.C. (1994). Difference and diversity: Gay and lesbian couples. *Social Services for Gay and Lesbian Couples,* 1, 5-31.

Murray, C.I. (1994, November). *Siblings of gay and lesbian people: Coming out, identity, and caregiving issues.* Paper presented at the annual meetings of the National Council on Family Relations, Minneapolis, MN.

Myers, M.F. (1981-1982). Counseling the parents of young homosexual male patients. *Journal of Homosexuality,* 7, 131-143.

Myers, M.F. (1989). *Men and divorce.* New York: Guilford.

Nabozny v. Podlesny, 92 F.3d 446 (7th Cir. 1996) [On–line]. Available at www. kentlaw.edu/7circuit/1996/jul/95-3634.html.

Nakajima, G.A., Chan, Y.H., & Lee, K. (1996). Mental health issues for gay and lesbian Asian Americans. In R.P. Cabaj & T.S. Stein (Eds.), *Textbook of homosexuality and mental health* (pp. 563-581). Washington, DC: American Psychiatric Press.

National Coalition of Anti-Violence Programs (1998). *Anti-lesbian, gay, transgender, and bisexual violence in 1998.* New York: New York City Gay and Lesbian Anti-Violence Project.

National Coalition of Anti-Violence Programs (2000). *Anti-lesbian, gay, transgender, and bisexual violence in 1999.* New York: New York City Gay and Lesbian Anti-Violence Project.

National Coalition of Anti-Violence Programs (2004). *National information from the 2004 report on anti-lesbian, gay, transgender & bisexual violence.* New York: New York City Gay and Lesbian Anti-Violence Project.

National Gay and Lesbian Task Force (1991). *Anti-gay violence, victimization and defamation in 1990,* Washington, DC: Author.

National Gay and Lesbian Task Force (2001). *GLBT civil rights laws in the U.S.* [Online]. Available at www.ngltf.org.

Neisen, J.H. (1987). Resources for families with a gay/lesbian member. In E. Coleman (Ed.), *Integrated identities for gay men and lesbians: Psychotherapeutic approaches for emotional well-being* (pp. 239-251). Binghamton, NY: Harrington Park Press.

Neisen, J.H. (1990). Heterosexism: Redefining homophobia for the 1990s. *Journal of Gay & Lesbian Psychotherapy,* 1, 21-35.

Nemeyer, L. (1980). *Coming out: Identity congruence and the attainment of adult female sexuality.* Doctoral dissertation, Dissertation Abstracts.

Newman, B.S. (1989). The relative importance of gender role attitudes to male and female attitudes toward lesbians. *Sex Roles,* 21, 451-465.

Newman, B.S., & Mazzonigo, P.G. (1993).The effects of traditional family values on the coming out process of gay adolescents. *Adolescence,* 28, 213-226.

Nguyen, N.A. (1992). Living between two cultures: Treating first-generation Asian Americans. In L.A. Vargas & J.D. Koss-Chioino (Eds.), *Working with culture: Psychotherapeutic interventions with ethnic minority children and adolescent* (pp. 204-222). San Francisco, CA: Jossey-Bass.

Nichols, M. (1988). Bisexuality in women: Myths, realities, and implications for therapy. *Women and Therapy,* 7, 235-252.

Nichols, M. (1989). Sex therapy with lesbians, gay men, and bisexuals. In S.R. Leiblum & R.C. Rosen (Eds.), *Principles and practice of sex therapy: Update for the 1990s* (2nd ed.) (pp. 269-297). New York: Guilford.

Nichols, M. (1990). Lesbian relationships: Implications for the study of sexuality and gender. In D.P. McWhirter, S.A. Sanders, & J.M. Reinisch (Eds.), *Homosexuality/heterosexuality: Concepts of sexual orientation* (pp. 350-364). New York: Oxford University Press.

Norris, W.P. (1992). Liberal attitudes and homophobic acts: The paradoxes of homosexual experience in a liberal institution. In K. Harbeck (Ed.), *Coming out of the classroom closet: Gay and lesbian students, teachers, and curriculum* (pp. 81-120). Binghamton, NY: Harrington Park Press.

Obear, K. (1991). Homophobia. In N.J. Evans & V.A. Wall (Eds.), *Beyond tolerance: Gays, lesbians, and bisexuals on campus* (pp. 39-78). Alexandria, VA: American College Personnel Association.

Ochs, R. (1996). Biphobia: It goes more than two ways. In Firestein, B.A. (Ed.). *Bisexuality: The psychology and politics of an invisible minority* (pp. 217-239). Thousand Oaks, CA: Sage.

Off Pink Collective. (1988). *Bisexual lives.* London: Off Pink Publishing.

Olson, E.D., & King, C.A. (1995). Gay and lesbian self-identification: A response to Rotheram-Boras and Fernandez. *Suicide and Life-Threatening Behavior, 25,* 35-39.

Orzek, A.M. (1992). Career counseling for the gay and lesbian community. In S. Dworkin & F. Gutiérrez (Eds.), *Counseling gay men and lesbians: Journey to the end of the rainbow* (pp. 23-24). Alexandria, VA: American Association for Counseling and Development.

Otis, M.D., & Skinner, W.F. (1996). The prevalence of victimization and its effects on mental well-being among lesbian and gay people. *Journal of Homosexuality,* 30, 33-56.

Outland, O. (2000). *Coming out: A handbook for men.* Los Angeles: Alyson Books.

OutProud, The National Coalition for Gay, Lesbian, Bisexual, and Transgender Youth and Oasis Magazine (1998, 2001). OutProud internet survey of queer and questioning youth.

Owlfeather, M. (1988). Children of grandmother moon. In W. Roscoe (Ed.), *Living for the spirit. A gay American Indian anthology* (pp. 97-105). New York: St. Martin's.

Pamela, H. (1989). Asian American lesbians: An emerging voice in the Asian American Community. In Asian Women United of California (Eds.), *Making waves: An Anthology of writings by an about Asian American women* (pp. 282-290). Boston: Beacon.

Parés-Avila, J.A., & Montano-Lopez, R.M. (1994). Issues in the psychosocial care of Latino gay men with HIV infection In S.A. Cadwell, R.A. Burnham Jr., & M. Forstein (Eds.), *Therapists on the front line: Psychotherapy with gay men in the age of AIDS* (pp. 339-362). Washington, DC: American Psychiatric Press.

Parks, C. (1999). Lesbian identity development: An examination of differences across generations. *American Journal of Orthopsychiatry, 69,* 347-361.

Patterson, C.J., & Chan, R.W. (1996). Gay fathers and their children. In R.P. Cabaj & T.S. Stein (Eds.), *Textbook of homosexuality and mental health* (pp. 371-393). Washington, DC, US: American Psychiatric Association.

Pattison, E.M., & Pattison, M.L. (1980). "Ex-gays:" Religiously mediated change in homosexuals. *American Journal of Psychiatry, 137,* 1553-1562.

Paul, J.P. (1984). The bisexual identity: An idea without social recognition. *Journal of Homosexuality, 9,* 45-65.

Paul, J.P. (1988). Counseling issues in working with a bisexual population. In M. Shernoff & W. A. Scott (Eds.), *The sourcebook on lesbian/gay health care* (2nd ed.) (pp. 142-150). Washington, DC: National Lesbian/Gay Health Foundation.

Paul, J.P. (1996). Bisexuality: Exploring/exploding the boundaries. In R.C. Savin-Williams & K.M. Cohen (Eds.), *The lives of lesbian, gay men, and bisexuals: Children to adults* (pp. 436-461). Ft. Worth, TX: Harcourt Brace.

Pearlman, S. (1992). Heterosexual mothers/lesbian daughters: Parallels and similarities. *Journal of Feminist Family Therapy,* 4, 1-21.

Peplau, L.A., & Cochran, S.D. (1990). A relational perspective on homosexuality. In D.P. McWhirter, S.A. Saunders, & J.M. Reinisch (Eds.), *Homosexuality/heterosexuality: Concepts of sexual orientation* (pp. 321-349). New York: Oxford University Press.

Peters, D.K., & Cantrell, P.J. (1993). Gender roles and role conflict in feminist lesbian and heterosexual women. *Sex Roles,* 28, 379-392.

Peterson, J.L. (1992). Black men and their same-sex desires and behaviors. In G. Herdt (Ed.), *Culture in America: Essays from the field* (pp. 147-164). Boston: Beacon.

Peterson, J.W. (1989, April). In harm's way: Gay runaways are in more danger than ever, and gay adults won't help. *The Advocate,* pp. 8-10.

Pilkington, N.W., & D'Augelli, A.R. (1995). Victimization of lesbian, gay, and bisexual youth in community settings. *Journal of Community Psychology,* 23, 33-56.

Plummer, K. (1975). *Sexual stigma: An interactionist account.* London: Routledge & Kegan Paul. Ltd

Plummer, K. (1995). *Telling sexual stories: Power, change and social worlds.* London: Routledge.

Ponse, B. (1976). Secrecy in the lesbian world. *Urban Life,* 5, 313-338.

Ponse, B. (1980). Lesbians and their worlds. In J. Marmor (Ed.), *Homosexual behavior: A modern reappraisal* (pp. 157-175). New York: Basic Books.

Pope, M. (1995). The "salad bowl" is big enough for us all: An argument for the inclusion of lesbians and gay men in any definition of multiculturalism. *Journal of Counseling & Development,* 73, 301-304.

Pope, M. (1996). Gay and lesbian career counseling: Special career counseling issues. *Journal of Gay & Lesbian Social Services,* 4, 91-105.

Pope, M. (1997). Sexual issues for older lesbians and gays. *Topics in Geriatric Rehabilitation,* 12, 53-60.

Pope, R.L., & Reynolds, A.L. (1991). Including bisexuality: It's more than just a label. In N.J. Evans & V.A. Walls (Eds.), *Beyond tolerance: Gays, lesbians and bisexuals on campus* (pp. 205-212). Alexandria, VA: American College Personnel Association.

Poussaint, A. (1990, September). An honest look at black gays and lesbians. *Ebony.* 124,126,130-131.

Pusey, A. (2003, June, 27). New day for gay Americans. *Dallas Morning News,* A1.

Quam, J.K. (1993). Gay and lesbian aging. *Siecus Report,* 21, 10-12.

Rachlin, K. (2001, August 20-24). *Transgender individuals' experiences of psychotherapy.* Paper presented at the 109th annual convention of the American Psychological Association, San Francisco.

Radonsky, V.E., & Borders, L.D. (1995). Factors influencing lesbian's direct disclosures of their sexual orientation. *Journal of Gay & Lesbian Psychotherapy,* 213, 17-37.

Rafkin, L. (Ed.). (1987). *Different daughters: A book by mothers of lesbians.* Pittsburgh, PA: Cleis.

Ragins, B.R., & Cornwell, J.M. (2001). Pink triangles: antecedents and consequences of perceived workplace discrimination against gay and lesbian employees. *Journal of Applied Psychology,* 86, 1244-1261.

Ragins, B.R., Cornwell, J.M., & Miller, J.S. (2003). Heterosexism in the workplace: Do race and gender matter? *Group & Organization Management,* 28, 45-74.

Ramos, J. (1994). *Companeras: Latina lesbians.* New York: Routledge.

Rand, C., Graham, D.L., & Rawlings, E. (1982). Psychological health and factors the court seeks to control in lesbian mother custody trials. *Journal of Homosexuality,* 8, 27-39.

Read, K. (1980). *Other Voices.* Toronto: Chandler & Sharpe, 1980.

Rehman, J., Lazer, S., Benet, A.E., Schaefer, L.C., & Melman, A. (1999). The reported sex and surgery satisfactions of 28 postoperative male-to-female transsexual patients. *Archives of Sexual Behavior,* 28, 71-89.

Reid, J.D. (1995). Development in late life: Older lesbian and gay lives. In A.R. D'Augelli & C.J. Patterson (Eds.), *Lesbians, gay, and bisexual identities the over the lifespan: Psychological perspectives* (pp. 215-240). New York: Oxford.

Reis, B. (1998). Will you be there for every child? Reports of violence against lesbians and gays. *Siecus Report,* 26, 9.

Remafedi, G. (1987). Male homosexuality: The adolescent's perspective. *Pediatrics,* 79, 326-330.

Remafedi, G., Farrow, J.A., & Deisher, R.W. (1991). Risk factors for attempted suicide in gay and bisexual youth. *Pediatrics,* 87, 869-875.

Reyes, M. (1992). *Women's studies programs in Latin America: A source of empowerment.* (Doctoral dissertation, University of Massachusetts, 1992). Dissertation Abstracts International, 53, (6-A) 1819.

Rhoads, R.A. (1993, November). *Toward a critical postmodern view of student identity.* Paper presented at the annual meeting of the Association for the Study of Higher Education, Pittsburgh, PA.

Rhoads, R.A. (1994a, February). *College lives and identities: Selves in transition.* Paper presented at the 15th Annual ethnography in Education Research Forum, University of Pennsylvania, Philadelphia.

Rhoads, R.A. (1994b). *Coming out at college: The struggle for a queer identity.* Westport, CT: Bergin & Garvey.

Rhoads, R.A. (1995). Learning from the coming-out experiences of college males. *Journal of College Student Development,* 36, 67-74.

Rhoads, R.A. (1997). Implications of the growing invisibility of gay and bisexual male students on campus. *NASPA Journal,* 34, 275-266.

Ridge, D., Minichiello, V., & Plummer, D. (1997). Queer connections: Community, "the scene" and an epidemic. *Journal of Contemporary Ethnography,* 26, 146-181.

Robinson, B.E., Walters, L.H., & Skeen, P. (1989). Response of parents to learning that their child is homosexual and concern over AIDS: A national study. *Journal of Homosexuality,* 18, 59-80.

Rodriquez Rust, P.C. (2000). *Bisexuality in the United States: A social science reader.* New York: Columbia University Press.

Rodriquez Rust, P.C. (2001). Two many and not enough: The meanings of bisexual identities. *Journal of Bisexuality,* 1, 31-68.

Rodriquez Rust, P.C. (2002). Bisexuality: The state of the union. *Annual Review of Sex Research,* 133, 180-240.

Rofes, E. (1989). Opening up the classroom closet: Responding to the educational needs of gay and lesbian youth. *Harvard Educational Review,* 59, 444-453.

Rofes, E.E. (1983). *"I thought people like that killed themselves": Lesbians, gay men and suicide.* San Francisco: Grey Fox.

Rofes, E.E. (1993/1994). Making our schools safe for sissies. *The High School Journal,* 77, 37-40.

Rogers, S.M., & Turner, C.F. (1991). Male-male sexual contact in the U.S.A.: Findings from five sample surveys, 1970-1990. *Journal of Sex Research,* 48, 491-519.

Rohrbaugh, J.B. (1992). Lesbian families: Clinical issues and theoretical implications. *Professional Psychology: Research and Practice,* 23, 467-473.

Roothbart, M., & John, O.P. (1985). Social categorization behavioral episodes: A cognitive analysis of the effects of intergroup contact. *Journal of Social Issues,* 41, 81-104.

Rosario, M., Meyer-Bahlburg, H.F.L., Hunter, J., Exner, T.M., Gwadz, M., & Keller, A.M. (1996). The psychosexual development of urban lesbian, gay, and bisexual youths. *Journal of Sex Research,* 35, 113-126.

Rosario, M., Rotheram-Borus, M.J., & Reid, H. (1992). *Personal resources, gay-related stress, and multiple problem behaviors among gay and bisexual male adolescents.* Unpublished manuscript, Columbia University, New York.

Rosenfeld, C., & Emerson, S. (1998). A process model of supportive therapy for families of transgender individuals. In D. Denny (Ed.) *Current conceptions of transgender identity* (pp. 391-400). New York: Garland Publications.

Rosenfeld, D. (2003). *The changing of the guard: Lesbian and gay elders, and social change.* Philadelphia: Temple University Press.

Ross, M.W. (1983). *The married homosexual man.* Boston: Routledge & Kegan Paul.

Roth, S. (1985). Psychotherapy issues with lesbian couples. *Journal of Marital and Family Therapy,* 11, 273-286.

Roth, S. (1989). Psychotherapy with lesbian couples: Individual issues, female socialization and the social context. In M. McGoldrick, C. Anderson, & F. Walsh (Eds.), *Women in families: A framework for family therapy* (pp. 286-307). New York: Norton.

Roth, S., & Murphy, B.C. (1986). Therapeutic work with lesbian clients: A systematic therapy view. In M. Ault-Riche (Ed.), *Women and family therapy* (pp. 78-89). Rockville, MD: Aspen Press.

Rothblum, E.D. (1994). Introduction to the special section: Mental health of lesbians and gay men. *Journal of Consulting and Clinical Psychology*, 67, 211-212.

Rothblum, E.D., & Brehony, K.A. (1993). *Boston marriages: Romantic but asexual relationships among contemporary lesbians.* Amherst, MA: University of Massachusetts Press.

Rothblum, E.D., Mintz, B., Cowan, D.B., & Haller, C. (1995). Lesbian baby boomers at midlife. In K. Jay (Ed.), *Dyke life: A celebration of the lesbian experience* (pp. 61-76). New York: Basic.

Rotheram-Borus, M.H., Hunter, J., & Rosario, M. (1994). Suicidal behavior and gay-related stress among gay and bisexual male adolescents. *Journal of Adolescent Research*, 9, 498-508.

Rotheram-Borus, M.J., Rosario, M., & Koopman, C. (1991). Minority youths at high risk: Gay males and runaways. In M.E. Colton & S. Gore (Eds.), *Adolescent stress* (pp. 181-200). New York: Adline.

Rowden, T. (2000). African American gay culture. In G.E. Haggerty (Ed.), *Gay histories and cultures: An encyclopedia* (pp. 19-20). New York: Garland Publishing.

Rubenstein, W.B. (1996). Lesbians, gay men, and the law. In R.C. Savin-Williams & K.M. Cohen (Eds.), *The lives of lesbian, gay men, and bisexuals: Children to adults* (pp. 331-343). Ft. Worth, TX: Harcourt Brace.

Rupp, L.J. (1997). "Imagine my surprise:" Women's relationships in historical perspective. *Journal of Lesbian Studies*, 1, 155-175.

Russell, G.M., & Bohan, J.S. (1999). Implications for clinical work. In J.S. Bohan & G.M. Russell (Eds.), *Conversations about psychology and sexual orientation* (pp. 31-56). New York: New York University Press.

Russell, S.T. (2005). Beyond risk: Resilience in the lives of sexual minority youth. *Journal of Gay and Lesbian Issues in Education*, 2, 5-18.

Rust, P.C. (1992). The politics of sexual identity: Sexual attraction and behavior among lesbian and bisexual women. *Social Problems*, 39, 366-387.

Rust, P.C. (1993). "Coming out" in the age of social constructionism: Sexual identity formation among lesbian and bisexual women. *Gender & Society*, 7, 50-77.

Rust, P.C. (1995). *The challenge of bisexuality to lesbian politics: Sex, loyalty, and revolution.* New York: New York University Press.

Rust, P.C. (1996). Sexual identity and bisexual identities: The struggle for self-description in a changing sexual landscape. In B. Beemyn & M. Eliason (Eds.). *Queer studies: A lesbian, gay, bisexual, and transgender anthology* (pp. 64-86). New York: New York University.

Rust, P.C. (2000). Bisexuality: A contemporary paradox for women. *Journal of Social Issues*, 56, 205-221).

Rust, P.C. (2003). Finding a sexual identity and community: Therapeutic implications and cultural assumptions in scientific models of coming out. In L.D. Garnets & D.C. Kimmel (Eds.), *Psychological perspectives on lesbian, gay, and bisexual experiences* (pp. 227-269). New York: Columbia University Press.

Rutter, V., & Schwartz, P. (2000). Gender, marriage, and diverse possibilities for cross-sex and same-sex pairs. In D.H. Demo, K.R. Allen, & M.A. Fine (Eds.), *Handbook of family diversity* (pp. 59-81). New York: Oxford University Press.

Safe Schools Coalition of Washington State (1996, January). A report on the five year anti-violence project of the Safe School Coalition of Washington State [On-line]. Available at www.safeschools-wa.org. Safe Schools Coalition of Washington, 1999. Information from web site: www.safeschoolscoalition.org/safe.html.

Saghir, M.T., & Robins, E. (1973). *Male and female homosexuality.* Baltimore: Williams & Williams.

Saghir, M.T., & Robins, E. (1980). Clinical aspects of female homosexuality. In J. Marmor (Ed.), *Homosexual behavior* (pp. 280-295). New York: Basic.

Sakai, C.A. (2003). Identity development in female-to-male transsexuals: A qualitative study. Dissertation Abstracts International: Section B: The Sciences and Engineering, Vol. 64(3-B), 2003, p. 1505.

Saltzburg, S. (2004). Learning that an adolescent child is gay or lesbian: The parent experience. *Social Work, 49,* 109-118.

Sanders, G.L., & Kroll, I.T. (2000). Generating stories of resilience: Helping gay and lesbian youth and their families. *Journal of Marital and Family Therapy, 26,* 433-442.

Sanford, N.D. (1989). Providing sensitive health care to gay and lesbian youth. *NursePractitioner, 14,* 30-47.

Sauerman, T.H. (1984). *Coming out to your parents.* Los Angeles, CA: Federation of Parents & Friends of Lesbians and Gays.

Saulnier, C.F. (2002). Deciding who to see: Lesbians discuss their preferences in health and mental health care providers. *Social Work, 47,* 355-365.

Savage, D.G. (1996, May 21). Supreme Court strikes down law targeting gays. *Los Angeles Times,* A1, A14.

Savin-Williams, R.C. (1989-1990). Parental influences on the self-esteem of gay and lesbian youths: A reflected appraisals model. *Journal of Homosexuality, 17,* 93-109.

Savin-Williams, R.C. (1990a). Coming out. In W.R. Dynes (Ed.), *Encyclopedia of homosexuality.* (pp. 251-254). New York: Garland.

Savin-Williams, R. (1990b). *Gay and lesbian youth: Expressions of identity.* New York: Hemisphere.

Savin-Williams, R.C. (1990c). Youth. In W.R. Dynes (Ed.), *Encyclopedia of homosexuality* (pp. 1409-1415). New York: Garland.

Savin-Williams, R. (1995a). An exploratory study of pubertal maturation timing and self-esteem among gay and bisexual male youths. *Developmental Psychology, 31,* 56-64.

Savin-Williams, R.C. (1995b). Lesbian, gay male, and bisexual adolescents. In A.R. D'Augelli & C.J. Patterson (Eds.), *Lesbian, gay, and bisexual identities over the lifespan* (pp. 165-189). New York: Oxford University Press.

Savin-Williams, R.C. (1996). Ethnic- and sexual-minority youth. In R.C. Savin-Williams & K.M. Cohen (Eds.), *The lives of lesbian, gay men, and bisexuals: Children to adults* (pp. 152-165). Ft. Worth, TX: Harcourt Brace.

Savin-Williams, R.C. (1998a). *". . . and then I became gay": Young men's stories.* New York: Routledge.

Savin-Williams, R.C. (1998b). Lesbian, gay, and bisexual youths' relationships with their parents. In C.J. Patterson & A.R. D'Augelli (Eds.), *Lesbian, gay, and bisexual identities in families: Psychological perspectives* (pp. 75-98). New York: Oxford University Press.

Savin-Williams, R.C. (2001). *Mom, dad, I'm gay: How families negotiate coming out.* Washington, DC: American Psychological Association.

Savin-Williams, R.C. (2003). Lesbian, gay, and bisexual youths' relationships with their parents. In L.D. Garnets & D.C. Kimmel (Eds.). *Psychological perspectives on lesbian, gay, and bisexual experiences* (pp. 299-326). New York: Columbia University Press.

Savin-Williams, R.C. (2005). *The new gay teenager.* Cambridge, MA: Harvard University Press.

Savin-Williams, R.C., & Diamond, L.M. (1999). Sexual orientation. In W.K. Silverman & T.H. Ollendick (Eds.), *Developmental issues in the clinical treatment of children* (pp. 241-258). Boston: Allyn & Bacon.

Savin-Williams, R.C., & Diamond, L.M. (2000). Sexual identity trajectories among sexual-minority youths: Gender comparisons. *Archives of Sexual Behavior,* 29, 607-627.

Savin-Williams, R.C., & Dubé, E.M. (1998). Parental reactions to their child's disclosure of a gay/lesbian identity. *Family Relations,* 47, 7-13.

Savin-Williams, R.C., & Ream, G.L. (2003). Sex variations in the disclosure to parents of same-sex attractions. *Journal of Family Psychology,* 17, 429-438.

Scasta, D. (1998). Issues in helping people come out. *Journal of Gay & Lesbian Psychotherapy,* 2, 87-98.

Schaefer, S. (1977). Sociosexual behavior in male and female homosexuals. *Archives of Sexual Behavior,* 6, 355-364.

Schippers, J. (1990, August). *Gay affirmative counseling and psychotherapy in the Netherlands.* Paper presented at the meeting of the American Psychological Association, Boston, MA.

Schmitt, J.P., & Kurdek, L.A. (1987). Personality correlates of positive identity and relationship involvement in gay men. *Journal of Homosexuality,* 13, 101-109.

Schneider, B. (1984). Peril and promise: Lesbian's workplace participation. In J.T. Darty & S. Potter (Eds.), *Women-identified women* (pp. 211-230). Palo Alto, CA: Mayfield.

Schneider, B. (1986). Coming out at work: Bridging the private/public gap. *Work and Occupations,* 13, 463-487.

Schneider, M. (1986). The relationships of cohabiting lesbian and heterosexual couples: A comparison. *Psychology of Women Quarterly,* 10, 234-239.

Schneider, M.S., Brown, L.S., & Glassgold, J.M. (2002). Implementing the resolution on appropriate therapeutic responses to sexual orientation: A guide for the perplexed. *Professional Psychology: Research and Practice,* 33, 265-276.

Schoenberg, R. (1989, April). *Unlocking closets in the ivory tower: Lesbian/gay identity formation and management in college.* Paper presented at the meeting of the American College Personnel Association, Washington, DC.

Schope, R.D. (2002). The decision to tell: Factors influencing the disclosure of sexual orientation by gay men. *Journal of Gay & Lesbian Social Services,* 14, 1-21.

Schope, R.D., & Eliason, M.J. (2000). Thinking versus acting: Assessing the relationship between heterosexual attitudes and behaviors toward homosexuals. *Journal of Gay & Lesbian Social Services,* 11, 69-92.

Scott, R.R., & Ortiz, E.T. (1996). Marriage and coming out: Four patterns in homosexual males. *Journal of Gay & Lesbian Social Services,* 4, 67-79.

Sears, J.T. (1989). The impact of gender and race on growing up lesbian and gay in the South. *National Women's Studies Association Journal,* 1, 422-457.

Sears, J.T. (1991). *Growing up gay in the South: Race, gender, and journeys of the spirit.* Binghamton, NY: Harrington Park Press.

Sears, J.T., & Williams, W.L. (Eds.). (1997). *Overcoming heterosexism and homophobia.* New York: Columbia University.

Seil, D. (1996). Transsexuals: The boundaries of sexual identity and gender. In R.P. Cabaj & T.S. Stein (Eds.), *Textbook of homosexuality and mental health* (pp. 743-762). Washington, DC: American Psychiatric Press.

Sell, R.L. (1996). The Sell assessment of sexual orientation: Background and scoring. *Journal of Gay, Lesbian, and Bisexual Identity,* 1, 295-310.

Seltzer, R. (1992). The social location of those holding antihomosexual attitudes. *Sex Roles,* 26, 391-398.

Serovich, J.M., Skeen, P., Walters, L.H., & Robinson, B.E. (1993). In-law relationships when a child is homosexual. *Journal of Homosexuality,* 26, 57-75.

Service Members Legal Defense Network (1999). *Clemency hearing for gay sailor's killer* [Online]. Available at www.sldn.org.

Shachar, S.A., & Gilbert, L.A. (1983). Working lesbians: Role conflicts and coping strategies. *Psychology of Women Quarterly,* 7, 272-284.

Shallenberger, D. (1994). Professional and openly gay: A narrative study of the experience. *Journal of Management Inquiry,* 3, 119-142.

Shilts, R. (1987). *And the band played on.* New York: St. Martin's.

Shively, M. G., & De Cecco, J. P. (1977). Components of sexual identity. *Journal of Homosexuality,* 3, 41-48.

Shively, M.G., Jones, C., & De Cecco, J. (1983-1984). Research on sexual orientation: Definition and methods. *Journal of Homosexuality,* 9, 127-136.

Shon, S.P., & Ja, D.Y. (1982). Asian families. In M. McGoldrick, J.K. Pearce, & J. Giordano (Eds.), *Ethnicity and family therapy* (pp. 208-229). New York: Guilford.

Silverstein, C. (1991). Psychological and medical treatments of homosexuality. In J.C. Gonsiorek & J.D. Weinrich (Eds.), *Homosexuality: Research Implications for public policy* (pp. 101-114). Newbury Park, CA: Sage Publications.

Silverstein, C. (1996). History of treatment. In R.P. Cabaj & T.S. Stein (Eds.), *Textbook of homosexuality and mental health* (pp. 3-16). Washington, DC: American Psychiatric Press.

Simon, W., & Gagon, J.H. (1967). Homosexuality: The formation of a sociological perspective. *Journal of Health and Social Behavior,* 8, 177-185.

Simoni, J.M. (1996). Pathways to prejudice: Predicting students' heterosexist attitudes with demographics, self-esteem, and contact with lesbians and gay men. *Journal of College Student Development,* 37, 68-78.

Singerline, H. (1994). OutRight: Reflections on an out-of-school gay youth group. *The High School Journal,* 77, 133-137.

Slater, B.R. (1993). Violence against lesbian and gay male college students. *Journal of College Student Psychotherapy,* 8, 177-202.

Smith, A. (1997). Cultural diversity and the coming-out process: Implications for clinical practice. In B. Greene (Ed.), *Ethnic and cultural diversity among lesbians and gay men* (pp. 279-300). Thousand Oaks, CA: Sage.

Smith, B. (Ed.). (1983). *Home girls: A black feminist anthology.* New York: Kitchen Table.

Smith, B. (1992). Toward a Black feminist criticism. In G. Hull, P. Scott, & B. Smith (Eds.), *All the women are white, all the blacks are men, but some of us are brave* (pp. 157-175). Old Westbury, NY: Feminist Press.

Smith, J. (1988). Psychotherapy, homosexuality, and homophobia. *Journal of Homosexuality,* 5, 59-74.

Smith, N.G., & Ingram, K.M. (2004). Workplace heterosexism among lesbian, gay, and bisexual individuals: The role of unsupportive social institutions. *Journal of Counseling Psychology,* 51, 57-6.

Smith, Y.L.S., Van Goozen, S.H.M., Kuiper, A.J., & Cohen-Kettenis, P.T. (2005). Sex reassignment: Outcomes and predictors of treatment of adolescent and adult transsexuals. *Psychological Medicine,* 35, 89-99.

Snyder, M., & Uranowitz, S.W. (1978). Reconstructing the past: Some cognitive consequences of person perception. *Journal of Personality and Social Psychology,* 36, 941-950.

Socarides, C.W. (1978). *Homosexuality.* New York: Jason Aronson.

Sohier, R. (1985-1986). Homosexual mutuality: Variation on a theme by E. Erikson. *Journal of Homosexuality,* 12, 25-38.

Sophie, J. (1985-1986). A critical examination of stage theories of lesbian identity development. *Journal of Homosexuality,* 12, 39-51.

Sophie, J. (1987). Internalized homophobia and lesbian identity. *Journal of Homosexuality,* 14, 53-65.

Spaulding, E. (1982). *The formation of lesbian identity during the "coming out" process* (Doctoral dissertation, Smith College, 1982). Dissertation Abstracts International, 43, 2106A.

Stanley, J., & Wolfe, S. (1980). *The coming out stories.* Watertown, MA: Persephone.

Stark, L. (1991). Traditional gender role beliefs and individual outcomes: An exploratory analysis. *Sex Roles,* 24, 639-650.

Stein, E. (1999). *The mismeasure of desire: The science, theory, and ethics of sexual orientation.* New York: Oxford University Press.

Stein, M., Tiefer, L., & Melman A. (1990). Follow up observations of operated male-to-female transsexuals. *Journal of Urology,* 143, 1188-1192.

Stein, T.S. (1993). Overview of new developments in understanding homosexuality. *Review of Psychiatry,* 12, 9-40.

Stein, T.S. (1997). Deconstructing sexual orientation: Understanding the phenomena of sexual orientation. *Journal of Homosexuality,* 34, 81-86.

Stein, T.S., & Cohen, C.J. (1984). Psychotherapy with gay men and lesbians: An examination of homophobia, coming-out, and identity. In E.S. Hetrick & T.S. Stein (Eds.), *Innovations in Psychotherapy with Homosexuals.* Washington, DC: American Psychiatric Association.

Stewart, T.A. (1991, December 16). Gay in corporate America. *Fortune,* 43-56.

Stokes, J., & Damon, W. (1995). Counseling and psychotherapy for bisexual men. *Directions in Mental Health Counseling,* 5, 4-15.

Stokes, J.P., Damon, W., & McKirnan, D.J. (1997). Predictors of movement toward homosexuality: A longitudinal study of bisexual men. *Journal of Sex Research,* 34, 304-312.

Storms, M.D. (1980). Theories of sexual orientation. *Journal of Personality and Social Psychology,* 38, 783-792.

Strommen, E.F. (1989). "You're a what?" Family members' reactions to the disclosure of homosexuality. *Journal of Homosexuality,* 18, 37-58.

Strommen, E.F. (1990). Hidden branches and growing pains: Homosexuality and the family tree. *Marriage & Family Review,* 14, 9-34.

Swann, S.K., & Spivey, C.A. (2004). The relationship between self-esteem and lesbian identity during adolescence. *Child and Adolescent Social Work Journal,* 21, 629-646.

Talamini, J.T. (1982). *Boys will be girls: The hidden world of the heterosexual male transvestite.* Washington, DC: University Press of America.

Tarver, D.E. (2002). Transgender mental health: The intersection of race, sexual orientation, and gender identity. In B.E. Jones & M.J. Hill (Eds.), *Mental health issues in lesbian, gay, bisexual, and transgender communities* (pp. 93-108). Washington, DC: American Psychiatric Publishing.

Taylor, H.E. (2000). Meeting the needs of lesbian and gay young adolescents. *The Clearing House,* 73, 221-224.

Telljohann, S.K., & Price, J.H. (1993). A qualitative examination of adolescent homosexuals' life experiences: Ramifications for secondary school personnel. *Journal of Homosexuality,* 26, 41-55.

Tewksbury, R., & Gagné, G. (1996). Transgenderists: Products of non-normative intersections of sex, gender, and sexuality. *Journal of Men's Studies,* 5, 105-129.

Tewksbury, R., Grossi, E.L., Suresh, G., & Helms, J. (1999). Hate crimes against gay men and lesbian women: A routine activity approach for predicting victimization risk. *Humanity and Society,* 23, 125-142.

Thomas, K. (1999, April 15). Anti-trans violence. *Worker's World Newspaper,* A1.

Thompson, C.A. (1992). Lesbian grief and loss issues in the coming out process. *Women & Therapy,* 12, 175-185.

Tierney, W.G. (1992a). Building academic communities of difference: Gays, lesbians, and bisexuals on campus. *Change,* 24, 41-46.

Tierney, W.G. (1992b). *Enhancing diversity: Toward a better campus climate.* A report of the Committee on Lesbian and Gay Concerns, University Park, PA: Pennsylvania State University.

Timberlake, E.M., & Cook, K.O. (1984). Social work and the Vietnamese refugee. *Social Work,* 29, 108-113.

Tofoya, T.N. (1996). Native two-spirit people. In R.P. Cabaj & T.S. Stein (Eds.), *Textbook of homosexuality and mental health* (pp. 603-617). Washington, DC: American Psychiatric Press.

Tofoya, T.N. (1997). Native gay and lesbian issues: The two-spirited. In B. Greene (Ed.), *Ethnic and cultural diversity among lesbians and gay men* (pp. 1-10). Thousand Oaks, CA: Sage Publications.

Tremble, B., Schneider, M., & Appathurai, C. (1989). Growing up gay or lesbian in a multicultural context. *Journal of Homosexuality,* 17, 253-267.

Triandis, H.C., Kurowski, L.L., & Gelfand, M.J. (1994). Workplace diversity. In H.C. Triandis, M.D. Dunnette, & L.M. Housh (Eds.), *Handbook of industrial and organizational psychology* (2nd ed.) (Vol. 4) (pp. 769-827). Palo Alto, CA: Consulting Psychologists.

Troiden, R.R. (1979). Becoming homosexual: A model of gay identity acquisition. *Psychiatry,* 42, 362-373.

Troiden, R.R. (1988). Homosexual identity development. *Journal of Adolescent Health Care,* 9. 105-113.

Troiden, R.R. (1989). The formation of homosexual identities. *Journal of Homosexuality,* 17, 43-73.

Troiden, R.R., & Goode, E. (1980). Variables related to the acquisition of a gay identity. *Journal of Homosexuality,* 5, 383-392.

Trujillo, C. (Ed.) (1991). *Chicana lesbians: The girls our mothers warned us about.* Berkeley, CA: Third Woman.

Turner, J.S., & Helms, D.B. (1995). *Lifespan development* (5th ed.). Fort Worth, TX: Harcourt Bruce College Publishers.

Tvesky, A., & Kahneman, D. (1973). Availability: A heuristic for judging frequency and probability. *Cognitive Psychology,* 5, 207-232.

Udis-Kessler, A. (1996). Challenging the stereotypes. In S. Rose & C. Stevens (Eds.), *Bisexual horizons: Politics, histories, lives* (pp. 45-57). London: Lawrence & Wisehart.

Uribe, V. (1994). The silent minority: Rethinking our commitment to gay and lesbian youth, *Theory into Practice,* 33, 168-172.

Uribe, V., & Harbeck, K.M. (1991). Coming out of the classroom closet. *Journal of Homosexuality,* 22, 9-27.

Uribe, V., & Harbeck, K.M. (1992). Addressing the needs of lesbian, gay, and bisexual youth: The origins of PROJECT 10 and school-based intervention. *Journal of Homosexuality,* 22, 9-28.

Vargo, M.E. (1998). *Acts of disclosure: The coming-out process of contemporary gay men.* Binghamton, NY: Harrington Park Press.

Von Schultless, B. (1992). Violence in the streets: Anti-lesbian assault and harassment in San Francisco. In G.M. Herek & K.T. Berrill (Eds.), *Hate crime: Confronting violence against lesbians and gay men* (pp. 65-75). Newbury Park, CA: Sage Press.

Waldner-Haugrud, L.K., & Magruder, B. (1999). Coming out to parents: Perceptions of family relations, perceived resources, and identity expression as predictors of identity disclosure for gay and lesbian adolescents. *Journal of Homosexuality,* 37, 83-100.

Waldo, C.R. (1998). Out on campus: Sexual orientation and academic climate in a university context. *American Journal of Community Psychology,* 26, 745-774.

Waldo, C.R. (1999). Working in a majority context: A structural model of hetero-sexism in minority stress in the workplace. *Journal of Counseling Psychology,* 45, 218-232.

Waldo, C.R., Hesson-McInnis, M.S., & D'Augelli, A.R. (1998). Antecedents and consequences of victimization of lesbian, gay, and bisexual young people: A structural model comparing rural university and urban samples. *American Journal of Community Psychology,* 26, 307-334.

Walters, A.S., & Phillips, C.P. (1994). Hurdles: An activity for homosexuality education. *Journal of Sex Education & Therapy,* 20,198-203.

Walters, K.L. (1997). Urban lesbian and gay American Indian identity: Implications for mental health service delivery. *Journal of Gay & Lesbian Social Services,* 6, 43-65.

Warren, C.A.B. (1974). *Identity and community in the gay world.* New York: John Wiley & Sons.

Weinberg, G. (1972). *Society and the healthy homosexual.* New York: St. Martin's.

Weinberg, M.S., & Williams, C.J. (1974). *Male homosexuals: Their problems and adaptations.* New York: Oxford University Press.

Weinberg, M.S., Williams, C.J., & Pryor, D.W. (1994). *Dual attraction: Understanding bisexuality.* New York: Oxford University Press.

Weinberg, M.S., Williams, C.J., & Pryor, D.W. (1998). Becoming and being "bisexual." In E.J. Haeberle & R. Gindorf (Eds.), *Bisexualities: The ideology and practice of sexual contact with both men and women* (pp. 169-181). New York: Continuum

Wells, J.W., & Kline, W.B. (1987). Self-disclosure of homosexual orientation. *Journal of Social Psychology,* 127, 191-197.

Weston, K. (1999). *Render me, gender me: Lesbians talk sex, class, color, nation, studmuffin.* New York: New York University Press.

Whisman, V. (1996). *Queer by choice: Lesbians, gay men, and the politics of identity.* New York: Routledge.

Whitehead, H. (1981). The bow and the burden strap: A new look at institutionalized homosexuality in native North America. In S.B. Ortner & H. Whitehead (Eds.), *Sexual Meanings: The cultural construction of gender and sexuality* (pp. 80-115). New York: Cambridge University.

Whitman, J.S., Cormier, S., & Boyd, C.J. (2000). Lesbian identity management at various stages of the coming out process: A qualitative study. *International Journal of Sexuality and Gender Studies,* 5, 3-18.

Whitney, C. (1990). *Uncommon lives: Gay men and straight women.* New York: Plume.

Whittlin, W. (1983). Homosexuality and child custody: A psychiatric viewpoint. *Conciliation Courts Review,* 21, 77-79.

Williams, W.L. (1986). *The spirit and the flesh: Sexual diversity in American Indian culture.* Boston: Beacon.

Williamson, D.S. (1998). An essay for practitioners: Disclosure is a family event. *Family Relations,* 47, 23-25.

Wilson, B.D.M., & Miller, R.L. (2002). Strategies for managing heterosexism used among African American gay and bisexual men. *The Journal of Black Psychology,* 28, 371-391.

Winkelpleck, J.M., & Westfeld, J.S. (1982). Counseling considerations with gay couples. *Personnel and Guidance Journal,* 60, 294-296.

Winnecott, D.W. (1965). *The maturational process and the facilitating environment.* New York: IUP.

Wolf, T.J. (1985). Marriages of bisexual men. *Journal of Homosexuality,* 11, 135-148.

Wood, J.T., & Inman, C.C. (1993). In a different mode: Masculine styles of communicating closeness. *Journal of Applied Community Research,* 2, 279-295.

Wooden, W.S., & Parker, J. (1982). *Men behind bars: Sexual exploitation in prison.* New York: Plenum.

Wooden, W.S., Kawasaki, H., & Mayeda, R. (1983). Lifestyles and identity maintenance among gay Japanese-American males. *Alternate Lifestyles,* 5, 236-243.

Woodhouse, A. (1989). *Fantastic women: Sex, gender, and transvestism.* New Brunswick, NJ: Rutgers University Press.

Woods, J.D, & Lucas, J. (1993). *The corporate closet: The professional lives of gay men in America.* New York: Free Press.

Woolf, L.M. (2002). Gay and lesbian aging. *Siecus Report,* 30, 16-21.

Woolf, P.F. (1998). Mid-life transition to lesbian: Expanding consciousness of women. *Anthropology of Consciousness,* 9, 49-72.

Woolsey, C. (1991, October 7). Digital pioneers program to fight AIDS, ignorance. *Business Insurance,* p. 80.

Wren, B. (2002). "I can accept my child is transsexual but if I ever see him in a dress I'll hit him": Dilemmas in parenting a transgendered adolescent. *Clinical Child Psychology and Psychiatry,* 7, 377-397.

Wyers, N.L. (1987). Homosexuality in the family: Lesbian and gay spouses. *Social Work,* 32, 143-148.

Yarhouse, M.A. (1999). Social cognition research on the formation and maintenance of stereotypes: Applications to marriage and family therapists working with homosexual clients. *American Journal of Family Therapy,* 27, 149-161.

Year in review (2001, January). *The Advocate,* pp. 11-26.

Zerubavel, E. (1982). Personal information and social life. *Symbolic Interaction,* 5, 97-109.

Zuger, B. (1984). Early effeminate behavior in boys: Outcome and significance for homosexuality. *Journal of Nervous and Mental Disorders,* 172, 90-97.

Index

Acculturation, model of coming out and, 66
Adams, C.L., 87
Adelman, M., 96
Adolescents. *See* Youths
Adult victims of violence, 14
Advocate, The, 165
African Americans, disclosure and, 87-88, 106-108
Affirmative action, advances in, 18-22
Allen, M.W., 48
Allen, P.G., 136
American Airlines, 166
American Psychiatric Association (APA), 18
Anderson, S.C., 28, 85
Androgyne, 3
Anhalt, K., 52
"Anti-gay ideology," perpetrators, 167
"Anti-Homophobia Training for School Staff and Students," 162
Asian American families, disclosure and, 110-111
Assault, school violence, 12
Avoidance, coping style, 8, 125
Awareness phase, model of coming out, 49-50

Balsam, K.F., 10
"Be silent and invisible," family norm, 107
Beals, K.P., 136
Beauchaine, T.P., 10
Beeler, J., 119, 155
Ben-Ari, A., 149
Berger, R.M., 93
Berkey, B.R., 26
Berrill, K.T., 10

Bias crime, 17
Bibliotherapy, 134
Biodyke, 3
Bisensual, 3
Bisexual
    coming out as, 53-56, 137-140
    identity and, 33-34
    term, 3
Bockting, W.O., 27
Bodlund, O., 36
"Boston marriage," 29
Boxer, A.M., 98
Bozett, F.W., 74, 118
Bradford, J., 84-85, 92
Bradford, M., 55
Brady, S., 47
Brown, L.B., 93, 105
Brown, L.S., 96
Busse,W.J., 47
Button, S.B., 124
Byrne, J.S., 125

Cain, R., 90, 120
Campus, violence and, 13-14
Cass, V.C., 43, 132-133
Charbonneau, C., 85
Childbearing, before coming out, 74
Children, disclosure to one's own, 117-118
Chism, N., 121
Chronic illness, model of coming out and, 65
Ciro, D., 11
Climate-setting incident, violence, 12
Cohler, B.J., 66, 74-75, 93
Coleman, E., 115
College, disclosure at, 120-121, 162-163
Collins, J.F., 55

Coming Out and Disclosures
© 2007 by The Haworth Press, Inc. All rights reserved.
doi:10.1300/5423_13